The People of

DEVON

in the First World War

The People of
DEVON
in the First World War

DAVID PARKER

For Pamela, my wife.
Without her love and support,
especially during my severe illness,
this book would not have been written

First published 2013

The History Press
The Mill, Brimscombe Port
Stroud, Gloucestershire, GL5 2QG
www.thehistorypress.co.uk

British Library Cataloguing in Publication Data.
A catalogue record for this book is available from the British Library.

ISBN 978 0 7509 5289 7

Typesetting and origination by The History Press
Printed in Great Britain

CONTENTS

INTRODUCTION

Themes, sources and acknowledgements

THEMES

Three wooden boards adorn the base of the tower inside the little church of St Petrox at Dartmouth Castle in southern Devon. Upon them in white letters are written the names of twenty-eight men from the parish who perished as a result of the First World War. Unlike most such memorials, though, it records more than names. Five of the men, it says, died on HMS *Monmouth* on 1 November 1914, the day she was sunk at the Battle of Coronel, off the coast of Chile. Another died on HMS *Defence* on 31 May 1916, the day she blew up at the Battle of Jutland. Several more, soldiers probably, are mentioned as 'killed in action', but one could be recorded only as 'missing'. The dates are scattered across every year of the war, and so are those for others who are recorded as dying from 'wounds' and 'disease'. One, a 'prisoner of war', died on 9 November 1918, just two days before the war ended. Another succumbed to 'exposure' on 23 November 1918 after serving on his 'last ship HMS *Oppossum*', one of a class of early destroyers renowned for their unhealthy all-pervading wetness. The last man did not die until 13 November 1919, a year after the Armistice was signed.

As this sombre memorial signifies, the war went on for nearly four and a half desperate years, men died in many places and in many ways, and the Armistice on 11 November 1918 did not end the suffering. Across Devon hundreds of granite crosses and brass plaques record similar heavy losses that families and their communities somehow had to bear. The conflict began in August 1914 in a blaze of patriotic fervour, as crowds gathered to cheer army reservists off to a war that most expected to be won within a few weeks, after glorious cavalry charges on the northern plains of Europe and a triumphant new Battle of Trafalgar at sea.

Many men thought themselves fortunate to have joined local Volunteer and Territorial Army battalions in earlier years. They had enjoyed peacetime training in rifle drill, life under canvas and basic manoeuvres, and now anticipated being called upon to defend the kingdom from possible invasion, or even, perhaps, agreeing to service overseas. Hundreds of thousands

St Petrox Church at Dartmouth Castle. (Author's collection)

more flocked to recruiting stations across the land. Some no doubt were caught up in the heady excitement of the moment, some believed the war was one of national honour in the defence of Belgium against remorseless German brutality, and others saw enlistment as an escape from lives of monotony, misery or poverty; or perhaps all three.

All these initial feelings were soon dashed as the brief open conflict in southern Belgium and across its border into France settled down into the prolonged war of attrition between millions of troops in hundreds of miles of opposing trenches winding across the plains, valleys and hills of Flanders, Picardy, Champagne, Lorraine and Alsace to the Swiss border. There was a never-ending need for more men on this Western Front as one indecisive battle after another consumed tens of thousands of lives, and Devon was repeatedly scoured first by recruiting parties and then by conscription and accompanying tribunals as the initial rush died away. And all the while families looked with horror as a succession of railway trains arrived with the wounded to fill local hospitals, and never-ending lists of casualties filled the newspapers.

As the memorial in St Petrox reveals, the war took Devon soldiers and sailors across the world. They served in the battleships, cruisers, destroyers, minesweepers, armed trawlers and submarines of the Royal Navy, and in a host of regiments in India, Africa, the Middle East and Italy, as well as the trenches of the Western Front. A few flew rickety aeroplanes into increasingly lethal dogfights. These men are far from forgotten in this book, not least because their experiences exerted an immediate and often lasting impact upon those they left at home. Primarily, though, the book is about those men, women and children who were left behind, and how those in the cottages, terraces and mansions, farms and factories, churches and chapels, hospitals and schools across Devon responded to the demands and pressures of this totally unprecedented war.

The book has adopted a thematic approach rather than a chronological one. Each chapter therefore identifies and expands upon a key theme throughout the war, with succeeding chapters supported by ideas and arguments in preceding ones where cross-referencing is appropriate. Such an approach, it is hoped, minimises the number of sharp breaks in the overall story, and makes its component parts more readable. This Introduction identifies the themes, comments on the sources and offers my thanks to the many people who have helped me. Chapter One sets the geographical and historical scenes. It identifies the curious mix of ancient and modern apparent in Devon in 1914, and argues that the county was far from being a social or economic backwater. Chapter Two concentrates upon Devon's response to the demands of active service, from the initial rush of volunteers to the intensive recruitment marches, and the mounting controversies surrounding the introduction of compulsion. It looks, too, at the nature of the news that families received from abroad. Chapter Three describes Devon's reaction to 'outsiders' – notably the host of Belgian refugees, real and imagined enemy spies, 'aliens' at Buckfast Abbey and those whom contemporaries called 'conscientious objectors'. Chapter Four discusses the hurried establishment of numerous war hospitals, the work of medical staff and dozens of voluntary organisations, and the response of local communities to the wounded in their midst. It analyses the roles of women, and contemporary views on their ability to cope with wartime demands and emergencies. Chapter Five identifies the war-related activities of schoolchildren, and follows the marked changes in wartime attitudes towards the health and education of the rising generation. Chapter Six looks at rural and urban communities under pressure – the war economy, industrial unrest, farmers wrestling with labour issues, the arrival of new and unusual groups of workers, and the imposition of draconian central controls. Finally Chapter Seven draws the threads of these themes together, and explores how key issues and stories unfolded in the 1920s.

SOURCES

It is a curious but common mistake to think that people back home knew little of the lives of the men at war. Devon's newspapers were full of news about the war, and although most reports, and especially the headlines, were up-beat about the fighting qualities and successes of the Allied forces, the small print often noted heavy losses, minimal advances and grim retreats in the face of the enemy's determined resistance. The initial breathless and often wildly inaccurate reports of successful battles were usually followed by those that added cautious amendments and more measured claims. As the interminable casualty lists appeared, only the most optimistic of headline readers could believe in a stream of Allied successes and imminent Allied victory as the months and years of relentless warfare ground on. Without doubt, though, regular newspaper readers could easily gain a reasonably accurate picture of the unfolding campaigns on land and sea across the world. Certainly the locations of battles were not kept secret for very long, and sometimes, a little carelessly perhaps, incidents that were part of a bigger battle were reported before that bigger battle had run its course. All in all censorship of any news about the build-up to battles was tight, but it bordered on the loose once those battles had been joined. And no doubt just as army and naval commanders tended to put self-justifying 'spins' in their reports, and accentuate successes while diminishing reverses, so newspaper editors freely padded out articles with patriotic comments and added favourable details to particular incidents. Editors were well aware what was expected of them as purveyors of news at a time of unprecedented national crisis, and of course too much talk of defeat, and associated pessimism, could easily lead to prosecution under the draconian clauses of the wartime Defence of the Realm Act. Nevertheless, by and large everyone knew how well or badly the war was going.

Countless letters have survived from Devon servicemen to their families, employers, and old schools. Some are matter of fact, some highly emotional, some fervently patriotic, some deeply religious and some alarming in their accounts of life in war zones. Although all were censored, many do not spare the feelings of their readers about narrow escapes from death, the hideousness of artillery bombardments, ghastly wounds and the sudden deaths of colleagues, and the sorry plight of refugees. Far from sparing loved ones these gruesome experiences, they wanted to share them. Some recipients of letters let local editors publish extracts in newspapers, and some servicemen wrote directly to newspapers in response to war-related articles they had read. Perhaps from time to time local editors may have invented letters to suit the edition they were currently planning, and indeed one is suspicious of letters published without a name, address and date, but the vast majority are accredited by reference to the local serviceman's name, rank, regiment or ship, and the name and address of the person to whom it was sent.

Several wartime diaries kept by Devon servicemen, and one by a south Devon farmer, have survived, and so have a number of memoirs composed in later times, including those by Captain Gamblen, a gentleman-farmer's son who enlisted as a private and rose to a captaincy; Alfred Gregory, the local newspaper editor and wartime mayor of Tiverton; Ruth Whitaker, an Anglican clergyman's daughter who served as a Voluntary Aid Detachment (VAD) nurse in Exeter; Dick Pym, a mariner and sportsman from the small port of Topsham; and Devon's influential Lord Lieutenant, Earl Fortescue, whose privately printed manuscript is particularly illuminating. Generally speaking the soldiers' diaries are matter of fact, but the very ordinariness of most of the entries reveals the events and routines, such as the meals, illnesses, news from home and visits to local towns, that mattered most to the writers. As many Devon men served in India and the Middle East, their entries reveal the striking impact that long sea voyages and the sights and sounds of foreign cultures had upon them. The memoirs are different. They were compiled with a wider readership in mind, and invariably pass more comment upon events and personalities the writers selected as significant; the immediacy of the diary is lost, but the reflections can reveal much about the writers' character, attitudes and times.

A variety of sources illuminate social issues during the traumatic years of war. The minutes of Devon County Council, Exeter City Council and Plymouth Borough Council and their various subcommittees have survived, although mainly they limit themselves to decisions finally reached rather than giving any flavour of the contributory discussions. Fortunately local newspapers contain almost verbatim accounts of many county and city council meetings, and often, too, they include the deliberations of major subcommittees, notably the key ones of education, public health and agriculture. Adding interest, the editors were frequently disposed to write comments on these debates, thereby revealing their social assumptions and political leanings.

Newspapers also devoted a great deal of space to meetings convened by religious bodies and charitable organisations, and to discussions by editors and correspondents about women's physical, spiritual, moral and financial well-being while so many menfolk were away from home. Detailed and sometimes salacious reports of court cases arising from drunkenness and prostitution fuelled wider fears for the fragility of women and their inherent inability to cope alone – despite the mountain of evidence to the contrary. The equally detailed accounts of juveniles brought before the courts for theft and vandalism added to the wartime panic about the collapse of civil discipline, the decay of family life and declining standards of elementary education. Despite the fines and imprisonment imposed on the women, and the birching and dispatch to reformatory schools handed out to young offenders, newspapers constantly bemoaned the failure to stem the tide of criminality.

Yet notwithstanding the largely unwarranted panic, women and children were also perceived as having key roles to play in the war effort. The same newspapers that derided the weaknesses of women on one page often contained adjacent reports and correspondence about their determined and capable work having replaced men in a range of occupations, and as efficient and energetic organisers of war-related charities. Certainly, as a variety of records show, the numerous Devon hospitals caring for the wounded could not have succeeded without the volunteer nurses and the host of female support staff. The concept of women of all social classes as the providers of devoted care and loving comfort, and giving wholehearted support to men at war whatever the cost in personal worry, was of supreme importance to the nation's morale, and was consistently appealed to in recruiting meetings and advertisements.

Children's needs, and the nation's needs of its children, moved from the shadows towards the limelight as the war progressed. The headteachers of all elementary schools – those provided by the state and churches for the vast majority of children up to the age of fourteen – were obliged to keep logbooks in which they recorded important details such as attendance rates, holidays, epidemics, visits by school medical staff, inspectors, school managers and local dignitaries, holidays, changes to staff and syllabuses, and other activities and incidents thought worth recording, such as school repairs, prize days, outings and confrontations with parents. Although rarely discursive, they are a mine of information, and accumulatively the numerous logbooks consulted for this book significantly supplement newspaper reports and the generally terse minutes of council meetings. As one year of war followed another the logbooks reveal changes that took place as schools became increasingly subject to the needs of the war effort. Several schools were requisitioned by the army, a high proportion of eligible male teachers enlisted, and there were drastic economies in staffing, equipment and building repairs. Attendances nearly everywhere dropped sharply because of the increased demand for child labour and tacit relaxation of attendance by-laws. The schools were very much subject to the exigencies of the times, and children were expected to do their utmost to promote the war effort. Many lessons were linked to the war and to the inculcation of greater patriotism, and schools were perceived as major promoters of local war charities.

Nevertheless, records reveal longer-term changes in attitudes towards children as the war progressed. The appalling casualty rate, coupled with the havoc wreaked upon the nation's international commerce, started to focus attention upon the means of ensuring the physical health, mental well-being and carefully honed manual skills of the rising generation, upon which would rest responsibility for the restoration and future defence of the nation's imperial supremacy and economic strength. Extended child healthcare and broader educational opportunities were suddenly serious items for discussion and, more importantly, political action.

The war led to the creation of emergency committees with specific local functions, and some records of these have survived. The intensive activities and internal controversies of the Exeter Committee for the Relief of War Refugees and its successor, the Devon and Cornwall War Refugees Committee, are well recorded in minutes, letters, reports and printed pamphlets. Some records of the wide-ranging activities of Devon's branch of the Red Cross, notably in connection with the numerous war hospitals and their hard-pressed supply depots, have survived to reveal both the struggles and triumphs of its members. Devon's War Agriculture Committee records are extant, although latterly it was largely superseded by the County Executive Food Production Committee, with its remit to radically enhance agricultural production, a task it carried out with a vigour bordering on ruthlessness. Some records survive of the remarkably determined women's war service committees in Devon, which reveal the difficulties they experienced in breaking down male prejudices. In addition there are the papers of special committees responding, or not responding, to the government's grant-backed invitation to create a network of maternity and infant welfare centres.

Each event, trend and opinion in this book stems from evidence in one, and very often more than one, of these many sources. As space was severely limited in this publication, and the vast number of references would overwhelm the text whether they were long lists at the end of each chapter or the book, it was decided to limit the information on sources to the itemised bibliography. However, via the publisher the author will furnish any reader who wishes to pursue particular points with the detailed references.

A NOTE ON CURRENCY

Pounds '£', shillings 's' and pence 'd' (from the Latin *denarius*, for penny) were the currency of the day, with 12d making a shilling and 20s making a pound. There were also farthings, of which 4 made a penny. Thus, five pounds, twelve shillings and sixpence farthing would be written as £5 12s 6¼d. A guinea (shortened to 'gn') was £1 1s 0d. There was no single coin for this value, and it was usually reserved for expensive goods that were primarily the preserve of the rich.

A strict conversion to decimal coinage is easy: 6d is 2½p in decimal coinage, 1s is 5p, 2s and 6d is 12½p, 5s is 25p, 10s is 50p, and 20s or a pound is £1 – the only similar figure. A 1914 penny is less than half a modern 1p; a farthing beyond comparison. At the other end of the scale 5gns is £5.25, and 20gns is £21.

However, the relative value of money is far more difficult to calculate. At the start of the twentieth century, around 25s was a southern counties farm labourer's weekly wage – £1.25 today – although he probably occupied a cheap or even free farm cottage with a sizeable vegetable patch. Approaching 40s, or £2, was what a skilled local building worker might expect. In real terms, rents today are far higher, while most everyday items are much cheaper. Approximately £1 in 1914 would be worth over £75 today, if the retail price index is used, but nearer £300 if average earnings are the basis for calculation. According to the first formula, 6d then would be £3.75-£4.00 today. For many families in 1914 6d, or 2½p, was a coin to be stored away and spent wisely.

As the modern amounts appear so small and historically meaningless, it seemed pointless to accompany every £ s d amount in the text with the decimal equivalent.

ACKNOWLEDGEMENTS

This book does not, of course, eschew the local histories of Devon's numerous towns and villages, or those describing and analysing specific trades and industries. These are wonderfully informative. However, as intimated here, this book draws largely upon primary sources – county and city council papers, school logbooks, various war charity and committee files, numerous local newspapers, selected private papers, and unpublished memoirs and diaries. It is apposite here to give my thanks to the staff of archives, museums and libraries who have been so generous with their assistance in identifying sources and providing documents: Axe Valley Museum, Seaton; Barnstaple & North Devon Museum; Bicton Gardens Countryside Museum; Bovey Tracey Heritage Centre; Brixham Heritage Museum; Cookworthy Museum, Kingsbridge; Dartmouth Museum; Devon & Exeter Institution, Exeter; Devon Record Office, Sowton, Exeter; Ilfracombe Museum; North Devon Record Office, Barnstaple; Plymouth Central Library; Plymouth & West Devon Record Office; Sidmouth Museum; Tiverton Museum of Mid Devon Life; Topsham Museum; Torquay Library; West Country Studies Library, Exeter, and West of England Newspapers, Newton Abbot.

Copyright owners of photographs have been generous in giving permission for their publication, and many made no charge. The citation against each of them in the text is given with gratitude. The majority of illustrations have not appeared previously in a published work. I am pleased to record here my deep appreciation of the expertise and time devoted by Tony Ovens to reproducing the majority of the photographs and preparing them, especially the numerous low definition originals, so expertly for publication.

CHAPTER ONE

DEVON IN THE SUMMER OF 1914

Ancient landscapes, traditional hierarchies, recent initiatives

As spring turned into early summer in the year 1914 there were many issues for the people of Devon to worry about, but imminent war with Germany and Austria-Hungary was not one of them. There had been intermittent sabre rattling over the past couple of decades, largely centred upon rival commercial ambitions in far-flung parts of the world, but flurries of diplomatic activity had always settled things down. Germany's belated attempts in the last decades of the nineteenth century to create a few colonies in Africa had led to irritating moments in its relationship with Britain, but realistically Kaiser Wilhelm II seemed unlikely to seriously challenge the world-wide dominions and colonies of King George V. There appeared no chance of Germany's growing number of battleships attaining superiority over the Royal Navy, and as a military precaution Britain had recently signed a defensive Triple Entente with Russia to the east of Germany and France to its west. And besides, most European royal families were inter-related and visited each other amid splendid ceremonies apparently full of *bonhomie*. As a backup, though, the new International Tribunal at The Hague was ready to resolve disputes before they led to war. A few pessimists perceived ominous signs that mounting jealousies would inevitably tip over quite soon into armed conflict, but nothing much regarding international alarms presaging war appeared in the newspapers. The arrest and conviction of a German spy in Devon in 1911 no doubt thrilled readers, but local newspapers could not have done more to mock the amateurism of Ober-Leutnant Max Shultz, who had posed as a journalist and attempted to elicit information about Devonport Dockyard from some workers he invited onto his houseboat.

DOMESTIC WORRIES

There was far more to worry about at home, as local as well as national newspapers revealed. The bitter strikes in Glasgow, Liverpool, London and Manchester among the dockyard and transport workers, and the drafting of troops into the capital, were headline news in 1911, and on 2 September the *Exeter Flying Post* was sure that Socialist agitators were to blame. 'An epidemic of malignity reduced society to chaos', a leader thundered, and locking onto a favourite target added, 'of what use is it to boast of our universal education when underlying masses of sheer savagery suddenly burst forth amongst us'. The class war was ever present.

In 1912 the widespread coal strike quickly caused local difficulties. The Great Western Railway's goods yards and most branch lines were at a standstill, and Meldon, Teign Valley and Beer quarries, Silverton Paper Mills, and Messrs Willey's iron foundry in Exeter had to close. Exeter opened a soup kitchen, the Mayor's Poor Box was drawn upon, Lord Poltimore gave £50 to help relieve the city's poor, and the Earl of Devon allowed villagers to forage in his woods. Rumbles of industrial unrest and threats of national strikes continued well into 1914. In July that year a lengthy and sometimes violent strike brought production to a halt at Trusham quarries in the Teign valley; and at the end of that month the grievances of building workers in Exeter erupted into another strike.

The suffragettes were equally alarming, and certainly newsworthy. In 1912 and again in 1913 and 1914 the *Exeter Flying Post* was horrified at their actions – breaking the windows of key political opponents across London, smashing Kew Gardens' orchid house, putting tar in pillar boxes, cutting telegraph wires and, most shocking of all, interrupting a service in St Paul's Cathedral. More comfortingly, it noted that the Exeter meetings of the National League for Opposing Women's Suffrage were supported by both male and female members of the influential Fortescue, Buller, Acland and Kennaway families. To applause, at one of the meetings in 1913, the chairman asserted, 'The destinies of the country, of great imperial and commercial importance, must be managed by men', and a Mrs Greatbatch did women little service when she 'spoke from experience of life in an industrial district, and she knew that the women there did not want the vote and would not know what to do with it'. Another female speaker exclaimed that equal pay was nonsense as equal work was impossible.

In December 1913 Exeter was astir as news spread that the suffragette leader, Mrs Pankhurst, had been arrested on the liner *Majestic* just off Plymouth and taken to Exeter Prison. As she grew weaker on hunger strike, and endured forced feeding, suffragettes flocked to the prison gates and so did a crowd of local men who charged the female pickets. 'Much rough horseplay ensued', said

Trewman's Flying Post, and one suffragette was barely saved from being thrown off the parapet of the nearby railway bridge. The agitation continued up to the outbreak of war. In January 1914 the wealthy Miss Rosalie Chichester hosted a non-militant pro-suffrage rally at Arlington Court in north Devon. In May similar meetings were held in Exeter and Newton Abbot, both of which were supported by the local press and a scattering of councillors and businessmen. Speakers steadfastly proclaimed the enrichment of women's lives through the extension of the franchise and their participation in political affairs.

The intractable problem of Home Rule for Ireland was equally high profile, as Irish Nationalists and Protestants geared themselves for violent civil war whatever political solution was forthcoming in Westminster. Tension was heightened by sensational news reports that caches of rifles and ammunition were being smuggled into the country. In December 1913 a train taking Sir Edward Carson, the fervent Protestant Unionist, to Plymouth stopped at Exeter St David's station and an appreciative crowd gathered to hear his brief impromptu talk. Exeter's Unionist MP, H.E. Duke (later Lord Merrivale), together with sympathetic editors, ensured that the Protestant and Unionist opposition to Home Rule was to the fore in numerous local meetings and extensive follow-up reports.

PROTECTING THE NATION

The times were indeed turbulent, with future social stability an uncertain prospect. Nevertheless, despite all this domestic turmoil, some key local figures tried to ensure that Devon was prepared for war, although of course not envisaging a global conflict. In the middle of May 1914 it was probably with mixed feelings of surprise, excitement and apprehension that families in several market towns and seaside resorts across east Devon witnessed a full-scale military exercise undertaken by the Royal Army Medical Corps, Red Cross and VAD nurses, orderlies, stretcher-bearers and drivers. It was based on the assumption that enemy forces had landed at nearby Bridport in Dorset and were being counterattacked by troops of the Wessex Territorial Division. Replicating assumed wartime conditions as much as possible, with boys from Exeter School acting as extra patients and numerous companies of Boy Scouts employed as assistant orderlies, 1,300 casualties were created, of whom 1,160 were deemed hospital cases. Huge quantities of bedding and stores were brought out, and temporary war hospitals were set up in Honiton, Ottery St Mary, Budleigh Salterton, Exmouth, Topsham and Exeter. Rest and receiving points were created at the railway stations in Honiton, Ottery St Mary and Exeter's Queen Street, a fully fitted ambulance train was used for severe cases, and an array of motor- and horse-drawn transport was used to take the wounded to and from the railway stations. War Office officials observed the massive event, and the newspapers rather blandly concluded that it was a great logistical success, much like the colourful annual manoeuvres of the Devon militia.

For centuries Devon had seen its ports and shores as likely landing points for continental invaders, and VADs for both men and women had been raised across Devon soon after the appointment in late 1909 of the first county director,

Earl and Countess Fortescue and Castle Hill. (Devon Record Office)

Mr J.S.C. Davis, immediately after the government had inaugurated the scheme. Their primary aim was to supplement the medical services of the nation's Territorial Forces in case of war. The influential Buller family, whose recently deceased and locally revered doyen had been General Sir Redvers Buller VC from Downes, near Crediton, had ensured that the initiative maintained a high profile, with the active support of Earl Fortescue, Devon's Lord Lieutenant and a key figure in the Territorial Force. Not surprisingly, Countess Fortescue was president of the county branch of the British Red Cross Society, and her committee represented a roll-call of notable county families, including Sir Ian and Lady Amory of Knightshayes Court near Tiverton, the Dowager Lady Churston of Churston Court near Brixham, Mrs Rennell Coleridge of Salston Manor near Ottery St Mary, Sir John Kennaway and Miss Kennaway from Escot near Ottery St Mary, Mrs Mildmay of Flete near Ivybridge, Lady Seaton of Buckland Abbey near Yelverton, and the Honourable Mrs Lionel Walrond of Bradfield House near Uffculme.

The Devonshire Regiment had a peacetime strength of three regular army battalions, and still retained close links with the county from which it customarily recruited most of its men. Formed in 1685 to help crush the Duke of Monmouth's western counties rebellion against his uncle King James II, the regiment won its fearsome nickname 'The Bloody Eleventh' in 1812 after its desperate struggle against the French at Salamanca in northern Spain during

Knightshayes, near Tiverton, seat of the Heathcoat-Amory family. (Devon & Exeter Institution)

the Napoleonic Wars. By 1914 several additional Territorial battalions had been created, based in various towns across the county. A sign of their popularity was the Military Tournament and Tattoo held at the County Ground on the outskirts of Exeter in June 1914. The infantry undertook a skirmish, the artillery unlimbered and prepared guns for firing, the engineers erected an observation tower and sent telegraph messages to the command post, the signallers laid cables 'at a gallop' and established contacts with various outposts, and the cavalry 'showed they were quite at home in the saddle'. More serious training by regular army units was undertaken from 1893 until 1914 at the Okehampton Field Artillery Practice Camp on Dartmoor, a vast expanse prohibited to the public which was fully equipped with barracks, stabling and gun stores.

The Territorial volunteers took part in annual training and manoeuvres, usually in tented camps on scrubland. In May 1914, 450 members of the Royal North Devon Hussars and their horses went for a fortnight to Ashwick, north of Dulverton in Somerset. That August, just a few days before war broke out, large crowds watched 3,371 officers and men of three Territorial battalions of the Devonshire Regiment, and two Territorial battalions of the Duke of Cornwall's Light Infantry, detrain at Exmouth and march the 4 miles to Woodbury Common accompanied by military bands and wagons drawing tons of equipment for two weeks of summer manoeuvres. Also active in the county under the umbrella of the Devonshire Territorial Force Association was the Royal Devon Yeomanry, first raised locally in 1794 by Sir Stafford Northcote of Pynes, Exeter, primarily to suppress civil disorder within the county – which it did on several occasions. By 1914 it had four squadrons spread across the southern half of the county with its overall headquarters in Exeter, and that May large crowds gathered as 430 men from the yeomanry and an accompanying transport column encamped at Lower Haytor Downs outside Bovey Tracey. Linked to all these forces were Territorial Transport and Supply Columns, Garrison Artillery, and Royal Army Medical Corps (RAMC) Ambulance and Hospital Units. Recruitment was good, the battalions were largely up to strength, and, of course, their officers were drawn from the ranks of the nobility and gentry. Earl Fortescue was colonel, and also president and chairman of the Devonshire Territorial Force Association, and his deputy was Lord Clifford of Chudleigh.

Holidaymakers and residents of Devon's seaside resorts such as Ilfracombe and Westward Ho! in the north and Seaton, Sidmouth, Exmouth, Dawlish, Teignmouth, Torquay and Paignton in the south were often treated to the impressive sight of British battleships gliding slowly past or moored off shore. Such appearances were good public relations events for the Royal Navy and summer tourist attractions for the towns. In June 1914 the elderly HMS *Commonwealth*

HMS *Conqueror*, moored off Ilfracombe, July 1914. (Ilfracombe Museum)

Capstone Parade, Ilfracombe. (Author's collection)

visited Ilfracombe, and crowds flocked to Capstone Hill, the Pier and the Parade to see it. Local people and the crew put on a sports day in the public park and a concert in Alexandra Hall, and parties of schoolchildren had the awesome experience of visiting the ship and viewing its four 12in guns at close quarters. A month later the warm welcome and mutual visits were repeated, and the sights were even better, when two modern sister ships, HMS *Conqueror* and *Thunderer*, moored off the resort, each massively armed with ten 13.5in guns. During three months of summer 1914 Ilfracombe Pier recorded 33,179 paying entries; 'the battleships were responsible' remarked a council member – 'but don't forget the bands' added another.

On the southern coast Devonport was a major naval port, employing thousands of local people not only servicing, repairing and rebuilding warships of all types, but also building new ones. Launches were occasions for local celebration, especially if the ships were large, such as the battleships HMS *King Edward VII*, *Queen* and *Royal Oak*, and the cruisers HMS *Arrogant*, *Aurora*, *Cleopatra*, *Furious* and *Minotaur*, launched and completed there between

Torquay harbour, with warships anchored off shore. (Author's collection)

1898 and 1915. After stiff competition from other ports, and interminable delays, the small Devon town of Dartmouth was chosen as the site for a new naval college to replace the Dart's ancient floating hulk *Britannia*. Eventually completed in 1905, the imposing new Royal Naval College high above the deep water estuary dominated the town, and the annual passing-out parades, royal connections, annual regattas and visiting warships helped ensure naval affairs maintained a high local profile.

THE HEIGHT OF THE AGE OF STEAM

Just as the Territorial battalions on their way to Woodbury Common had travelled across Devon to Exmouth by train, and the pre-war VAD exercise had relied upon the railways, so the naval dockyards and numerous commercial ports were coming to rely on the speedy communications provided by increasingly powerful steam locomotives. In addition, the growing prosperity of many Devon farms and seaside resorts would have been impossible without the steadily expanding network.

Amid great public excitement, the first Great Western Railway (GWR) train arrived in Exeter from Paddington via Bristol, Taunton and Tiverton Junction on 1 May 1844. In due course branch lines fanned out from Tiverton Junction east to the rural communities around Hemyock and west to Tiverton itself. The substantial market town of Tiverton was also halfway along a later GWR line that wound its way from just outside Exeter through the countryside to Bampton, a few miles later joining the equally winding GWR line from Taunton through South Molton to Barnstaple. From Exeter the main GWR line reached Plymouth via the southern coastal and market towns of Dawlish, Teignmouth, Newton Abbot, Totnes and Ivybridge in May 1848, before winding on to Penzance by 1859. Substantial branches were later built from Newton Abbot north to Bovey Tracey and Moretonhampstead, and south to Torquay and Paignton and then onwards to Brixham and Kingswear. Others went north from Totnes to Ashburton and south from Brent to Kingsbridge. Among the lines serving Plymouth and its hinterland was one that stretched to Princetown, the location of Dartmoor Prison.

The London and South Western Railway's (LSWR) more southerly route from Waterloo via Salisbury, Yeovil and Axminster reached Exeter in 1860, and then laboriously skirted the northern and eastern slopes of Dartmoor via Crediton, Okehampton, Lydford and Tavistock to reach Devonport and Plymouth in 1890. To the south of Exeter one short branch line connected with Topsham and Exmouth, and later on Budleigh Salterton. A few miles to the east a second went to Ottery St Mary and Sidmouth, and a third to Seaton. A far longer LSWR line wound northwards from Exeter through Crediton and a dozen villages in the Yeo and Taw valleys to Barnstaple Junction. From here three short lines branched out to Ilfracombe, Bideford and Lynton, again each one passing through several villages. Further west, a line wandered from Okehampton through agricultural communities to reach Halwill Junction, where further rural lines continued westwards to Holsworthy and Bude or turned north towards Hatherleigh, Great Torrington and Bideford. With just a few miles of line to be completed in the 1920s, notably between Hatherleigh and Torrington, by 1914 the county network was virtually at its peak.

The railways made many towns and villages more accessible, thereby encouraging new developments and enabling the produce of farms and factories to be sent to new and distant customers far more quickly and in greater bulk than ever before. Admittedly many subsidiary lines curved back and forth across the countryside taking routes involving the fewest cuttings, embankments or bridges, and often the daily number of trains were few, the rolling stock far from new and the journeys full of stops and starts, but they represented a liberating advance on the horse-drawn coaches, wagons and carts that had lurched along dusty and uneven roads in summer and waterlogged ones in winter. And, of course, mainline services had cut the travelling time to major cities outside the region to hours rather than days. The fastest horse-drawn coach between Exeter and London had taken sixteen and a half hours, but very few could afford seats on it, while the mid-Victorian express trains took only four and a half hours

An advertisement for Moorland Hotel, Ilsington, Dartmoor. (Devon & Exeter Institution)

and charged lower fares. As old railway photographs reveal, even the smallest rural stations possessed a siding or two with animal pens and ramps for loading and unloading goods wagons. Superior hotels in holiday resorts ensured their carriages or motor cars were waiting for their clients as trains arrived, while local private carriers were there for less socially elevated visitors. Lilian Wilson, born in Ilfracombe in 1896, recalled the 'very smart affair drawn by two horses' that conveyed visitors to and from the Royal Clarence Hotel, and the way residents and ordinary holidaymakers gawped at wealthy visitors.

The steam locomotive significantly enhanced Devon's economy, and was to play a major role in the war.

TOURISTS AND THE RESORTS

The railways seriously eroded the services of the sea-going packet steamers that brought visitors from London and Southampton to the southern resorts, although the paddle-steamers offering trips up and down the coast with stop-off points for walks, meals and entertainment proliferated alongside the seaside hotels and guesthouses. In the summer of 1907 a young boy from Euston in London, probably aged about twelve, kept a diary of his family holiday in north Devon.

It reveals both the attractions and frustrations that the locality afforded visitors. He and his family travelled on the 11.10 a.m. train from Waterloo to Exeter and then on to Barnstaple and their final destination, Ilfracombe, arriving at 5.20 p.m., an hour behind schedule. One day they took a trip on the SS *Gwalia* to Clovelly, and on another went by train to Mortehoe, where they took a carriage ride to Woolacombe. Fortunately, the boy wrote, the return train from Morthoe was thirty minutes late or they would have been stranded. A coastal steamer trip to Lynmouth proved frustrating. It started forty-five minutes late, and as there was no pier it took an hour to unload the passengers by two small boats. Towards the end of their stay a carefully planned railway outing took them to Barnstaple Junction, where they changed trains for Bideford. They took lunch there, and went on by train first to Westward Ho! and then to Appledore, where they crossed by ferry to Instow. Typically, the weather was invigorating but variable, the diarist concluding that Devon was 'exceedingly pretty but very damp'.

Today the line from Exeter to Barnstaple still exists, but all the other north Devon lines have long closed. In the early twentieth century, though, trains were probably far more crowded than the roads. Lilian Wilson recalled that Ilfracombe children 'used to play happily in the street, traffic went round them and no-one thought it dangerous'. The streets, she said, were merely dirt with quarried stones pressed into it from time to time by a steamroller. On particularly hot days they required the town's water cart to dampen down the choking dust.

Writing in 1745, a century and a half earlier, Robert Fraser had noted how the wildness of Devon's remote high moors, deep valleys, looming cliffs and hidden bays had combined with their enduring reputation for enhancing physical health and mental well-being to attract wealthy visitors who were prepared to put up with the discomfort of the overland or coastal journey and the generally high cost of accommodation. In 1879 the publisher John Murray thought it commercially worthwhile to issue *A Handbook for Travellers in Devonshire*, which combined eulogies about the scenery and historic sites with full details of the fast growing rail network and recommended inns and hotels. A couple of contrasting quotations give the flavour of this and many other guidebooks designed to entice Victorian and Edwardian travellers. In southern Devon between the rivers Tamar and Teign, it advises the visitor, 'From the cliffs of the coast, when requiring relief from the glare of the sun and water, he can hasten to the skirts of the moors, there to wander through shady dells, amid mossy rocks and mossy trees, or along the banks of pellucid streams …' At Devonport the county 'contains the greatest Naval and Military Arsenal combined, in the British Empire, planted on the shores of a harbour not to be surpassed for spaciousness, security, and scenic beauty'. Its docks, fitting yards,

A paddlesteamer and tourists at Totnes. (Author's collection)

Paignton beach before the war. (Author's collection)

barracks, granite forts, gun wharfs, and, 'above all, the floating Armaments of iron and wooden war ships floating peacefully on the bosom of the Hamoaze, combine to display to the fullest, the power of Great Britain, and present along a spectacle worth coming far to see'. Awesome scenery and awesome Imperial power were in close proximity in Devon.

By the end of the nineteenth century the middle classes and even many artisan families from across the country were flocking to the county's burgeoning resorts, those blessed with sandy beaches not surprisingly prospering commercially far more than those burdened with shingle. As the early twentieth-century visitors' lists in local newspapers reveal, the wealthy and titled still patronised luxury hotels in resorts such as Ilfracombe, Torquay and Sidmouth, but Devon was not nearly as exclusive as it had once been. Indeed the wealthy owners of coastal land had contributed to the change. The Cary and Palk families had developed much of Torre and Torquay as an upper-class winter resort but a middle-class summer one, and the Rolle family agreed a multitude of leases that allowed the almost unchecked growth of Exmouth and Withycombe.

By 1914 many locals were holidaymakers themselves. Day trips became popular as families took advantage of the introduction of cheap excursion trains on bank holidays and weekends. On Whit Monday 1890, 3,000 day tickets were issued from Exeter to sandy Exmouth, and numbers grew year by year; far fewer, though, went to pebble-strewn Budleigh Salterton. Piers were built, military bands played, tennis, golf and archery clubs abounded, horses and bicycles could be hired, swimming baths were opened, and trips by buses, charabancs and pleasure steamers were heavily advertised. Catering for thousands of holiday-makers was already big business, and the war would hit that business hard.

THE CHANGING COUNTRYSIDE

In contrast, agriculture had dominated the Devon landscape for centuries, but it had also undergone great changes in recent years as it strove to recover from the deep depression that had blighted farming since the 1870s. The picture of the Devon farming countryside outside the moors drawn by John Murray's 1879 *Handbook* is one of 'exuberant vegetation, the results of rich soil and favourable climate, warmed by mild sea breezes on two sides, resulting in products of the garden approaching those of the shores of the Mediterranean'. It adds, 'The lanes are

A pre-war postcard of a Devonshire lane. (Author's collection)

The market at Holsworthy. (Author's collection)

steep and narrow, and bordered by tangled hedges, often thirty feet above the road … In the deep shadowy combes villages lie nestled, with ruddy walls of clay and roofs of thatch, and seldom far from one of those crystal streams which enliven every valley.' The descriptions, affected though they appear, are little different from those of the traveller and commentator Robert Fraser in 1745, mentioned earlier.

The exotic phrases in Murray's *Handbook*, although not untrue, took no account of the mounting economic pressures upon landowners, working farmers and their labourers as bulk grain started to pour into the country from the vast plains of America, seriously undercutting local prices. Farmers were forced to adapt, and in the county between 1870 and 1895 the acreage devoted to wheat diminished by a massive 65 per cent, and barley by 36 per cent, as they were replaced by a concentration upon lamb, beef and dairy production for national as well as local markets.

By 1914 there were 800,000 sheep in Devon, 300,000 dairy and beef cattle, and 92,000 pigs; they were big business. Around a quarter of a million livestock were leaving the county from numerous town and country railway sidings each year. Based on acreage, in 1914 oats were Devon's most prevalent cereal crop, with wheat and barley still substantial but lagging far behind. There were sizeable crops of turnips, swedes, potatoes, mangolds and rape. Vast quantities of apples were produced, and a minority of favourably sited farmers continued to cultivate cherries, plums and soft fruit, such as strawberries, raspberries, currants and gooseberries. A huge acreage was put down to permanent pasture, and also to clover, sainfoin and grass. Hay harvesting was a great annual event in many rural communities. In addition over 168,000 acres of Devon's heath and moorland was used for grazing.

As well as livestock, by 1914 many tons of south Devon fruit and Taw and Teign valley potatoes were dispatched by train to London and other major cities. Nevertheless Exeter and the three adjacent towns of Plymouth, Devonport and East Stonehouse were large customers for locally produced food, and the huge number of holidaymakers added to local demands. Small farms everywhere were diversifying, and by 1914 many farmhouse dairies were producing cheese, butter and clotted cream for local sale to supplement family incomes. As a pre-war schoolboy in Topsham on the Exe estuary, Dick Pym remembered that animals were regularly driven down the main street to market, and the irresistible horror of peering through the cracks in the high gates of the local slaughterhouse.

Greater productivity also involved the efficient use of labour, however, and by 1914 the county's agricultural workforce had declined dramatically since 1870. Calculated at 1.8 for every 100 acres, it was well below the national average of 2.43. Wages were low. Pre-war advertisements offered a skilled adult labourer about 15*s* to 16*s* a week with a cottage and a garden, and boys aged fourteen to sixteen could expect around 7*s*.

Many advertisements sought men with the ability to handle horses, which in 1914 remained the major source of motive power on the county's farms and roads. Across Devon the 43,000 working horses provided mounts for business and pleasure, and for pulling the host of carriages, carts, wagons, ploughs, harrows and

A 1907 advertisement picturing a Tavistock District Laundry motor van. (Devon & Exeter Institution)

drills, and delivery vans, omnibuses and charabancs. They were often used to shunt single goods wagons in station sidings. Nevertheless the internal combustion engine was making an appearance, and by 1914 the first Devon motor haulage company was operating, along with forty-six motor engineering companies, forty-three garages, seven motor car proprietors, six builders, six repairers and five accessory companies. In his memoirs Earl Fortescue mentions that although Castle Hill, his mansion, had no telephone in 1914, he did possess a motor car.

Despite these changes, the structure of Devon farms remained little altered, with small family-worked enterprises dominating the landscape. In the 1790s William Marshall had observed that most farms were between 20 and 40 acres, with very few over 200 acres. In 1913 the situation had not changed greatly. There were 6,536 holdings of 20 acres or less, 6,150 between 21 and 100, 4,1781 between 101 and 300, and only 315 that were more than 300 acres. The typical Devon farming family had its farmhouse and yard surrounded by a series of small varyingly shaped fields, each a few acres in size and surrounded by a hedge. Occasionally the historical vagaries of ownership and tenancies, and perhaps local custom, led farmhouses to be integral components of large villages, such as in Broadhembury, Otterton and Ugborough, with their fields scattered in no particular pattern outside them.

GREAT HOUSES AND ESTATES

Beneath this traditional appearance, however, the ownership of the land was beginning a gradual revolution that would not reach its peak until after the war. In the 1870s most Devon farmers were tenants, with many of their holdings part of the vast estates, several well over 20,000 acres, owned by the Duke of Bedford, Earl Fortescue, the Earl of Devon, the Earl of Portsmouth, Sir Charles Dyke Acland, Lord Clinton, the Honourable Mark Rolle and the Duchy of Cornwall. It has been calculated that in mid-Victorian times over half the land in Devon was owned by just 198 families. By 1914 the sale of estates in part or in whole was beginning to enable an increasing number of farms to be owner-occupied, a process that was accelerated, as will be seen, during the First World War. A notable event occurred in 1911 when the Duke of Bedford sold up much of his estates in and around Tavistock, wherever possible to tenants. It was part of his policy of concentrating his holdings around Woburn and Endsleigh, but other factors prompted his action. The ownership of land was losing its political importance, and income from agriculture had fallen for a generation. On top of this, David Lloyd George, the pre-war Liberal Chancellor of the Exchequer, imposed a land tax, and threatened even more punitive measures in his populist campaign against the largely Conservative landed aristocracy. In June 1914 the last of a series of sales of the Earl of Portsmouth's Eggesford estate took place. There were eighty-four lots totalling 2,763 acres of small farms, cottages and woodland across the parishes of Wembworthy, Winkleigh, Coleridge, Chawleigh and Eggesford itself. Nearly all were sold to tenants, although no-one wanted Eggesford House – which had been abandoned in 1911.

Nevertheless a large house and plenty of land were still linked to significant social status and local authority. In 1907 a richly covered and copiously illustrated book was published, describing in deferential terms the nobility, gentry, senior army and naval officers, and grander clergy, gentlemen farmers and businessmen of Devon, together with their houses and estates. Nearly 450 major properties scattered across the countryside are featured. Most of their owners were Justices of the Peace, and the majority served on county, city or local councils, Boards of Guardians or the committees of charitable institutions or societies – such as the illustrious members of Countess Fortescue's Red Cross Committee mentioned earlier. Among the other dignitaries scattered across the county were Sir Charles Dyke Acland of Killerton House, Broadclyst, Charles Calmady-Hamlyn of Leawood, near Bridestowe, Miss Rosalie Chichester of Arlington Court, north Devon, Lord Clifford of Chudleigh at Ugbrooke, Lord Clinton of Bicton House, near Budleigh Salterton, and Heanton Satchville, near Petrockstowe, the Earl of Devon of Powderham Castle, George Lambert MP of Cofyns, Spreyton, Lord Leith of Fyvie of Lupton, Sir Henry Lopes of Maristow, Tamerton Foliot, the Earl of Morley of Saltram, near Plymouth, Sir Robert Newman of Mamhead Park, Starcross, Lord Poltimore of Poltimore House near Exeter and Court Hall, North Molton, and Colonel Hugh Acland Troyte of Hunstham Court.

Mamhead Park, Starcross, seat of Sir Robert Newman. (Author's collection)

There were a few impressive mansions, such as Earl Fortescue's Castle Hill and the Earl of Devon's Powderham Castle, although none were on the scale of palatial residences such as Blenheim in Oxfordshire, Castle Howard in Yorkshire or Hatfield House in Hertfordshire. A few more were Georgian creations or recreations, such as Saltram, Ugbrooke, Arlington and Killerton, but the great majority are better described as substantial Victorian country houses in rambling mock-Gothic style, complete with sizeable entrance halls, panelled reception rooms, cavernous kitchen suites, courtyard carriage and stable blocks, and walled kitchen gardens. Every approaching visitor would glimpse the house through an array of shrubs and trees, and admire the manicured lawns, terraces and parterres while attending garden parties. These houses were showpieces and reception centres ensuring the social standing of the owners, as well as mere places in which to live. Nearly all were characterised by pointed arch doorways and numerous bay windows, patterned brickwork, complicated roofs and skylines, carved gables and finials, and a host of tall chimneys.

In 1914 many of the families in these houses still dominated the communities in which they were situated. They owned much of the land and most of the cottages, employed a significant number of local people, held the right to nominate the local Anglican parson, and were benefactors of village schools, halls, charities and societies. Most people in most rural communities still acted deferentially towards the socially superior family in the 'big house' – whether it was through well-earned respect or the traditional due owed by the grateful or vulnerable worker to his powerful employer.

In Anne Acland's history of her family she records a cousin of Sir Thomas Dyke Acland (1842–1919), who succeeded as 12th baronet in 1898, being struck by his 'patriarchal appearance and attitude towards his tenants and lesser members of his family'. On Lady Day and at Michaelmas his tenants appeared dressed in their best to pay their rents, and those living on the Killerton estate were expected to attend the Sunday service in the family's Killerton chapel. Mrs Simcoe of Dunkeswell was a generous benefactor to the school and village, and with an accepted sense of social hierarchy her uniformed servants preceded her to church on Sundays; she expected to see her tenants and their families there too. About 300 people lived in Filleigh in north Devon. The great majority worked on Earl Fortescue's Castle Hill estate, including the head gardener, head gamekeeper, clerk of works, land steward, foreman carpenter and forester, or were Fortescue's tenant farmers and their employees. The earl was the sole landowner, and his family had built the village school, provided the library and appointed the rector.

In 1914 the ties of paternalism and patronage remained strong across Devon, if sometimes creating tension, and both the ties and the tensions were to play

The Heathcoat-Amory staghounds. (Devon & Exeter Institution)

their part in the county's response to war. One example stemmed from that classic event in the English countryside – the hunt. For many decades the Amory family's renowned pack of staghounds had hunted each Wednesday and Saturday in season, and scattered across the county there were twelve packs of foxhounds and ten packs of harriers. They provided employment, sporting enjoyment and popular spectacle, as well as signifying a major landowner's wealth and devotion to upper-class rural life. Nevertheless, even the traditional sights and sounds of the well-patronised stag and fox hunts were to come under critical scrutiny by 1916, being increasingly seen as the unfairly protected and unacceptably labour-intensive indulgence of the wealthy.

LIFE IN THE VILLAGE

Life for most villagers was hard, if not quite as hard as in earlier centuries; even in the early and middle years of the nineteenth century the yeomanry had been called out to control food rioters in several Devon country towns. Family cottages were usually built of cob, which is local subsoil mixed with straw and water and pressed into a sticky mass. The reputation of the county's rural homes was low. In 1913 Bampton's medical officer of health recorded that 'generally speaking, the buildings were very antiquated, with low walls, small windows and badly ventilated'. Many, he said, fell just short of condemnation. A typical cottage had two or three lime-washed rooms downstairs, one a store, which were divided by interior walls usually created from timber frames filled with reeds or lathes and plastered over. One or two upstairs rooms provided sleeping facilities. An open fire in the main room, or perhaps a small range, was used for cooking, heating and light. By 1914, though, paraffin wax candles were affordable and some families were aspiring to paraffin lamps, but the poorest still resorted to making spluttering rushlights. Some villages had piped water and cesspits, and even sewers, but most outlying cottages relied on springs or pumps and wells for water, and outside soil closets for toilets. Food included bread, salt fish, a little mutton, with luck some home-produced eggs and chicken, and eked-out portions of preserved ham, bacon and black or white pudding from the family pig, together with vegetables from the cottage garden. Tea was a treasured commodity, cider was a common drink and public houses plentiful. Lasting health and security were precarious. Much depended on the seasonal crops, the health of the animals and the strength of the cottagers, who had to work long hours, usually for six days a week.

Devon's villages might have seemed buried in the country, but *Kelly's Directory* for 1914 reveals that they contained many skills and services. King's Nympton lay 2½ miles from South Molton Road station (later renamed King's Nympton) on the GWR's Exeter to Barnstaple line, and 5 miles from South Molton itself. It had fewer than 500 inhabitants, but possessed a school, a post office with several collections and deliveries six days a week, an Anglican church and a United Methodist chapel. In the parish tradesmen included a bootmaker, butcher, carpenter, carrier, dairyman, draper and grocer, farmer and dealer in poultry, eggs, cream and butter, insurance agent and valuer, mason, watermiller, sawmiller, two publicans, shoemaker, general shopkeeper, tailor, thatcher and wheelwright. Sheepwash was even smaller, with just 284 inhabitants. It lay 5 miles from Hatherleigh, 10 miles from Great Torrington and 6 miles from Halwill and Beaworthy station on the

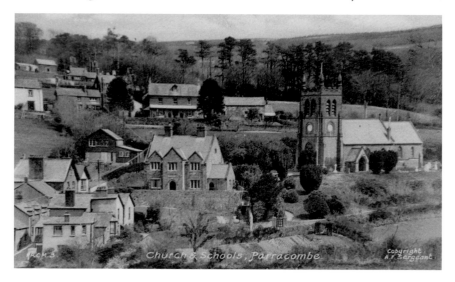

Parracombe, with its church and, in the centre, its school. (Author's collection)

LSWR line from Okehampton to Bude. Nevertheless, it had a post office, an elementary school, an Anglican church with a resident vicar, and Baptist and United Methodist chapels. The commercial addresses included several farmers, two shopkeepers, a grocer, butcher, publican, a shoemaker who doubled as the newsagent, a dressmaker, thatcher, corndealer, watermiller, two stonemasons, carpenter, wheelwright, cycle repairer, midwife and the sub-postmaster, who was also a blacksmith.

In 1916 the villagers in Butterleigh, a few miles south-east of Tiverton, were so incensed at being described as living in a 'one-eyed place' that they secured an article in the *South Molton Gazette*, which itemised the range of easily available services and facilities for the eighty-three inhabitants. They had, they pointed out, a church, a chapel, a day school, two Sunday schools, a post office with morning and evening deliveries, a shoemaker, a blacksmith, a dairy farm selling local produce, a dressmaker, a carpenter, a grocer's shop, three people who cut hair, two public houses, bread delivered five days a week, a pig-killer, a butcher who called twice a week, and a miller who delivered several types of flour to people's doors.

Villages also created their own enjoyment and engaged successfully in self-help initiatives. In 1913 the Exe valley village of Silverton, perhaps a partic-ularly active community, put on a flower show, several dances, a fete, a jumble sale to aid the local Nursing Association, a parade in support of the Royal Devon & Exeter Hospital, involving friendly societies, the Territorials and local Sunday schools, a horticultural show, a temperance fete, a harvest festival, and a carnival for the Exeter Eye Hospital. The village possessed a rifle club, choir, cricket club and a men's Bible class, and its debating society was prepared to tackle major contemporary themes including 'Compulsory Military Service', 'Abstinence', 'Female Suffrage', 'Tramps', 'Home Rule', 'We Live Too Fast', 'Collections for Olympic Games', 'The World is Not Growing Wise', and, poignantly, 'War is better now than in a few years' time'.

POPULATION AND OCCUPATION

The decennial censuses reveal the extent of change in the sizes of Devon's towns and villages, and also in employment across the county. Overall Devon's population growth was much below the national average throughout the nineteenth and early twentieth centuries. In 1801 it was the fourth largest county in population, but in 1901 it had dropped to fifteenth, primarily because the lack of coal meant that the main initiatives of the Industrial Revolution passed it by. Between 1801 and 1901 the population fell just short of doubling, to 662,196, whereas the rest of England and Wales grew three and a half times. Between 1901 and 1911 it rose by 5.7 per cent to 699,703, compared with 10.9 per cent nationally. Within that decade the populations of the urban and rural districts of Devon moved very little either up or down, with the notable exceptions of Newton Abbot, an expanding railway centre, Plympton St Mary, adjacent to expanding Plymouth, and the still developing coastal resorts of Exmouth, Paignton, Sidmouth, Teignmouth and Torquay. The three conjoined towns of Plymouth, Devonport and East Stonehouse – which were to amalgamate under the expanded Borough of Plymouth in 1914 – were the largest conurbation. Their combined totals were 193,171 in 1901, 208,430 by 1911 and 219,926 by 1921. The cathedral city of Exeter was much smaller. It grew from 54,217 in 1901 to 59,092 by 1911 but only to 59,582 by 1921, and that final figure included the Urban District of Heavitree which had been absorbed into the city in 1913. In both Plymouth and Exeter ribbons of standard pattern late Victorian and Edwardian terrace houses, some simple and plain fronted and some embellished with bay windows and a little fancy brickwork, had crept out along the approach roads away from the historic mix of grander houses, compact slums, assorted commercial sites and public buildings in their centres.

The fortunes of a number of Devon industries and trades were changing, and of course the availability of jobs significantly affected local populations. Succeeding censuses changed the way they grouped some prominent occupations, and this makes exact comparisons difficult, but nevertheless a number of trends can be discerned. The greatest rise occurred in the notable category 'Defence of the Realm', with 17,420 soldiers, sailors and marines stationed in Devon in 1901 and 26,913 in 1911. Other areas of employment were largely static. Domestic service, including the array of indoor and outdoor staff in houses, hotels and other hostelries, was the greatest employer, occupying 45,168 women and 7,204 men in 1901, and 45,374 women and 9,825 men in 1911. Agriculture was a close second, employing 40,597 men and 2,131 women in 1901, rising to 42,609 men and 5,055 women in 1911. In 1911 other major categories spread across the county were the 2,438 men and 15,720 women making and selling an array of clothing, and the 16,681 male and 9,496 female shopkeepers, innkeepers and their assistants. Again often found in rural areas, as well as in Plymouth and Exeter, were the 17,054 men and 197 women employed in a host of metalwork concerns in 1911, including blacksmiths, wheelwrights, turners and fitters, and shipwrights, boilermakers and ironfounders.

Transport was big business. The railways occupied 5,588 men and 24 women in 1911, and 6,751 men and 26 women were involved in road transport, most as stable-keepers, grooms, wagoners, carriers and horse bus drivers. As a sign

Trams and shops in Plymouth Old Town. (Author's collection)

of the times, though, the transport figures included 1,641 who were working with motor cars, lorries, vans, buses and trams. In 1911, 9,708 men worked on rivers, the sea or in dockyards as merchant seamen, harbour staff, warehousemen, coal heavers and bargemen, together with 79 women; most were telegraphists or telephone operators but a few women went to sea. Another 1,725 men were commercial fishermen. Coastal trade kept many small ports busy, such as Exmouth, Topsham, Exeter itself, Teignmouth, Dartmouth, Ilfracombe, Northam and Bideford, and of course Plymouth. In Exeter, for example, the first week of April 1914 saw six ships arrive with timber from Sweden, potatoes from Scotland, limestone from Berry Head and Babbacombe, and cement from London.

Other occupations had been in marked decline for decades. By 1911 the once thriving wool industry was holding onto several mills, but reduced to 494 men and 675 women, and lacemaking still occupied 357 men and 1,343 women, but machine production was fast replacing the traditional hand worked designs. Mining was a shadow of its former self, with the vast majority of the once prosperous copper, iron, silver, lead and manganese workings deserted. Just 559 men worked in them in 1901 and 163 in 1911. Quarrying for stone, slate and limestone (for burning in the numerous kilns to reduce the acidity in much of Devon's soil) remained comparatively buoyant, employing 1,353 people in 1911.

CHILDREN, SCHOOLS AND CONTROVERSIES

For many decades before the war social welfare issues, notably health and education, had been mired in long-standing financial and ideological controversies. During the nineteenth century there were marked advances, with legislation barring young children from industrial employment and ensuring they had a modest amount of what was termed elementary education. The fruits were to be seen in the host of barrack-like urban schools and church-like village schools across the county. Despite persistent opposition from those hostile to state intervention in people's lives, or who challenged the actual need for mass education, or criticised the cost, by 1899 all children up to the age of twelve had to attend school full-time, and by then elementary schooling was provided free of all charges.

Of course most families who could afford to do so sent their children to fee-paying private schools, grammar schools or even the expensive 'public' schools, where a superior education was assumed to be gained, and where there was no contact with a host of children from the working classes. There were great differences between the curriculum of the free elementary schools and the fee-paying ones. The latter could freely engage in the subjects and syllabuses thought appropriate by their proprietors or headteachers, and pander

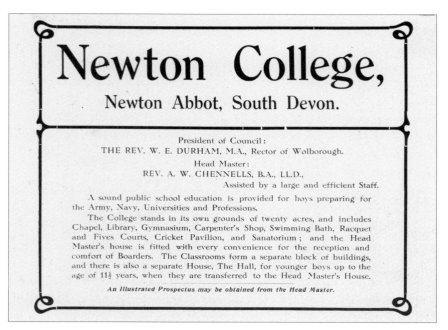

An advertisement for Newton College, Newton Abbot. (Devon & Exeter Institution)

to the reputation they sought to achieve and the degree of exclusivity their fee levels could maintain. Most, though, sought distinction by an emphasis upon the elevating influence of Latin and team games, with other key subjects being mathematics, English literature, English and Classical history, religious education, and perhaps some French and science. Equally important was the school's ability to secure for its leavers good social connections and careers.

Elementary schoolchildren were channelled down different routes. Many believed the highly disciplined teaching of basic reading, writing and arithmetic accompanied by regular religious instruction and a modicum of patriotic tales from English history to be an adequate means of training for the lower classes, who were expected to become the next generation of dutiful domestic staff, farm labourers and factory hands. By 1914, though, a significant number of elementary schools included laundry work, cookery and housewifery for girls, gardening and handwork for boys, and structured physical exercises for both. As always, arguments centred on balancing the cost of the extra facilities with the thought that children might be better prepared for their menial but essential roles. But there was also the consideration, attractive to some but anathema to others, that the wider training might inspire some children to seek out careers beyond the normal expectations of their social class. When a slightly wider

An urban double-decker elementary school building containing separate boys' and girls' schools: Heavitree, Exeter. (West Country Studies Library)

scattering of private and publicly funded scholarships became available in the early twentieth century to enable a few more of the ablest elementary pupils to transfer to the prestigious grammar schools at the age of eleven or twelve, the controversy over crossing the boundaries of social class intensified. The war brought all these social, educational and ideological tensions to the fore.

Elementary education was also a centre of religious controversy. Many schools had been founded throughout the Victorian era by either Anglican parishes or various Nonconformist congregations, or wealthy benefactors of each persuasion. The mutual hostility that had led so many places to possess rival churches and chapels had spilled over into the provision of competing Sunday schools, and sometimes day schools, in efforts to ensure that the rising generation adopted a particular version of the Christian faith. As the churches and chapels mentioned earlier in King's Nympton, Sheepwash and Butterleigh bear witness, Devon was no exception to this rivalry.

From 1870 another school provider entered the arena. Although the state had made grants since 1833 to Anglican and Nonconformist schools if they met specific standards, the controversial 1870 Education Act obliged localities without voluntarily funded schools to create School Boards, which would build and maintain wholly publicly funded schools. This secured state school places for many more children, while at the same time raising deep suspicions in church groups about the quality of religious education that went on in them. Another equally controversial Education Act in 1902 abolished the local School Boards, and made county and borough councils the local education authorities for all elementary schools, and bestowed upon them wider powers to maintain and expand secondary grammar schools. In matters of religious education and the maintenance of buildings, though, the voluntary schools retained significant powers.

All this was still new in 1914, and many issues remained in the melting pot. These included the educational facilities to be provided, the by-laws governing attendance and leaving school, and whether the school health service could offer free treatment. Every advance was controversial. For example, in 1911 Alderman John Stocker, chairman of Exeter Education Committee, proclaimed 'with delight … the fact that any poor boy could now work his way from the elementary schools to the great Universities', but the Archdeacon of Exeter believed the future 'had a very black cloud over it, for in many of the secondary schools now being built by public authorities there was practically no religious instruction at all'. Both were overstating their cases, as controversialists do. Very few secondary school scholarships were available, and the archdeacon was really bemoaning the lack of Church of England-biased teaching in the new secondary schools. The war did not halt the acrimony. In 1916 a Diocese of Exeter meeting applauded Sir Thomas Acland for arguing 'that there was practically no recognition of God or of religion whatever in the educational system of the country as far as the State was concerned'.

Another age-old issue lay largely hidden, however. The 1901 census for Devon shows that 2,245 boys and 1,054 girls aged between ten and fourteen were in full-time employment, most as farm labourers, indoor and outdoor domestic servants, textile workers, shop assistants, errand boys and street hawkers. The 1911 census does not itemise occupations, but records that 274 boys and 33 girls aged eleven to thirteen, and 993 boys and 409 girls aged between thirteen and fourteen were in full-time work. By-laws allowed children aged between thirteen and fourteen to leave school if they satisfied a combination of attendance regulations and academic standards, but one must suspect that many young children were working illegally. Early leaving, and also excessive hours of employment before and after school, were issues raised time and time again during the war, and certainly headteachers and school medical officers believed many parents and employers were ignoring the attendance laws with impunity.

Attendance rates varied widely between schools, and from week to week within each school. Logbooks show that each year most schools managed several periods lasting a few weeks when attendance was satisfactorily high (90 per cent or more), but many factors contributed to bringing these welcome periods to an abrupt end. By far the most dramatic were the frequent epidemics blighting schoolchildren's lives, sending attendance rates plummeting and closing schools – from rampant colds and coughs to mumps, chicken pox, impetigo and measles, and the frightening outbreaks of ringworm, scarlet fever and diphtheria. Diphtheria was, perhaps, the most feared contagious disease, but as one school medical officer wrote, ringworm 'is one of the most obstinate diseases, and, in spite of the assiduous application of ointments and lotions, will remain to depress the spirits of its victim, to make him taboo to his school fellows, spoil his education, worry his parents, and be the bête noir of the doctor'.

During bouts of foul weather attendances remained low for days, even weeks, at a time as footpaths and lanes became blocked with snow or were turned into quagmires. Many children did not possess waterproof shoes or coats, or a change of clothing to bring to school, and most village schools had no drying facilities beyond a single open fire or coke stove. When hay, corn, fruit and potatoes needed harvesting many older boys were absent, and so were girls when domestic emergencies cropped up, such as the illness of their mothers or younger siblings. And then there were the irresistible attractions of the circuses, shows and menageries that toured Devon, and the seaside and naval regattas, and the famous markets and fairs at Bampton, Barnstaple, Newton Abbot, Okehampton, South Molton and Tavistock. Numerous headteachers lamented the low attendances at these times. The great fairs combined numerous sideshows and entertainments with sales and auctions of farm animals and chattels, and local farmers often paid boys to help out at these events. The school medical officers and nurses offered their best advice, the school attendance officers tried to chase up the worst absentees, and school managers used up their 'special holiday' quotas when particularly exciting local events loomed large, but the war would make things far worse before they started to get better.

A number of orphaned or otherwise destitute boys were accommodated and trained at the British Seamen's Orphan Boys' Home in Brixham and also on the training ship *Mount Edgcumbe*, which was moored off Saltash. In 1907 St Boniface's Home for Boys had been established in Sampford Peverell by the Church of England Society for Waifs and Strays. A substantial orphanage for girls had existed in Plymouth since 1834. Other children were in the care of the county's Boards of Guardians. Many of these still lived in workhouses, but the 1911 census shows that 163 boys and 122 girls in Newton Abbot and Plymouth were accommodated in ten or so 'Scattered Homes'. These were large houses, rented or purchased, where children lived in relatively small groups under the care and control of wardens in an environment reminiscent of a house, and attended local schools, although still under the overall supervision of the Guardians. The 'Scattered Homes' concept was new, and the unproven novelty, with its additional financial and administrative burdens, was viewed with considerable suspicion by most other Devon Boards. Reactionary Exeter preferred to build a single large children's home in institutional style, which opened in 1913. The war was to highlight a number of workhouse scandals.

THE GROWTH OF HEALTH AND WELFARE INSTITUTIONS

In addition to the large hospitals in Plymouth and Exeter, and the smaller cottage hospitals in market towns, funded by benefactions, subscriptions and fees, determined voluntary efforts had led to the foundation of several institutions for the care and training of those whom contemporaries termed physical, mental and moral defectives. Public support and the favourable views of wealthy benefactors and local authorities who contributed towards the cost of inmates were important, and therefore reports by the institutions always argued that the benefits of incarceration in terms of physical and moral care were infinitely preferable to any alternative ways of life. Great emphasis was placed on the value-for-money training that kept the residents in a firmly secure environment away from the outside world and its temptations, and gave them useful manual work to undertake which often contributed to the running of the institution, and might, if all went very well, fit a few of them to become reasonably responsible members of society.

These foundations included the Devon County Lunatic Asylum in Exminster (1845) for adults, and the Western Counties Asylum in Starcross (1877) for boys and girls whose mental deficiency was moderate enough to suggest they were to some extent educable. The Lunatic Asylum had a troubled history. Nearly always overcrowded as families and workhouses became increasingly unwilling to care for troublesome and apparently incurable cases, the Asylum found it hard to find and keep satisfactory staff, and it was only from 1897 that any specialist training was given. Twice enlarged, by 1906 the Asylum had 1,352 inmates. Here, as in other crowded and difficult to manage institutions, infectious diseases spread alarmingly quickly. Yet so great was the demand for such institutions that as early as 1874 the city of Exeter had been obliged to build its own asylum at Digby, just outside the city.

Starcross admitted children as young as seven, and many of its 270 residents were 'paupers', dispatched by Boards of Guardians. A key feature of the regime was the inculcation of manual skills coupled with the moral qualities of patience, perseverance, self-discipline and self-fulfilment that contemporaries associated with this training. To the gratification of staff, governors and local authorities the end products of the carpentry, tailoring, basket making, brush

The Western Counties Institution at Starcross, near Exeter. (Author's collection)

making, shoemaking, wood carving, weaving, and gardening classes undertaken by the boys, and the dressmaking, knitting, lacemaking, and straw hat classes provided for the girls, contributed significantly to Starcross's finances. Typical of local attitudes was Dr J. Mitchell Clarke's lecture on heredity in Exeter in 1912 under the auspices of the National Union of Women Workers, in which he asserted that the 'feeble-minded' should be 'isolated in colonies where they could do no harm to anybody.' He lavished praise on Starcross, and criticised the existing and planned day schools for mentally defective pupils in Plymouth, Devonport, Exeter and Torquay for unduly prolonging the adverse influences of parents; such children should be permanently removed from their families. These asylums would not be immune from the pressures of war.

This was also true of the Devon House of Mercy for the Reception of Fallen Women in Bovey Tracey and the several homes organised by the Exeter Diocesan Association for the Care of Friendless Girls (St Olave's Trust). The alleged ease with which women of weak intelligence or promiscuous character in the lower classes were held to succumb to the temptations of sex and drink had aroused Victorians to create charitable institutions dedicated to restoring them to more respectable lives, through prayer, disciplined daily routines and training in useful skills. Although struggling financially, in 1914 the Exeter Diocesan Association supported several homes, one offering girls who seemed in danger of going astray training for domestic service, another offering temporary shelter in a Home of Refuge, and a third providing a home, again temporary, for those already 'fallen' into pregnancy. In most cases the babies were quickly boarded out. The women and girls came from their own, perhaps threatening or unwelcoming, homes, applied from off the streets, were sent by workhouse Guardians, or were recommended by magistrates who were offering an alternative to custodial sentences. Some girls made good, but some went on to the far stricter Devon and Exeter Industrial School and a few others continued a downward spiral, which led to prison. A similar charitable foundation, the Friendless Girls' Help Association, served Plymouth.

In a typical display of Victorian aristocratic and religious humanitarianism, the House of Mercy had opened in 1863 through the efforts of the Revd the Honourable Charles Courtenay, son of the 10th Earl of Devon, and vicar of Bovey Tracey, and his network of upper-class connections. Women entered the House of Mercy for many reasons. Most were aged between fifteen and twenty-one, although a few were younger. Usually it was on the recommendation of the police courts, the Exeter Diocesan Association or Boards of Guardians. The entrants were termed 'penitents', and stayed for up to two years. Some were single mothers, others were prostitutes or habitual drinkers or both.

The House of Mercy at Bovey Tracey. (Devon & Exeter Institution)

Some had been abused by family, erstwhile lovers or employers, and others had become thieves. Many were orphans or had been abandoned by parents. In the autumn of 1914, with so many families being disrupted and so many servicemen in local garrisons and ports, it was feared that many more women would become the moral casualties of war.

ISSUES IN THE TOWNS

The reports from Exeter's police court and city council give a flavour of contemporary issues and attitudes. Certainly antisocial behaviour was not new, but it was constantly challenged. In 1912 city councillors wrestled with various civil annoyances, and eventually passed by-laws banning the handcarts covered with assorted advertisements for shops and services that blocked the narrower streets, and making throwing bottles and broken glass, 'orange peels, banana skins or any other dangerous substances' onto the roads an offence. They backed down, though, from trying to ban the incessant shouting, ringing of bells, clanging of gongs and use of 'other noisey (*sic*) instruments' to attract customers. The apparent proliferation of hawkers with barrows and women with prams blocking pavements were other perennial nuisances, and in 1916 the city council came close to restricting the former to two traditional market areas and banning the latter from the High Street during the heart of some shopping days. The arguments of trade and commerce, though, overrode those of public convenience and safety. The increasing presence of motor vehicles was worrying too, with a never-ending string of court cases centred on inadequate lights, excessive speed and overturning on corners. Motor vehicles were wonders, but also widely feared. In January 1912, for example, one Exeter driver was convicted for driving recklessly at 14–16mph in and out of stationary carts. All these contentious issues suggest that the plethora of picture postcards of peaceful early twentieth-century high streets could be misleading.

Far more serious, though, were the numerous cases of drunkenness and violent behaviour on the streets and in the home. Detailed reports of child neglect cases appeared regularly, and the courts were often at a loss to decide whether to impose fines mellowed by offers of advice and support through local charities, or send one or both parents to prison and place the children in the care of a Board of Guardians. Sad stories surrounding the discovery of the bodies of newly born babies raised grave suspicions of infanticide. Although this was rarely proven conclusively in court, the intermittent

High Street, Exeter.
(Author's collection)

cases received huge newspaper coverage, and alongside the far more frequent child neglect cases heightened public fears for the physical and moral health of thousands of families living in poverty within the county, and especially in the crowded tenements of Exeter and Plymouth.

While many people in positions of influence accepted that welfare reforms were urgent, many also refused to accept that public funds, as opposed to charitable sources, should be used, and some denied the problems were as bad as they were made out to be. In 1913 Dr Stirk, Exeter's medical officer of health, presented to the city council an alarming report on the evils of the city's poor West Quarter, largely located in St John's Ward just a few minutes' walk from the Cathedral Close. He had found tenements with steep and dark staircases, little light or ventilation, and full of single rooms in which whole families lived by day and slept by night. Ceilings were falling down, damp and cracked walls had been unrepaired for years, and sanitary conditions were appalling. In the ensuing debate one councillor said that the city council had no authority over private landowners except in sanitation, and another believed that things were 'not so shockingly bad'. Eventually a more sympathetic member secured agreement for several colleagues to join him on a West Quarter tour. It was all to no avail. The group reluctantly agreed that a few tenements needed improving and that the landlords should be told, but bearing in mind that the population there had fallen from 978 in 1901 to 724 in 1911 and there had been no epidemics, except one of measles, for five years, they said no further action was needed – and nor was any taken. With, one suspects, a marked degree of cynical disbelief, a councillor retorted 'it was most satisfactory to hear that St John's Ward was as sweet and pure as any in the city'. It was, as the 1921 Census revealed, by far the most overcrowded ward in Devon, exceeding the poorest quarters of Plymouth, although they were more extensive and incited equally frustrating council debates. St John's Ward, Exeter, had a population density of 161.5 per acre in 1921. Several others in Exeter and especially Plymouth exceeded 100 per acre. In marked contrast, across Devon the Urban Districts averaged just 3.8 an acre, and the generally sparse Rural Districts were 0.2 an acre.

CONCLUSION

In 1914, therefore, Devon was in a state of flux. Within the last quarter of a century or so its farmers had changed ancient practices successfully in the face of a deep depression, its seaside resorts had achieved new prosperity with tens of thousands of visitors descending upon them each year, and the railways had linked most towns and many villages to markets and suppliers way beyond the locality. Although pockets of great poverty and distress still existed, a variety of social reforms were taking place in the teeth of bitter controversies between those advocating greater state intervention in people's lives and those convinced of the sufficiency of charitable support for the genuinely needy together with the safety blanket of the Poor Law administered by the Boards of Guardians. It is salutary to note that the 1911 census recorded as many as 2,238 men and boys and 1,762 women and girls in the care of Devon's Guardians. And throughout all these changes and controversies the greater and lesser houses of wealthy and influential families remained scattered surprisingly thickly across the landscape. Their owners still dominated their localities socially and economically, and occupied most positions of civil and military authority across the county.

The high summer of 1914 was like many summers before it, with final preparations being made for a host of popular events on and around the Bank Holiday, Monday 3 August. Advertisements were appearing for horse and pony shows at Bideford, Bratton Fleming, and Lynton, regattas at Appledore, Beer, Paignton and Seaton, horticultural shows at Bovey Tracey, Hartland, Heavitree, Moretonhampstead, Seaton and Shute, flower shows at Alphington, Braunton, Broadclyst, Chagford, Dawlish, Lustleigh and North Tawton, and sports days at Clyst Honiton, Manaton, Okehampton, Sandford and Whimple. There was beautiful weather for everything held the week before Bank Holiday, and on

Schoolchildren coming ashore after visiting the battleships moored off Ilfracombe, July 1914. (Ilfracombe Museum)

29 July the aviator Marcus Manton enthralled crowds outside Exeter with his aerobatics. On 3 August, though, the skies were as ominous as the European news, and the following day heavy showers combined with the announcement of the British ultimatum to Germany to dampen the remaining summer festivities, and signal the end of most of them.

As the news of the outbreak of war filtered through east Devon, Stoodleigh Court was hosting the annual cricket match against its near neighbour, Knightshayes Court. The players were a mix of aristocratic family members – the Money-Coutts of Stoodleigh and the Heathcoat-Amorys of Knightshayes – and their estate workers. As the match ended Hugh Burdett Money-Coutts brought out glasses of their best champagne for the teams. With dark humour, and more truth than he could possibly know, he toasted that as they might not be alive to celebrate the war's end they had better enjoy it now.

CHAPTER TWO

GOING TO WAR

Joining up, life in uniform, facing the enemy

THE CALL TO ARMS

News of the imminent prospect of war reached the village of Broadclyst in east Devon on the evening of Sunday 2 August 1914. Ruth Whitaker, the young daughter of the local vicar, was attending evensong in the parish church when she noticed the verger looking at his daughter, who had appeared in the open doorway with a piece of paper in her hand. He was a Naval Reservist, and a telegram had arrived. 'He got up noiselessly,' she recalled, 'hung his cassock on its peg in the tower vestry, and left. By the time we came out he was on his way to the depot in Exeter.'

Throughout Devon thousands of others with military and naval training received similar calls. In Plymouth Royal Marine buglers marched briskly through the city's streets sounding the recall. In Silverton Charles Saunders, a National Reservist, was married on 29 July, received a telegram on 2 August, and left to join his regiment the following day. Excursion trains were cancelled and ordinary timetables abandoned as the sudden movements of troops, horses, wagons and equipment intensified. On Bank Holiday Monday holidaymakers at South Molton station wanting a day at the seaside were told, 'We will take you there but we cannot guarantee to bring you back.' In Exmouth the 'usual gaiety was almost entirely absent', with people asking each other for information; in Exeter and Plymouth crowds waited anxiously outside the *Gazette* and *Western Herald* offices for the latest news. In Ilfracombe 1,000 people attended a Bank Holiday concert in Victoria Pavilion. After the National Anthem the audience responded with cheers and boos when someone called out 'Three Cheers for Old England' and 'Down with Germany'. The following day many visitors curtailed their holidays and returned home.

In Crediton a gentleman-farmer's son, the future Captain Gamblen, saw the recall notice pinned to the post office door on Sunday, and while playing a Bank Holiday cricket match he glanced up at several trains with military equipment steaming south from north Devon. A week later, on Monday 10 August, Crediton's Market Street was full of horses, wagons and harnesses requisitioned from local farmers by the army. The farmers had been badly inconvenienced at a particularly busy time of the year, but few protested. Butchers in Kingsbridge issued a public notice that deliveries would stop as they had lost all their horses, and no doubt similar disruptions to routine were experienced across the county. It was not 'Business as Usual' as some tried to proclaim.

As the British Government had feared, on 3 August Germany declared war on France and its armies immediately invaded Belgium and Luxembourg on their way through to Paris and their planned swift victory. On the morning of 4 August the British Government, a guarantor of Belgian neutrality and always extremely wary of who controlled the Low Countries, sent an ultimatum to Germany to evacuate that country; by eleven o'clock in the evening there had been no reply, and by midnight Britain was at war. A frighteningly quick sequence of events had led to this final failure of diplomacy. The assassination of Grand Duke Franz Ferdinand, the heir to the Austro-Hungarian crown, in the Bosnian capital of Sarajevo on 28 June 1914 had gone largely unnoticed in British newspapers, but it brought to a head the swirling tensions following decades of territorial disputes, commercial rivalry and rampant nationalism

The interior of the Pavilion, Ilfracombe. (Author's collection)

The army purchasing horses at Kingsbridge, 1914. (Cookworthy Museum)

between the European nations. Austria-Hungary, with some justification, saw a Serbian plot behind the killing, aimed at destabilising the Balkan provinces in its ramshackle empire, and duly invaded Serbia despite Russia's opposition to such Austro-Hungarian advances in this region. Germany supported its ally Austria-Hungary, and declared war on Russia when the tsar refused to stop mobilisation. As France made loud warlike noises in support of its ally Russia, Germany declared war on France. Its immediate onslaught westwards was based on the fact that Russian mobilisation would be a long-winded affair, giving Germany time for a quick knock-out blow to France before it faced its eastern enemy. It was Germany's failure to achieve this decisive blow that led to the four and a half years brutal and bloody slogging match.

As the news of war spread through Devon, the *Torquay Times* claimed 'the great tension of uncertainty was relieved' and 'pent up feelings were let loose in expressions of loyalty and patriotism'. The promoters of late summer galas and fetes scrapped their plans, steamer companies received notices that their pleasure boats were requisitioned for naval use, and Anglican and non-conformist clergy lamented the failure of the their fervent petitions to the government to avoid war.

Over the August Bank Holiday the Devon and Cornwall Territorials continued their training in indifferent weather on Woodbury Common. Two days later they broke camp, marched to Exeter St David's station accompanied by numerous steam lorries and lumbering horse wagons, many requisitioned from local breweries, and amid cheering crowds boarded trains for Plymouth and garrison duty along the coast. Earl Fortescue recalled the men's uncomfortable night in the train, the lack of breakfast in Plymouth, and the long, hot, dusty marches to outlying fortresses, and blamed the incompetence of officers. The diary of Private May in the Devonshire Regiment reveals the importance soldiers attached to food and drink. When he arrived at Exeter's Queen Street Station from Topsham Barracks he was given lemonade, a sandwich, an apple and a packet of Woodbine cigarettes, at Salisbury he got tea, and at Larkhill Camp that evening he enjoyed bread, cheese and more tea.

Within a couple of days the Brixham trawlers in dock were deprived of one, two or three crew members when the 140 Royal Naval Reservists there were ordered to Devonport; those at sea followed immediately on their return to port. In Paignton the Royal Naval Reservists and Territorials left employers and families and marched to the station, with bands playing and crowds cheering, and accompanied by many requisitioned horses and 'two trade motor cars belonging to Messrs Deller's Ltd.'. A few days later the town witnessed the stirring sight of the officers and men of the 2nd Devon Artillery Battery assembling in the station concourse and eventually leaving for Salisbury Plain, with four guns, eight ammunition wagons, several general service wagons and 131 horses.

Departures were invariably prolonged when mountains of equipment and dozens of horses had to be loaded onto the trains. Barnstaple, Torrington and South Molton became hives of activity as the local squadrons of the Royal North Devon Hussars gathered, drilled and exercised, and a few days later joined up as a complete regiment at Barnstaple Junction station; they took a whole day to fill two complete trains, amid cheering crowds, patriotic music and tearful family farewells. The squires and gentlemen-farmers of north Devon had provided most of the officers and men, all the horses and many of the wagons. 'Mother, sister, sweetheart, father, brother, friend – all were there,' enthused the *South Molton Gazette*. 'Without exception the men were fine specimens of British manhood, strong, active, alert, and only too eager to place their services at the disposal of their country.'

In Ilfracombe crowds gathered on Capstone Hill to watch the signals passing between ships and the coastguard station, and successive groups of Reservists and Territorials were cheered to the station after processions, parades, speeches and church services in the town. On Sunday 9 August C Squadron of the Royal 1st Devon Yeomanry under Major Harold St Maur attended Totnes parish church. The hymns were 'Onward, Christian soldiers' and 'Soldiers of Christ, arise', and the lesson centred on the sentence 'And I heard the voice of the Lord saying: Whom shall I send and who will go for us? And I said: Here am I, send me.' The vicar assured his congregation that

Royal Naval Barracks, Devonport. (Author's collection)

Territorials departing from Kingsbridge station, 1914. (Cookworthy Museum)

the war had been forced upon the nation, the cause was just, and God would provide them with the necessary courage to win through whatever the difficulties. Like many clergy, he saw the most successful soldier as the purest one. 'The bravest soldier and the strongest upholder of right,' he concluded, 'was likely to be he who kept his body in temperance, soberness and chastity and who entered the conflict with the consciousness of sins forgiven.'

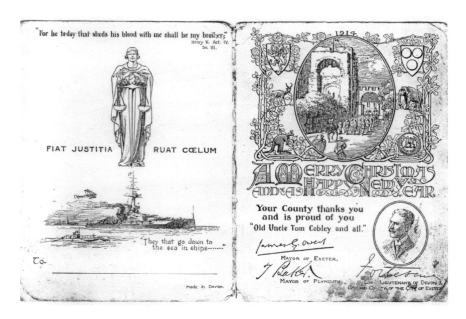

"For he to-day that sheds his blood with me shall be my brother."
Henry V. Act. IV.
Sc. III.

FIAT JUSTITIA   RUAT CŒLUM

"They that go down to the sea in ships......"

To

Made in Devon.

1914

A MERRY CHRISTMAS AND A HAPPY NEW YEAR

Your County thanks you
and is proud of you
"Old Uncle Tom Cobley and all."

James G. Owen
MAYOR OF EXETER.

J Baker
MAYOR OF PLYMOUTH.

Fortescue
LORD LIEUTENANT OF DEVON &
CITY AND COUNTY OF THE CITY OF EXETER

The Christmas card and message sent to locally recruited soldiers and sailors by the mayors of Exeter and Plymouth, and Earl Fortescue, the Lord Lieutenant. (Topsham Museum)

Early in October Territorial battalions departed for India. Tearful final farewells took place when the troop train called at Newton Abbot for the local contingent, and, the *Mid Devon & Newton Times* noted, 'proud smiles mingled with tears, and clenched hands helped to restrain quivering lips'. They steamed out to 'a continuous round of cheering and the waving of hands and handkerchiefs'. One soldier wrote to his old school in Ilfracombe, and another to his wife in Barnstaple, in wonderment at Port Suez and the sight of hundreds of Arabs covered in black dust recoaling the ships, children diving into the sea for coins thrown by the troops, the swarm of small boats selling strange food and souvenirs, the colours, smells and bustle of markets, the presence of British and French battleships, and the strange sensation of passing through the Suez canal with the desert so close each side. They arrived in Bombay on 10 November, and were sent to garrisons among the northern Indian tribes to deal with any signs of rebellion, possibly stirred up by German agents.

The recruiting rallies

On 7 August Lord Kitchener, the Secretary of State for War, called for 100,000 more men to create a 'New Army'. Despite the high numbers in Devon's Territorials, Fortescue asked local mayors to stimulate more recruiting and to identify reliable recruiting contacts in each parish.

Tiverton's mayor, Alfred Gregory, was enthusiastic, and so was the Heathcoat-Amory family whose textile mill was the town's main employer. At a mass meeting Gregory asserted that the Germans might land from airships nearby, and 'I should like to feel there are a dozen Englishmen here who know how to shoot them'. Immediately after the meeting forty men joined the Territorials, another forty the National Reserve, sixty-four the Civic Guard and twenty-six volunteered as dispatch riders. Their training began the following day.

In Torquay several recruiting processions wound from different parts of the borough to assemble in Princess Gardens. The speeches were typically hard-hitting. To repeated cheers, Captain Phillpotts spoke of the jealous Kaiser's 'dastardly' attack upon the liberty, integrity and prosperity of the British Empire, Admiral Sir William Acland warned that given the chance Germany would ravage Britain as it had brave Belgium, and the Revd J.T. Jacob, vicar of Torre, stated that 'those who had not taken their share of service would be branded as cowards, and would deserve the appellation'. P.J. Hanson, secretary of the Navy League, concluded with the fiery message that 'the British Empire was responsible for the continuance of liberty in almost every small community, and the progress of every quasi-civilized community in the world', and therefore all Britons 'should regard it as the greatest privilege of their lives to be allowed to stand up for the security and continued happiness of their country'. The twenty-six recruits were heartily cheered, and they brought the week's intensive drive there to over a hundred.

In Crediton an early recruiting rally was a huge event. Union Jacks, streamers and bunting adorned shops and houses; and a procession was headed by the Exonia Band from Exeter, followed by forty members of the Crediton National Reserve, forty members of the Crediton VAD, the town's fire brigade and its friendly societies, with the town band bringing up the rear. Thirty-eight recruits were secured, and whisked off for medical examination.

The early autumn saw a multitude of similar events across the county. Prominent among the speakers were the local aristocracy and squirearchy, chairmen of local councils, parish clergy and local military figures, often retired. In Ottery St Mary the stage party included Lord Coleridge, Sir John Kennaway, Sir Ernest Satow and Colonel Western, and in Holsworthy three Members of Parliament – Waldorf Astor, Sir John Spear and Christopher Addison – spoke at the same meeting. The Plymouth Recruiting Committee arranged for Waldorf Astor and Arthur Shirley Benn, the city's MPs, to address audiences during the intervals in Plymouth Argyle football matches and during entertainments at the Theatre Royal, Palace Theatre and Cinedrome.

Recruiting rallies were planned as dramatic occasions. Great banners were emblazoned with slogans such as 'Duty, Duty, Duty – Do It Now', 'Why Don't You Go?' and 'Our Brothers Are Calling For You'. Colourful and noisy processions headed by local bands incorporated as many local groups as possible to attract crowds. Once people had assembled, the mass singing of patriotic songs and the National Anthem stirred the emotions, after which speakers used the dire threats posed by a brutal aggressor, the patient suffering of innocent Belgians, the nobility of the British cause and the long line of British military and naval heroes to appeal to the honour and manliness of young men. The barbarism of Germany was invariably contrasted with Britain's Imperial altruism and sense of fair play. H.E. Duke, Exeter's MP, spoke in Exmouth of the inherent peacefulness of the British people and their love of liberty, but asserted that everyone recognised 'the present conflict was one of men against barbarians, a conflict of manhood and humanity against savagery, a conflict of liberty against military despotism'. Using a ploy most speakers resorted to, he trusted that Exmouth's men would come forward as freely as those from other local places he had addressed. In Exeter, Duke spoke scathingly of Germany's nineteenth-century record of brutality against Denmark, Austria and France as it established its dominance over central Europe, and its desire to destroy the British Empire. 'So long as there was a power guided by men whose inspiration seemed to come from hell,' he thundered, 'no State in Europe was safe.' In Bideford he worked the crowd into a frenzy with rhetorical questions such as, 'Was there a man in Bideford who was ready to be cuffed, hustled and spat upon by a Prussian drill sergeant? (Loud "No's") and Were they afraid (Many "No's"). Their fathers never were (Loud cheers). Please God, we never would be; and for his part, he would sooner see this kingdom of ours extinguished than see the curse of Germanism rampant here. Well, men of Bideford, are you of the same mind? ("Yes").' 'Amid a hurricane of cheering' forty recruits came forward.

At a Barnstaple rally on 11 September, Lord Fortescue publicised to rousing cheers the recruiting figures to date. The 1st and 2nd Battalions of the Devons had risen from 1,500 to 2,000 between them, the 3rd Devons from 400 to 2,000 and the new 8th Devons – recently permitted to call itself General Buller's Own complete with a bulldog mascot given by his daughter, Miss Georgiana Buller – was 1,100 strong. The next battalion, the 9th Devons, was at a similar strength, and soon a 10th would be created. The Territorials were at their establishment strength of 6,700 men, and they were all volunteers for overseas service. Reserve Territorial battalions would now be formed to match each one of those going abroad.

Georgiana Buller in later life. (*Journal of Bone & Joint Surgery*, Vol.35B.4, November 1953)

Some national figures in the trades union and suffragette movements supported the war, despite their earlier, often anti-government, agitation for reform. They urged enlistment with their own particular arguments. Speaking to an appreciative audience of Trade Unionist, Labour, Socialist and Co-operative associations in Plymouth in November 1914, Ben Tillett, leader of the vast National Transport Workers' Federation, asserted that he supported the war wholeheartedly, and emphasised that the working classes made up twenty-five out of every twenty-six men fighting it. Be watchful, he warned, as it was beholden to the State that wartime family allowances were generous, and social reforms should be similarly generous once victory was achieved. The same month saw Mrs Pankhurst in Exeter, speaking equally fervently in

Volunteers parade at Seaton before leaving for training, 1914. (Axe Valley Museum)

support of the war. She turned a key anti-suffragette argument on its head, saying, 'She had often been told that women should not have the vote because they had not to fight. And now the men were in the dock; the women were the jury and the judges, and were waiting to see how they were going to fight for them.' She said she could not understand why so many men were holding back when the new family allowances meant womenfolk could fill the men's jobs as well as run their homes. It was a facile argument, much like the vicar of Torre's cry that 'You can go to fight for your country comforted by the knowledge that your wives and families will receive loving care.'

Never enough men

For all the effort there were insufficient recruits. Such patriotic tales as the Exeter lad who was rejected as too short but stuffed his boots with newspaper before successfully applying again belied the truth that not everyone was rushing to the recruiting offices. In early September the editor of *Trewman's Flying Post* sourly claimed that 'There are some Little Englanders in Topsham who from fear of losing their work or of saving their lives still hold aloof from doing their duty to the Old Country.' In mid-October Holsworthy Urban District Council admitted 'with shame and regret' that the eighty-three volunteers from across the whole district represented only 3½ per cent of the local population and was the poorest response in the county. These percentages were the accepted measure of judgement for each locality's efforts, despite the fact they included the whole population, not just the number of eligible men, and they ignored the number who might be in the navy or regular army.

In October Kitchener sought another 100,000 men. Great efforts were made. A notable example was the Reserve Regiment of the 1st Devon Yeomanry billeted in Teignmouth. This increased its numbers by seventy-five in October, with many more expected, largely as a result of its determined integration with the townsfolk, including colourful public parades, well-publicised route marches and dutiful attendances at church services. By mid-November Southern Command estimated that Devon had contributed 4,414 men to Kitchener's New Army, but it represented just 0.62 per cent of the

Farewell card from Topsham.
(Topsham Museum)

population, way below Birmingham's 3.35 and Warwick's 4.07 and even lower than Dorset's 1.44 and Somerset's 0.82, although higher than Worcester's 0.51 and Cornwall's 0.28.

As early as 11 December the *Western Times* acknowledged that the rallies were failing. On four nights that week there had been military processions and rallies watched by cheering crowds in Exeter, but 'fewer than a score of volunteers have come forward'. The newspaper made great play of the alacrity with which it claimed Elizabethan Exonians had rallied to the beat of Sir Francis Drake's drum as the Spanish Armada approached. It highlighted, too, the poignancy of the 'Will they never come?' tableau in the Hippodrome, showing a British soldier, rifle in hand, standing over a wounded comrade and looking in the direction of England's southern shore. Speakers at rallies became more cynical. At one, Lieutenant the Hon. Lionel Walrond, the young MP for Tiverton, said 'he rather fancied that there were in this county some citizens who thought they were doing their duty to themselves and their country if they spent a shilling in cheering a faked war picture at a cinema palace or stood a soldier back from the front to a drink'. Devon was lagging behind, and 'every eligible man who had done nothing would be branded by women and children as a coward, a man shunned by patriotic men as a leper'.

Burdening men with potential shame, rather than filling them with immediate pride, became a common thread in rallies as winter approached.

Lord Fortescue did not mince his words at a cross-party planning meeting in Exeter at the end of November. Kitchener now needed a million men. This represented 6 per cent of the population, and 40,000 men from Devon. Only 10–12,000 had enlisted so far from the estimated 50,000 fit men aged eighteen to thirty-five available across the county. He intimated that farmers were stopping their sons enlisting, and hoped that non-conformists had got over their pacifism. Despite some demurring at his frankness, the meeting agreed to intensify recruitment through the creation of a Joint Parliamentary Recruiting Committee (PRC) for Devon, affiliated to the national body of the same name. Historian David Stevenson states that 2.4 million volunteers came from across the United Kingdom, and he confirms that the poorest responses came from the southern English and Irish agricultural counties.

With maximum publicity in newspapers and through numerous local meetings, several divisional PRCs were set up, each creating smaller district organisations within it. Fortescue addressed each divisional meeting, bluntly emphasising 'that Devon had not distinguished itself in the matter of recruiting' and pointedly criticising local figures. He cautioned members 'against stories which were circulated about the treatment of recruits as regarded food and accommodation', and urged them to encourage women to take up men's jobs. Women should be instructed, he added, to favour shops where they are served by women, not men. In March 1915 he went so far as to publicise figures from thirty mid-Devon parishes, showing widely varying recruitment rates from Widecombe's lowly 3.0 per cent, Throwleigh's 3.2 per cent and Buckland-in-the-Moor's 3.7 per cent to Kingskerswell's welcome 9.5 per cent, Moretonhampstead's 10.1 per cent and Chudleigh's 11.9 per cent. And all the time the newspapers listed the casualty figures.

THE 1915 RECRUITING MARCHES

Recruitment intensified, and advertisements and speakers aimed highly personal messages at every man. There was the famous picture of a grim Lord Kitchener pointing his finger at the reader and saying 'Your Country Needs You'. Another advertisement prominent in Devon was solemnly entitled 'An Englishman's Catechism' and brought the empire, royalty, the nation's heritage and family honour to bear in four challenging questions:

WHO made this little Island the greatest and most powerful Empire the world has ever seen?

Our Forefathers

WHO ruled this Empire with such wisdom and sympathy that every part of it – of whatever race or origin – has rallied to it in its hour of need?

Our Fathers

WHO will stand up to preserve this great and glorious heritage?

We will

WHO will remember us with pride and exultation and thankfulness if we do our duty to-day?

Our Children

> Justify the faith of your fathers, and earn
> the gratitude of your children
> **ENLIST TO-DAY**
> **GOD SAVE THE KING**

Its sequel, issued a few weeks later, was a hard-hitting attempt at self-reflection.

5 Questions to Men who Have <u>Not</u> Enlisted

1. If you are physically fit and between 19 and 38 years of age, are you really satisfied with what you are doing today?
2. Do you feel happy as you walk along the streets and see <u>other</u> men wearing the King's uniform?
3. What will you say in years to come when people ask you – 'where did <u>you</u> serve in the great War?'
4. What will you answer when your children grow up, and say – 'Father, why weren't you a soldier, too?'
5. What would happen to the Empire if every man stayed at home <u>like you</u>?

Your King and Country Need You
ENLIST TO-DAY!

Throughout 1915 Devon's PRC organised a series of week-long recruitment marches across wide stretches of the county. The twenty-five or so troopers and their bands, led by two lieutenants and a sergeant major, came from the 3rd Devonshire Regiment; most were wounded men almost ready to return to active service. Each day they covered 20 to 30 miles, and visited half a dozen villages and towns. They were not really marches, as the soldiers used the local

A recruiting party marches into Ilfracombe, 31 May 1915. (Ilfracombe Museum)

railways and patriotically decorated cars and wagons lent by local well-wishers to travel much of the distance between the advertised rallies. Unless the venues were within a few miles of each other, they actually marched from just outside the village or town to the advertised assembly point, with their band playing, before the speakers held forth. Although local dignitaries sometimes addressed the assemblies, far greater reliance was placed upon the virtuoso performances of the PRC's specially selected speakers, mainly experienced parliamentarians. Asked well in advance to provide colourful venues and to drum up audiences, local clergy, retired army officers and councillors were usually conspicuous on the public platforms, and the family at the 'big house' often provided copious refreshments and stop-over facilities for the soldiers. In many places schools broke off their lessons so the children could greet the troops, add their voices to the songs and fill out the crowds.

The marches were efficiently organised, but the effusive welcomes in many villages were usually limited to clergy, councillors, children and the families in the big houses. With the exception of a few large market towns, the audiences were modest, receptions subdued and hostility not uncommon; and overall the number of recruits, maybe four to five hundred, was hardly commensurate with the organisational effort and Lord Fortescue's assumed shortfall. The PRC provided the officers and speakers with details of each locality's population and recruitment figures to date. They did not hesitate to use them to praise past efforts and also to assert, sometimes to the disappointment of complacent platform parties, that they were not enough.

In January 1915 the recruiting parties visited villages around South Molton, in February those in far west Devon, in May mid-Devon and Torquay, in June north Devon and the south-east coast, in July villages surrounding Tiverton, in September the south-west coast, and in November the north coast. Newspaper reporters accompanied each march, and while noting the enthusiasm of the soldiers, speakers and schoolchildren, they expressed scornful dismay that so many young men were impervious to the appeals.

Sometimes mothers and girlfriends were blamed. At South Molton the mayor bluntly asserted that mothers who refused to let their sons enlist were doing their best to brand them as cowards, and told young women to tell their suitors they had a 'little job across the water you want done' before they returned to a place in their affections. Women's actions could prove counterproductive in other ways. At Sidmouth, as often elsewhere, once the speakers had finished a few women 'called the fellows who were hanging back a lot of cowards. Then the fat was in the fire. High words started, and some of the striplings proved the truth of the statement by hustling them.' The opportunity was lost: 'once insulted, the men would never volunteer', lamented the *Western Times*. The officers were particularly disgusted at some men coming forward 'to gain a cheap reputation for gallantry' and then insisting on a regiment they knew was up to strength.

On occasion the soldiers grew exasperated. During a west Devon tour one youth spoken to replied, 'I will go when they fetch me, and not before,' adding with a smirk, 'I bain't a fool like you.' Near Witheridge, 'at one cottage the frightened face of a young man could be seen peering from the window. Could it be that he was afraid to come out and face the music? Whatever the reason for remaining indoors, he did not escape without notice. He was spotted by "Tommy's" keen eyes, and the remarks passed must have made his ears tingle.' At Copplestone a group of unwilling youths had a 'bad quarter of an hour' with the soldiers who confronted them. At last an angry trooper presented one with a white feather, saying 'Here, this is what you want. Get home to mother.' At Colebrook a surly railwayman was told he needed a petticoat. The recently promoted Sergeant Thomas Rendle VC was an enthusiastic recruiter, and always enjoyed rounds of cheers. Nevertheless his rough banter with those impervious to his approaches, and his assertion that compulsion was the only way to deal with shirkers, were not always well received – and even resulted in correspondence in the *Torquay Times* objecting to his authoritarian 'Prussianism'. Occasionally the very lavishness of country house receptions soured the marchers. When Mrs Acland Troyte entertained them almost royally at Huntsham Court, a touring speaker could not help comparing it with the desperate situation at the Western Front, not so far away.

Often farmers were blamed. A Huntsham farmer told soldiers they were not welcome on his property, and a soldier retorted 'why should anyone fight for you slackers?' Unabashed, the farmer asserted he should be back in the trenches, not 'mucking about' here, adding, 'I don't care a ———— if the Germans do come.' At Bradninch a man called out, 'Us'll go when the varmer's sons go,' and soon afterwards Lieutenant Larder was moved to say in nearby Tiverton that 'The farmers are a rotten lot up here and I'm sorry to say they are just as rotten in East Devon.'

Perhaps some places should not have been visited. Not surprisingly, in Brixham 'the waiting crowd was not lavish with tumultuous cheering': 14 per cent of the population was already on war service, many in minesweepers and 250 in the dockyards. Buckfastleigh was also a special case, with its mills at full stretch producing khaki cloth.

A concluding, and of course partisan, comment on one tour probably summarises all of them: 'despite all the kindness of the villagers and all their genuine enthusiasm and desire to help recruiting, there will always remain a nasty taste as a result of last week'. The 'shirkers' angered many, but solutions short of conscription were difficult to find. At meetings of Torquay and Exeter employers, questions were raised about unmarried men rather than married ones being targeted for enlistment, and about the ability of women to replace male employers in commercial posts, but the discussions went round and round rather than reaching common agreement. The Devon Farmers' Union bitterly resented the accusations that farmers were stopping their sons enlisting, counter-attacking urban employers for protecting their male staff, and everybody else for misunderstanding the complexities of agricultural production and overestimating the capacity of women for arduous farmwork. Throughout 1915 Plymouth held numerous rallies with modest success, but there was a lingering undercurrent of resentment felt by those risking hardship and death in uniform towards the dockyard workers, and, conversely, muttered comments around the city by those asserting that this was a capitalist not a socialist war, and therefore no concern of theirs.

One patriotic incident completely masked a sad by-product of the war. In September 1915 the entrance gates of the Devon County Asylum in Exminster were specially decorated and the staff enthusiastically cheered a recruiting party as it marched past to a civic reception in Exeter. The mood, though, was far less cheerful inside the Asylum, caused partly by the unrestricted approach to volunteering. By December 1914 forty-seven staff had enlisted, and the number eventually rose to eighty-seven. Many of their replacements were old or inexperienced, and the institution became crowded with 140 extra inmates from Bristol Asylum, which was converted into a war hospital. Rations were reduced too, and the mortality rate rose alarmingly. Between 1915 and 1918, 944 inmates died, an annual average of 236 – a hundred more than the average between 1910 and 1913.

Letters home

From August onwards towns and villages were assailed with information about the war not only from impassioned speeches at rallies but also from sermons in churches and chapels, letters arriving home from relatives and reports of events in newspapers. All the sources were partisan, as one would expect, and accumulatively they create images of great bravery, stoic endurance and abiding black humour, underpinned by an undying conviction that the British occupied the high moral ground. It is only the letters, though, that add the first-hand description of life in the armed forces, the surreal existence in the trenches, the noise and confusion of battle, the arbitrariness of death, the hideousness of wounds, and the desolation of communities in the path of the German army.

In September a member of the Royal Army Medical Corps (RAMC) wrote ominously to his brother in Newton Abbot: 'we are waiting for the word to advance to collect the wounded. We do this in turn, and one lot will be just coming back. The roar of the guns is terrific. Just fancy, as I scribble this brave men are losing their lives and others are being frightfully maimed.' In mid-October Corporal Abbot, Royal Engineers, wrote to his wife in Ilfracombe: 'This is the 17th day of this great battle, and there appears to be very little change, only the Germans have been driven back in several places with heavy loss, and you can see dead Germans lying about everywhere, and often we have been working among them.' One day, he added, 'I was lying beside one of our wagons and it got hit in several places, but I did not get touched.' At the same time Corporal Dyer, 2nd Cavalry Division, wrote to his brother in Torquay: 'I tell you it has made my heart bleed more than once. Fancy, seeing pieces of men's bodies lying about in all directions, and other poor fellows groaning all around you.'

In December the parents of Private Bentley Moore in Totnes eventually received his letter graphically describing his experiences in the London Scottish Regiment during the Battle of Messines, in October:

> It is like a huge nightmare from beginning to end, shelling you all day long in the trenches, with Maxim and rifle fire, and then at night it starts again, and very often with an attack that means bayonet work. You can hear the shells coming, but where they are going to drop you never know. On the night we made the famous charge we lay on an open field with the Germans about 400 yards away behind a hedge. They thought we were entrenched, as we were in a dip, so they gallantly charged us – only about a few thousand against a few hundred of us. When they were 20 yards from us we got up and charged them. I know I got one fat German right in the stomach, and he went over, bayonet and all. Then they all turned and ran, squealing like pigs.

Some Devon men were at the defence of Antwerp. Lance-Corporal Redford wrote home to Crediton that his unit was helping Belgian troops man a trench, but 'on each side of me fellows were being blown to pieces. How I escaped was a marvel.' Forced to retreat, he saw the city was 'a seething furnace', and 'thousands of refugees, men, women and children, were fleeing in all directions, and hundreds were lying dead as we passed along, many of them with arms, legs or head blown off'.

The physical destruction of Belgian villages and towns shocked many British troops, as did the thought that given a chance the Germans would behave the same in Britain. In this context it was easy to believe the tales of appalling atrocities perpetrated by the invaders on helpless civilians, and, as the historian David Stevenson argues, the evidence suggests some of the tales were true. He cites a study based on German soldiers' diaries, Belgian refugees' reports and 'the more sober' Allied inquiries, which concludes the Germans deliberately killed 5,521 Belgian and 906 French civilians in the first few weeks of the war, usually on the assumption they were guerrillas, and used some as human shields during advances through difficult terrain. Certainly local newspapers played an active part in turning the war into a deeper ideological conflict founded upon Germany's complete rejection of civilised values and Christian behaviour. It had, many public speakers proclaimed, become the anti-Christ, the devil incarnate.

A wartime advertisement for Black Cat cigarettes, with a Louis Raemaker cartoon. (*Western Evening Herald*, 29 August 1916)

Some newspapers contained Black Cat cigarette advertisements that reprinted the company's cigarette card set of Louis Raemaeker's blood-chilling cartoons of individual German atrocities.

Reports of German heartlessness came thick and fast. Recuperating at home in Dawlish, Private Stanley Cook of the 1st Devons told a reporter how he was knocked unconscious outside Namur and eventually stumbled across 'a party of four ambulance men, but they were helpless, as the Germans had cut off their hands'. Wounded soldiers in hospital in Exeter recounted tales of atrocities to visiting *Express & Echo* reporters. One had seen a little girl with both hands and feet cut off, a second said German soldiers had disguised themselves and driven up in civilian transport to surprise and kill Belgian families, and a third claimed the advancing Germans bayoneted wounded British soldiers. The *Ilfracombe Gazette* publicised soldiers' stories of 'women with their hands severed at the wrists, with their teeth battered out by the butt of a rifle, with their knees deliberately broken that they might have to crawl before their torturers'. Trooper H.E. Seccombe wrote to his sister in Kingsbridge: 'The Germans caught a Canadian sergeant and crucified him on the door. They paid dearly for it too, because curiously enough we captured practically no prisoners after that.' A wounded soldier in Exeter gave a sworn statement to the city's mayor that he had seen crucified soldiers near Ypres. One can imagine hard-pressed German soldiers acting brutally as they pushed forward hurriedly across totally hostile territory, but one can also imagine relieved British soldiers regaling reporters, who were only too happy to believe them, with heightened tales of battle horrors.

With scant circumstantial evidence, *Trewman's Flying Post* highlighted the differences between German and British sailors when three British cruisers – HMS *Aboukir, Cressey* and *Hogue* – were torpedoed in less than an hour by the German submarine *U9* on 22 September: 'The *Hogue* crew cheered as they took the last plunge with a spirit worthy of Grenville of the *Revenge*', but the Germans behaved 'with miserable want of chivalry. They jeered at the British crews struggling in the water. They attempted to torpedo a harmless British trawler which went to the rescue of the victims.' Several Devonians were among the casualties.

Yet the story of the 1914 Christmas truce was true. In a letter thanking his old school in Ilfracombe for his Christmas card, Lance-Corporal Charles Brown described how on Christmas Day a German officer bravely stood above his trench and said they would not fire if we would not. Brown dashed off with a message to an officer, and on his return 'I was never more surprised in my life, as I found Devons and Germans all mixed up and having a fine time. I believe this lasted all day.' Boxing Day was the same. Brown had mixed feelings, and wondered what those at home would make of it. It did not occur in subsequent years.

Soldiers in our midst

The soldiers were undoubtedly admired, but their mass presence also raised worries about their impact upon local communities – and high on the list of things to worry about were drink, sex and violence. Early in August 1914 *Trewman's Flying Post* warned that 'when thousands of young men are dumped down among strangers and with very little to occupy their time, then social questions of the most urgent kind arise', an issue taken up soon afterwards by Canon McLaren, who urged the provision of games rooms, refreshment centres and libraries for the troops' 'wholesome recreation' in Exeter. Later that autumn speakers at the Exeter Diocesan Conference were quick to condemn wartime Plymouth as a particular den of vice fuelled by drink, and urged all parishes to support the work of the Young Men's Christian Association (YMCA). When a large and well-equipped YMCA recreational hut, 120ft long and 30ft wide, was opened in the Raglan Barracks in Devonport in 1915, Major-General Penton, the garrison commander, openly expressed his pleasure that his men were being protected from the 'tremendous number of temptations' in Plymouth. Despite the comforting work of the YMCA, fears lingered. In April 1915 the Archdeacon of Totnes was explicit that units of soldiers arriving in parishes would arouse excitement, 'with results, in the case of women and girls, which they must all deplore'.

Not everyone agreed. In October 1914 the vicar of Ilsham completely misjudged the views of many parishioners when he distributed letters urging householders to ensure their daughters and female servants adopted 'very high standards of Christian modesty and conduct in demeanour and dress' and ideally were confined indoors 'after sunset', now that so many soldiers were in the district. Numerous objections to his low view of men in uniform forced an abject apology. Another apology had to be made by the Revd Everard Digby, an army chaplain, when the residents of Dartmouth felt he had sullied the town's reputation by publicly cautioning troops newly stationed there against approaches by local women. Writing in the November 1914 parish magazine, the vicar of Topsham expressed his pleasure, and by implication his relief, that the troops there had 'won golden opinions from everybody'. They boosted trade, attended church, made full use of the Recreation Room, and appreciated the lantern shows, whist drives, sing-songs and French lessons put on for them.

Nevertheless in Exeter and Plymouth there was a succession of court cases involving soldiers brawling when drunk. Early on in the war Lord Kitchener urged people not to treat soldiers to alcoholic drinks, and in 1915 this was made a summary offence. Throughout the war brothelkeepers and prostitutes were regularly targeted by the police, especially in Plymouth, for importuning members of the armed forces. And as we have seen, in the autumn of 1914 Exeter's Home of Refuge believed it would be unable to accommodate all the women who might benefit from places.

In general householders welcomed the troops billeted among them. A sense of patriotism was fortified by the trade and the billeting allowances they brought with them. The length of stay varied widely, some units undergoing training while others were in transit and awaiting embarkation. The small town of Budleigh Salterton absorbed 400 RAMC personnel in December 1914, while 850 'tired and dirty' troops were billeted in Newton Abbot, all with little complaint and much appreciation. In May 1915 the *Salcombe Gazette* eulogised the behaviour of a succession of North Country recruits from the 10th Battalion King's Own (Royal Lancaster) Regiment, who were billeted in Kingsbridge while training in the surrounding countryside. Paignton felt much the same, and certainly Sidmouth hoped for more troops when various units left in January 1915. Around the same time, the *Torquay Times* praised the 700 men staying there: 'The soldier is not a plaster saint, neither is he the terror which some people, who never go outside their narrow circle, imagine.' It added, 'If well treated, what a wonderful advertising body for future seasons they will become.' Such harmony was a little tarnished when the resort's shopkeepers were accused of raising prices as soon as they knew landladies had the billeting allowances.

In November 1915 Dawlish UDC regretted the town had no immediate prospect of more troops arriving to boost its economy. In October 1916 a huge row broke out in Teignmouth when householders suspected that the 2,000 troops they were expecting had failed to turn up because the council had been negligent in offering its public facilities to the military authorities. In February 1915 Paignton was desperate for more troops to arrive; it had a thousand already but wanted twice as many to fill all the lodging houses and boost local traders who were suffering from the previous autumn's low visitor numbers. The town was jubilant when three trains brought the London Post Office Rifles there in January 1917. In 1915 Ilfracombe, too, petitioned the army for troops, but when none arrived rumours began to spread that its failure to attract them was because a group of local females had informed officers that the town was far too immoral in character to receive them.

A small minority of citizens grew so incensed at seeing local men apparently eligible for war service but obviously not volunteering that they took to humiliating them by sending white feathers and abusive cards anonymously through the post. Their actions were completely counterproductive. In September 1914 the *Crediton Chronicle* published two scathing letters about these actions. One correspondent identified sixty recipients of white feathers, of whom he knew seven; of these, two had been rejected by military doctors, two knew they would never pass the medical examination, two had businesses to run and several dependants to support, and one had onerous public duties. The other writer had been a recipient of a white feather, and condemned the cowardice of the anonymous senders and their ignorance of his difficult personal circumstances. Another spate of anonymous hatemail occurred in Newton Abbot in 1915, immediately after a particularly heated recruiting meeting held at a time when volunteering was fading fast and conscription was under daily debate. The vicar of Wolborough publicly condemned the insults and the ignorance associated with them, and contemptuously assumed that they stemmed from some ignorant and over-excited women who had attended the recent rally.

Not surprisingly, troops arriving from the Dominions were warmly welcomed; the nation was relieved and gratified that the empire remained loyal and supported the war. In October 1914 the U-boat threat in the English Channel led to thirty-three assorted Canadian liners and transport ships being diverted from Southampton to Plymouth, and over two days and nights crowds cheered and sirens boomed as one by one the ships entered the Hamoaze and were piloted slowly to their berths. There was 'an almost never-ending line of masts and funnels', and as they approached land 'the ships' rigging and decks were masses of khaki figures'. The 250 boys and band of the *Mount Edgcumbe* training ship had the privilege of going on board a Saltash steamer, and welcoming each ship with verses from 'O Canada' and rousing cheers. In all 32,000 men and 7,679 horses, together with dozens of guns, hundreds of wagons and a mountain of baggage, were unloaded, and then reloaded over the next three days onto ninety trains to be transported to Salisbury Plain. One of the Canadian officers was Major John McCrae, who later wrote the famous poem beginning 'In Flanders Fields the poppies blow, Between the crosses, row on row.' Rumours of the arrival of this fleet had proved accurate, and so were those regarding the arrival in Plymouth of a contingent of South Africans

Canadian troops at St Thomas, Exeter, on their way from Plymouth to Salisbury Plain. (West Country Studies Library)

on the liner *Kildonan Castle* in October 1914. However, a month earlier large crowds spent a fruitless night at Tiverton Junction station after believing stories that trains full of exotic Russian Cossacks would be passing through Devon on their way from Scotland to Plymouth.

DEVON'S SEAMEN AND SHIPS AT SEA

Particularly cheering news in August 1914 was the success of the Devonport-crewed light cruiser HMS *Highflyer* in trapping and sinking the German armed merchant cruiser *Kaiser Wilhelm der Grosse* off the west coast of Africa. However, the sinking of the British armoured cruisers HMS *Good Hope* and *Monmouth* and the loss of all 1,570 hands at the Battle of Coronel, off the coast of central Chile, on 1 November 1914 shocked and humiliated the nation. Emotions ran particularly high as the light cruisers HMS *Aboukir*, *Cressey* and *Hogue* had been lost only a few weeks earlier. Newspapers recorded the local deaths. Among them was Captain F. Brandt, the commander of HMS *Monmouth*, from Sidmouth. Three members of his crew were from Teignmouth. The last letter home from one of them, Seaman Alfred Parker, told of his excitement at chasing German ships near 'a place where England gets all her beef and sheep from'. Engine Room Artificer P.H. Shattock from Cullompton was lost on HMS *Good Hope*. In mid-October he had

River Dart and Britannia Naval College, Dartmouth. (Author's collection)

written home optimistically about an imminent battle and the possibility of returning home for Christmas. One seaman from Ilfracombe was lost on HMS *Aboukir* and another on HMS *Hogue*. The Revd G.H. Collier of Babbacombe was the chaplain on HMS *Cressey*, and was saved by clinging to a piece of timber for two and a half hours. At the outbreak of war 400 cadets still in training at Britannia Naval College in Dartmouth had been hurriedly, and controversially, allocated to various ships, and twenty-seven of them between fifteen and sixteen and a half years of age had died shortly afterwards on these five cruisers.

As soon as war broke out the seas around Devon became busier and more dangerous. German ships in or near British ports were seized. The liner *Belgia* and the cargo ship *Ullaborg* were seized in the Bristol Channel, and the liner *Tubantia*, spotted in the Western Approaches on its way to Amsterdam with 'a large number of German reservists', was forced into Plymouth. Many civilian ships were requisitioned by the Admiralty with little notice. At least thirteen of the White Funnel Company's paddlesteamers seen so frequently at Ilfracombe were converted to minesweepers. Spacious, fast and shallow-drafted, they were well suited to the dangerous work, and were dispatched to Scotland, the Irish Sea, the North Sea, the Thames Estuary, the English Channel and even Gallipoli, as well as the Bristol Channel itself. Two were sunk minesweeping

Paddlesteamers in Ilfracombe harbour. (Author's collection)

off Ostend, and a third, the *Barry*, had the distinction of being the last ship to depart from Sulva Bay, with the beachmaster and his staff aboard, after the disastrous Gallipoli campaign.

By May 1915, 1,004 commercial trawlers and drifters around the British coast had been taken into the Royal Navy, together with their crews. Many vessels had gone from Brixham and all six from Plymouth. After hurried conversion they were used as tenders, armed minesweepers and patrol vessels in the English Channel, North Sea and Western Approaches. Some were engaged in patrolling and tending the 20-mile-long mine barrier that closed off the Dover Strait to enemy submarines, a task constantly threatened by the lightning raids of German torpedo boat destroyers. On the night of 20–21 April 1917 several of these fast and well-armed ships ran into two British destroyers, HMS *Broke* and *Swift*. In a famous episode the *Broke* rammed the German destroyer *G42* and a fierce hand-to-hand battle ensued, reminiscent of the Napoleonic wars, until *G42* sank and a badly battered *Broke* took on board the survivors. A fortnight later Frederick Carder, a casualty from the *Broke*, was buried in his home town of Paignton.

Attacks at sea without warning became common in 1917. The P&O liner *Medina*, carrying meat and butter, copper, tin and gold from Australia, was torpedoed 4 miles off Start Point on 1 February 1917. Fortunately she had just called into Plymouth to offload the gold before continuing to London. The hospital ship *Asturias* was torpedoed without warning about 8 miles off Start Point on the night of 20–21 March 1917, although she was displaying the Red Cross and showing all navigation lights. Over 300 people were towed in lifeboats to Salcombe by a patrol vessel, but forty-three were killed and thirty-nine injured in the attack and during the difficult evacuation from the still moving but uncontrollable liner. The bodies were landed at Torquay and Plymouth. In the summer of 1917 the skipper of a Brixham trawler had an intriguing encounter with a German U-boat commander. The U-boat surfaced by the trawler, but before sinking it the commander sheared off to attack the far greater prize of a liner. Nevertheless the trawler skipper had time to ask the German commander how he knew the English language and coast so well, and received the reply that he had lived in Sidmouth for more than twelve years.

THE CHURCHES' VIEWS

Almost as soon as the war started clergy of all denominations sought to find within the relentless conflict some revelation of God's will, to strengthen national resolve. Their answers to the question 'Why does God allow war?'

The torpedoed hospital ship *Asturias* aground on the South Devon coast. (Cookworthy Museum)

were many and varied. In August 1914 Canon McLaren of Exeter Cathedral preached on a verse from Psalm 119, 'It is good for me that I have been in trouble that I may learn Thy statutes,' and used it to urge greater recruitment as a Christian duty to the nation and greater faith as the Christian debt to God. The Bishop of Exeter, the Right Revd Archibald Robertson, preached that 'the war came … only just in time to save their national character from rapid and terrible deterioration', and he listed 'self-indulgence, uncleanness, pride and avarice' as grievous national sins to be overcome.

In November 1914 the Revd David Walters of Totnes Congregational Church offered a chilling explanation why the nation had not yet won the war. 'Victory tarried, perhaps, because we were not yet fit to be victorious … why they needed much prayer was not merely to enlist God as their ally to conquer their enemy, but that He may enable them to see the need of it all, and that they may be fit for the day of victory.' The vicar of South Molton said that the war happened 'because man had been fool enough to let the devil get hold of his will, and use it for his own ends – to spoil God's world'. He also asserted that 'England was not fit to win yet; there was far too much selfishness in England yet for a victory to be thoroughly healthy for us'. The vicar of Totnes also upheld selfishness to be the cause of the war, but chose to rail against the selfishness of recent British strikers as much as the selfishness of the German nation. The Exeter Diocesan Missioner, the Revd A. Langford Brown, explained the war in terms of God's ultimate purpose for mankind.

He believed that 'it was because God saw in human nature the possibilities of a higher and more Divine life that He allowed this visitation to come'. Many others adopted similar positions, first arguing that the almost inexplicable crisis was the moment to engender greater Christian faith across the nation, and then personalising it to offer everyone the chance of redemption with its sure and certain contribution to victory.

The concept of the Christian warrior was eulogised. The Totnes Congregational minister said that Christ had never rebuked anyone for being a soldier, and every Christian must draw his sword against the Germans, 'whose actions were those of the murderer, the lunatic and the beast'. The Anglican Bishop of Crediton, the Right Revd Robert Trefusis, a grandson of Lord Clinton, asserted that there were two forces at work in the world, Christ and Anti-Christ, the latter currently Germany. Anti-Christ denounced Christianity as weak, obsolete and a hindrance to progress. It was 'a destroyer of peace, the murderer of the aged and the helpless, the outrager of women, the devastator of villages and towns and sacred buildings – cruel, barbaric, tyrannical'. Every Christian, Trefusis concluded, was a member of Christ's Church militant, dedicated to the struggle against evil, and committed 'to continue a faithful soldier until his life's end'. Complementing this, a Brixham clergyman wrote: 'There are few more beautiful and stirring sights than to see a young soldier about to leave home and country for the scene of battle, kneeling with his family and friends at God's altar.' He then goes forth, he said, 'as a Christian soldier'.

A few cautioned against the rampant hatred of Germans. A Dartmouth vicar argued that it 'confuses, distrusts and blinds, preventing those who give way to it from seeing things in their true perspective', and asserted that far from all Germans were brutes. The vicar of West Alvington acknowledged how hard it might be to pray for our enemies, but the 'whole law of Christ' must be followed. In general, though, the clergy gave sanction to the views of secular hardliners. Lord Leith of Fyvie, who chose to live in Devon rather than Fyvie Castle in Scotland for much of the war, represented the most extreme anti-German position. An outspoken member of the Anti-German League, he sought local support to ensure that any peace treaty confiscated Germany's overseas territories and kept it out of world affairs. He believed that Germans had long ago penetrated every aspect of British life – business, government, the Independent Labour Party and the Stop the War movement – and must be rooted out. From early 1916 the militant British Empire Union was active in Devon, arguing vehemently against any post-war trade with Germany and urging the creation of the strongest possible commercial union within the

British Empire. Although Exeter City Council voted narrowly 25–22 in favour of a post-war embargo on trade with Germany, the Union publicly condemned the substantial minority against it. 'Anyone calling himself an Englishman,' it thundered, 'who wished to trade with Germany again after the experiences of the past two years ought to be hung to (*sic*) a lamp-post and left there until he literally stank in the nostrils of the people.'

LATER LETTERS HOME

As the war dragged through 1915 and 1916 the servicemen's letters home mixed outpourings of the horrors of battle and the hardships of daily life with more sensitive appreciations of the anxieties their readers were enduring, and more wistful thoughts of the Devon countryside.

By then trench warfare was well established along the Western Front, and in March 1915 a 2nd Devons soldier from Torquay wrote: 'It is, I can assure you, very, very cold work, and the weather has been wet for the past few days. Standing as one does in about 8 inches of mud and water, makes one's feet frightfully cold; and when the night comes, it would be excusable if one's thoughts gently veered from Berlin to "England's home and beauty".' Quite often he heard the Germans call 'Good morning Tommy' from their trenches just 45yds away, but he feared their snipers too much to reply. Aerial warfare was getting in its stride as fighter planes became faster and better armed. Writing to his brother in Exeter in the summer of 1915, Private C. Kerslake described a dogfight he watched from his trench: 'Talk about a hawk and a pigeon, nothing could be copied more completely. The swoop down, the setting fire to the Hun aeroplane, which dropped like a ball of fire, the aviator jumping out in mid-air, while the observer stuck to the burning plane and fell into the lines of the Cornwalls, to be captured by them.' Just possibly Lieutenant Densham, the Master of the Dart Vale Harriers, brought some comfort to readers of the *Mid Devon Advertiser* when he eulogised the efficiency with which the wounded were collected and transported, the care they received and the warm billets and baths, good food and sports available to troops in rest areas behind the lines. Other soldiers' letters revealed that many supposedly safe areas were regularly targeted by German artillery and aeroplanes.

Various experiences reminded men of Devon. In a letter home to Dawlish, Private Bert Davies described how he survived a German shell exploding in his rest area – 'You should have seen the mess.' He also described the thick cloying mud: 'I have never come across its equal yet, and I have been through a few lanes in Devon.' The last letter Private Walter Vinnicombe sent home to Willand before his death in Gallipoli spoke of the fleet bombardments of Turkish positions and the imminence of battle, and then went on to say, 'I am wondering how the garden is this year, also the apples. My word, how it makes my mouth water when I picture the orchard. I am hoping one day to sample once more a few of the apples.' Trooper Tom Clark of Ilfracombe was another who felt completely alienated from his home by the vileness of the rocky Gallipoli landscape, the shortage of water, the terrible cold, the danger of snipers and the shells whistling over their exposed positions.

The themes of separation and the link of love were, of course, common in letters. Lieutenant Stanley Webber wrote home to Plymouth on the eve of his death on the Western Front on 1 July 1916: 'If it should be my fate to go under, do not grieve for me, for love stretches over death and makes it only a temporary separation. I have no fear of death. I am going into the fight with the assurance of God's goodness, and submit myself to his care.' Nevertheless, the sacrifices the men were making could bring anger too. In April 1915 Lieutenant J.R. Braddick wrote home to Silford distraught at the death of so many civilians and young soldiers, and bitter towards those refusing to enlist. 'I say close theatres, pubs and everything. I should like to have all unmarried fellows and shove them up in the first line.' He was all in favour of conscription, and in giving conscripts a different badge to volunteers.

CONSCRIPTION AND CONTROVERSIES

Much blood was being spilt, and as 1915 wore on that blood became a weapon of recruitment. That October an impassioned speaker in Barnstaple chillingly blended past glories, present sacrifices and personal pride when he 'asked if the manhood of the country were prepared to follow in the wake of the Devon heroes of the past, and the men whose blood had been spilt in Flanders and the Peninsula of Gallipoli and other bloody battles, or to forgo their birthright, and bow their heads to the iniquitous rule of the barbarian savages, and take lying down the atrocities committed against God and His creatures.' In December the prime minister informed the nation of the number of casualties incurred up to 9 November: 69,272 men and 4,620 officers had been killed, 240,283 men and 9,754 officers wounded, and 54,446 men and 1,583 officers were missing or prisoners of war. The total was fast approaching 400,000, in just fifteen months. Many families were already mourning, many others lived in fear of the approaching steps of a telegraph boy and many more were tormented by the relentless public pressure to enlist – and accompanying thoughts of violent death or mutilation.

Conscription was a controversial issue nationally, but a resolution became increasing urgent as voluntary recruiting plummeted. Although speakers at rallies threatened its introduction, trades unions and many within the Labour Party, and especially the more Socialist-inclined Independent Labour Party (ILP), were bitterly opposed to it. It was seen as a dictatorial Continental intrusion into British life and the precursor to government control of the labour market. The Newton Abbot branch of the ILP, supported by a few non-conformist clergy, district councillors and the National Amalgamated Union of Shop Assistants, Warehousemen and Clerks, resolved unanimously to oppose conscription, and promised widespread strikes if Parliament invoked it. At an ILP rally in the town speakers utterly condemned the slide to compulsion as the destruction of people's liberty, and 'an insult to the memory of those who had given their lives to crush Prussianism'. Feelings ran high. 'Today,' it was claimed, 'the dirtiest gang that England was ever cursed with were trying to rivet upon the working classes the yoke of slavery.' In Exeter the Working Men's Association warmly applauded County Alderman Sir Robert Newman's hostility to conscription.

The nervous Liberal government initially adopted a compromise. The Earl of Derby, Director of Recruiting, came up with a scheme that avoided compulsion but sought to attract men into 'attesting', whereby they formally agreed to serve in the armed forces if and when called upon to do so. The Derby Scheme tried to introduce a sense of fairness by pledging not to call up married men until all available unmarried men had been taken. In addition, all adult males were divided into age bands, with younger men called before older ones. Special tribunals were created across the country that could exempt an attested man from service when he was called if he presented a good enough case that his job was crucial to the war effort, or vital in supporting a large and dependent family.

The excessively complicated and frequently misunderstood scheme got under way in November 1915. Detailed leaflets tried to guide tribunals: one, for example, differentiated between carriers of heavy goods, including coal, who could be exempted, from carriers of light goods who could not. Canvassers were trained to encourage men to attest and then grade them according to how their health and circumstances might affect their capacity or willingness to serve. It proved a tortuous and time-consuming task, as Devon newspapers quickly found out. Stories of muddles and mistakes abounded, and Lord Fortescue was forced to admit that 'the canvassers obtained were unfortunate selections or else they had been unfortunate in regard to the people they had been up against'. Many men were suspected of accentuating the difficulties in the way of their active service, and many married men feared they would be called up long before the pool of unmarried men had been drained.

Numbers willing to attest quickly dropped off. The scheme's success depended upon enough men attesting and the tribunals acting even-handedly – and being seen to do so. It failed on all counts, and understandably some historians believe it was meant to fail, thereby providing the excuse for fully fledged conscription to be introduced, which is exactly what occurred a few months later in May 1916, when a universal Conscription Act was passed by a sullen House of Commons.

As Devon's newspapers highlighted, most tribunals remained confused about the detailed changes and the prevailing rules for many months to come. Henceforth exemptions tended to depend upon two factors. The first was the skill with which applicants, and sometimes their employers, could plead that their post was crucial to the war effort or to the local economy, or both, or that their large families would be impoverished without their income, or that their businesses would collapse without them, or that they were physically unfit for service. The second was the degree to which the tribunal believed them, and certainly some panels were stricter than others in their interpretation of the regulations. Few exemptions were permanent. Most had a time limit of three or six months tied to pledges that every effort would be made to find a substitute – perhaps a woman or a school-leaver, or possibly a man too old or unfit for active service. At the end of the exemption period another tribunal appearance was necessary.

A scattering of cases drawn from the many hundreds reported give the tone and attitude of the tribunals, and their decisions. Overall it seems that an applicant's chances of success were gravely threatened if any suspicions arose that he was neither the sole breadwinner nor vital for his employer's continuing business, especially if it was not a war-related concern. In June and July 1916 the Plymouth tribunal exempted a watch and clock repairer because five dealers relied on him, a maker of naval uniform caps, the sole engraver in Devonport, and a fruit and potato merchant supplying the garrisons. With regard to large businesses this tribunal does seem to have been careful to exempt a few key younger men if their employers had genuinely taken on women and older men as substitutes for earlier volunteers or more recent conscripts. In December 1916 the Torquay tribunal exempted a married baker, a newspaper machinist whose departure would close the office as no substitute could be found, and a builder's yardman who had recently suffered injury. In 1917 Crediton tribunal gave three months exemption certificates to one of the few remaining local thatchers, the sole harness maker serving Lapford, Newton St Cyres and Copplestone, a mechanic looking after several doctors' cars and local farm machinery, and a coal delivery man covering a particularly wide area. In the same year Newton

Abbot tribunal exempted the proprietor of the popular Crediton tribunal, Newton Abbot exempted the proprietor of the popular Empire Theatre and Imperial Electric Theatre, and Teignmouth's tribunal was convinced by a grocer's assistant's argument that he was the only assistant left and women could not lift whole cheeses and sides of bacon. A ploughman, though, aroused little sympathy when he said he had accidentally shot off a finger just before being called up.

Some evidence of widely varying practice exists in the well-publicised accusation that South Molton was the place to go to avoid being in the army. In March 1916 it was claimed the tribunal had had 111 claims and made 51 absolute, 26 conditional and 17 temporary exemptions. When serving soldiers heard the news several wrote expressing their disgust, at both the applicants and the tribunal. Exemption was a very sensitive subject. Sir Ian Amory was criticised for opposing the exemption of hunt workers elsewhere while keeping his own horses and hounds intact. Tremayne Buller was angered at the public slur on his character when he sought exemption for his forty-year-old groom and chauffeur who, he claimed, was one of very few estate workers left, and on many days took his wife and daughter to work in Crediton VAD Hospital.

DESERTERS AND CONFIDENCE TRICKSTERS

It is not surprising that Devon's police forces were alert to the problem of deserters. One was arrested at his house in Dartmouth despite his family trying to cover up his presence, another was caught in a filthy condition hiding in Okehampton, two were found at Kenn, two in Ilfracombe, another two at Willand, and four were caught at Exeter without tickets on a train back home to Derby. All of them admitted their offence, and the common factor seems to have been an inability to cope with army life even though many of them had been volunteers. As one Territorial said, he 'could not get on with the drills and other work. He objected to being bullied by young officers and non-coms.' In court Sir Ian Amory had little sympathy, asserting 'he looked just the sort of man to do well in France and when he came back he would like the army'. *Trewman's Flying Post* found it 'the most amusing case'.

In 1916 a number of men were arrested for failing to present themselves for armed service when required, and were sent under armed escort to a barracks. The system was chaotic enough in late 1916 for the police and military authorities to descend upon a popular boxing tournament at Plymouth's Cosmopolitan Gymnasium and to take the details of 200 young men without obvious exemption certificates. Many young men attending Barnstaple Fair that year were also stopped and questioned.

A number of confidence tricksters saw the large transient population of servicemen in Devon as an opportunity to enrich themselves by posing as war heroes. In the summer of 1915 magistrates convicted a trickster dressed as an imposing naval officer with his arm in a sling, who had successfully sought money from several residents in Crediton. He claimed that he was visiting Lady Audrey Buller, allegedly a friend of his, at nearby Downes, but when he found out she was away he realised with embarrassment that he had arrived in the town without any funds to stay at a local inn. That September a bogus Black Watch officer was convicted of cashing fraudulent cheques at Torquay Hydro, after a lengthy spree posing with Distinguished Service Order and Legion of Honour medal ribbons and a recent letter announcing the award of his Victoria Cross. He was, in fact, an RAMC deserter. In November a trooper was found guilty in Cullompton of posing as a wounded war hero with a Distinguished Conduct Medal. He had ingratiated himself with locals in public houses, gained free drinks and lodgings and even regaled a local school with his deeds. A celebrated case was that of Edward Trelawney Clarence Ansell, who was sentenced to three years in prison at Exeter Assizes in January 1918. A repeated deserter, he had posed as an officer and stayed in the expensive Royal York Hotel in Sidmouth and Clarence Hotel in Ilfracombe. After living well in each one at other people's expense, he said he was called back to his military base in the Curragh, Ireland, and paid his bills with worthless cheques while asking for second cheques to be cashed. A year earlier he had been imprisoned for six months for doing exactly the same thing in Ottery St Mary. His list of frauds long predated the war, when he had specialised in embezzling large deposits from prospective agents for non-existent upper-class employment companies and trainee guides for non-existent London tour operators.

Returning heroes

The well-publicised award of medals for bravery probably evoked many thoughts of the horrors of warfare as well as engendering pride in British valour and, perhaps, a tinge of envy of other men's heroism and glowing reputations. A number of awards were made to injured soldiers in Devon hospitals. Bandsman, but soon to be Sergeant, Thomas Rendle and Private William Young were in Exeter war hospitals, and Lance-Corporal William Kenny was in Newton Hall Hospital when they all heard they had been awarded the Victoria Cross for supreme courage in rescuing wounded men under heavy fire. Rendle was born in Exeter, although later lived in Bristol, Young was Scottish and Kenny was Irish. Lieutenant Bernard Cox RN received his

Distinguished Service Order for gallantry during minesweeping operations in the Dardenelles from King George V, during his visit to Plymouth Royal Naval Hospital in September 1915.

Corporal Theodore Veale of the Devons won the Victoria Cross on 20 July 1915 for saving an officer's life under heavy fire on the Western Front. As he arrived home in Dartmouth schoolchildren thronged Kingswear station, and when the ferry reached the other side of the river six colleagues carried him shoulder high through the crowds to a civic reception. In October 1917 Private Tom Sage of Tiverton won the Victoria Cross near Ypres for rescuing a wounded colleague while serving in the Somerset Light Infantry. He, too, was accorded a civic reception when he returned home as his wounds healed. Mayor Gregory said: 'Through the mercy of God he was not killed, but for the rest of his days, be they long or short, he will bear on his body scars more honourable than all the adornments of rank or wealth.' Eight men of the Devonshire Regiment won Distinguished Conduct Medals at the costly Battle of Loos in September–October 1915.

A ceremony to mark the achievements of the Devons took place in Exeter in November 1915. It was meant to boost local pride and enlistment but it was as much a wake as a celebration. Two German howitzers captured by the 8th and 9th Battalions advancing on Hulluch during the Battle of Loos were drawn through the main streets by a team of black horses and ceremonially presented to the city in Northernhay, on a perhaps suitably dull and damp November day. Heroism, sacrifice and gratitude were key points in the speeches of Lord Fortescue and the mayor. Most of the officers and more than half the men had been killed in the attack on 26 September, but units had gathered around the few survivors to seize the guns and hold them overnight until relieved. Some of the wounded formed part of the military procession through the city. A little later the guns were loaned to Plymouth and put on display in the Guildhall Square. Enemy trophies were not always welcome, though. A sharp disagreement erupted in Moretonhampstead when its rector placed in the church, inappropriately it was thought, a German flag captured at Bagamoji Fort in East Africa and presented to him by a local serviceman.

Cheering audiences, civic addresses, illuminated certificates and celebratory teas were the order of the day for many returning medal winners, a few of whom were Sapper Arthur Ayre at Torrington, Sergeant Walter Martin at North Tawton and Sergeant Walter Potter at Exeter, who won Distinguished Conduct Medals, and Private W. Raymont at Chudleigh and Sergeant G. Mitchell at Kingskerswell, who won Military Medals. Lieutenant Jack Mills, a Newton Abbot cricketer but in 1915 an airman, became a celebrated

An Exeter Man's Terrible Vengeance.

Lance-Corpl. WOOD.

Second-Lieut. WRIGHT.

L.-CORPL S. W. WOOD, whose mother resides at 16, East John St., Exeter, and who has won the Medal of St. George, has a brother in the Army, besides four in the Navy. The circumstances under which the Medal was won were: At the battle of Neuve Chapelle he volunteered with an officer and three other men to bomb the Germans out of their front line trench. This party captured the German front line for about 250 yards, taking between 70 and 80 prisoners, including an officer, also a machine gun, besides inflicting other casualties on them. With reference to L.-Corpl. Wood's exploit, it may be added that the officer accompanying the party, Sec.-Lieutenant G. C. Wright, of Shrewsbury, was fatally shot by a wounded German, whose condition excited his sympathy, but was avenged by Wood, who threw a bomb that blew the treacherous German to bits.

'An Exeter Man's Terrible Vengeance.' (*Western Times*, 12 January 1917)

local figure when he and Lieutenant Jack Wilson won Distinguished Service Crosses for destroying a Zeppelin at its base in St Evere by hand-throwing bombs out of their aircraft. In February 1918 thousands waited in the rain at Torrington station to welcome home Captain George Hackwell, an RFC Flight Commander, who had been awarded a Military Cross for shooting down a Gotha bomber over Essex. Wounded soldiers from the local Red Cross hospital made an arch of walking sticks for him to pass under on his way to the civic reception. Five Ilfracombe men on the battleship HMS *Jupiter* were among those awarded medals by the last Tsar of Russia when their ship helped refloat a stranded steamer early in 1915.

TRAWLERS, SCHOONERS AND CARGO SHIPS

During the early hours of 1 January 1915 the elderly battleship HMS *Formidable* was sunk by *U-24* off the Isle of Portland, with the loss of 547 of the 780 crew. In rough seas off Berry Head the *Provident*, a Brixham trawler out fishing under Skipper William Pillar, came across a drifting open boat with seventy-one freezing survivors crowded aboard. Very skilfully Pillar brought the trawler alongside to rescue them all. His superb seamanship was greatly admired, and he and his crew were feted locally with receptions and presentations. The skipper, his two senior hands and a young apprentice received Board of Trade Silver Medals from the king at Buckingham Palace. Afterwards Pillar said, 'It was a regular beano', and when the king spoke to Daniel, the apprentice, he 'was proud as a peacock and blushed like a baby'. In appreciation of Brixham's readiness to feed, clothe and shelter the survivors whom Pillar brought ashore, the largely West Country crew of HMS *Colossus* formally presented the port with an inscribed photograph of their battleship. Another seventy crew members of the *Formidable*, adrift in an open boat, were not so lucky. Only forty-eight survived their twenty-two hours at sea before beaching at Lyme Regis.

In June 1917 Brixham skippers William Mead and William Brewer were awarded Distinguished Service Crosses, and deck hands James Knowles and Walter Vickers Distinguished Service Medals for an unspecified act of bravery at sea. Much later it was made public that they had served aboard the armed schooner HMS *Prize*, which disguised itself as an unarmed vessel – a 'Q-ship' – in order to lure an enemy submarine close enough to engage in battle. On 30 April 1917 this ploy had worked successfully, but both the submarine and schooner were badly damaged in the intensive exchange of fire and eventually drifted away from each other to limp home to their respective ports. Lieutenant William Sanders, the *Prize*'s captain, was awarded the VC. At least two other local vessels were fitted with hidden guns in great secrecy at Appledore shipyard.

On 16 July 1917 two other Brixham fishermen, Second Hand William Brett and Bosun Leonard Pillar, gained Distinguished Service Crosses when a U-boat surfaced and attacked their armed trawler *Asama* while it was fishing, and guarding a Belgian trawler. The *Asama*, under A.L. Petheridge of the Royal Naval Reserve, returned fire, and despite losing its mizzen mast and receiving damage to its engine room, which killed the engineer, it kept the submarine at bay for an hour and three-quarters, thereby allowing the Belgian ship to escape. The *Asama* eventually sank but the crew were rescued by a British destroyer. One night in February 1917 another requisitioned trawler was sailing in worsening seas off the Scillies under Skipper T.F. Farley when he spied a light bobbing ahead in the water. Next he heard distant calls, and eventually numerous crowded open boats appeared in the swell. A U-boat had sunk seven Dutch trawlers, and Farley and other trawlers on his patrol rescued 400 grateful seamen. He was mentioned in dispatches, and received a silver life-saving medal from the Dutch government. Other Brixham trawlermen risked their lives minesweeping in the Dardenelles, and often endured shelling from the Turkish shore batteries. 'How both boats came out undamaged was a marvel as the shells burst continually around them', said a sailor home on leave describing one mission. In two separate incidents trawlers were blown up in, and under constant fire Brixham men were involved in the hazardous rescues of survivors.

Another act of bravery involved twenty-year-old Ella Trout. She was out with her ten-year-old cousin in a small rowing boat off Hallsands, lifting crab pots, when they saw a steamer coming from the west. Suddenly the steamer disappeared in an explosion, probably torpedoed. As the wind was in the wrong direction Ella lowered her sails, and they rowed three-quarters of a mile to people swimming amid the wreckage. They pulled aboard a fireman, while a motor boat arrived to rescue the other survivors. In the House of Commons Colonel Mildmay, MP for Totnes, successfully sought an award for her, and in due course Lord Fortescue formally presented her with a medal for bravery at a ceremony in Plymouth.

The war saw many other U-boat incidents off the Devon coast. In February 1915, as the collier *Devereaux* approached Plymouth Sound, its crew saw and heard a huge explosion further out at sea. As the *Brixham Western Guardian* said, everyone hoped it was a lurking U-boat striking a mine. In March the tug *Dencade* landed twenty-nine survivors at Plymouth from the steamer *Adenwen*, sunk in the English Channel by *U-29*. Soon afterwards the collier *Bengrove* sank off Ilfracombe after a mysterious explosion, but without loss of life, watched by thousands lining the shore. In April the *U-24* stopped the French cargo ship *Frederick Franck* off Start Head, and although the bombs placed on board badly damaged her she did not sink, and was eventually brought safely into Plymouth by two tugs. In 1916 the bodies of five Greek sailors were washed ashore in Plymouth Sound. They proved to be from the steamer *George M Embirocos*, which had been stopped in heavy seas and sunk by a U-boat in the Channel with, the survivors claimed, little time allowed by the German captain to abandon ship. The local trawlers were in constant danger from the U-boats, as well as the weather. In November 1916 one surfaced among a group of Brixham trawlers some miles off Portland Bill and sank seven of them; one of them was Skipper Pillar's *Provident*. A dozen trawlers escaped, but only after cutting their nets. Eventually Devonport became the base for several American-built 'submarine chasers', which were called into action when sightings of U-boats were reported in the Channel.

MILITARY FAILURES AND SUCCESSES

With victory proving elusive, the lists of casualties were never-ending. In January 1916 the Allies finally evacuated Gallipoli after completely failing to dislodge the Turks from the rocky Peninsula to allow British and French warships through the Dardenelles. The eight month disaster caused over 200,000 Allied casualties – dead, wounded, sick and missing – and hundreds of local men were among them. In June the largest and most controversial naval battle of the war took place in the North Sea off Jutland. After initial dispatches suggested a British victory – perhaps another Trafalgar – euphoria turned to disbelief and sorrow as the news crept across the country of the fourteen British ships sunk and 6,097 casualties, compared with German losses of ten ships, mainly far smaller ones, and 2,551 casualties. Local newspapers sombrely listed the dead on the battle cruisers HMS *Queen Mary*, *Indefatigible* and *Invincible*, the cruisers HMS *Defence*, *Warrior* and *Black Prince* and the eight destroyers. Twenty-six men from Exeter alone died in the battle. Soon after the battle a crew member on HMS *Tiger* wrote to his Ilfracombe headmaster that although Admiral Beatty had claimed 'a brilliant victory … one will have to admit it was dearly won'. On 9 July 1917 an internal explosion, probably caused by the perennial problem of defective ammunition, blew up the modern battleship HMS *Vanguard* in Scapa Flow, killing 804 officers and men, among them William Ellis Lee, the son of the headmaster of Willand School. The *Vanguard* had been at Jutland, and Lee had written home that 'the happiest moment of my life was when the good ship Vanguard loosed the first salvo'.

In July 1916 optimistic reports appeared regarding Allied advances during the massive battles between the rivers Somme and Ancre, but three months later continuous lists recorded the heavy casualties and highlighted the desperate nature of the fighting. Eventually the failure to achieve the objective, the capture of Bapaume, had to be acknowledged. There had been 400,000 British casualties, and among them were many men from the 2nd Devonshire Regiment who had taken part in the bitterly contested attack on Pozières. 'The severe and prolonged struggle has demanded on the part of our troops very great determination and courage' was the bland acknowledgement in one of the final reports on the Somme offensive from General Headquarters in France, and dutifully reprinted in local newspapers. After the offensive had died away an officer wrote home that the 11 officers and 149 men of the Devon Regiment killed in their July attack were all buried:

in the Devon Cemetery in the front line trenches which they had left at 7.30 that morning. It is unusually placed at this point, in the right angle crowning the corner of a little wooded bluff – trees all shattered of course, but some undergrowth of thorn and elm still living. There's a valley in front, leading down to a large valley on the right, through which run a road and a railway, and up the hill to the west and south is a gentle slope. It all reminds very much of Dartmoor – easy gentle slopes – but is rich land, though now foul with thistles.

Not all the casualties were suffered abroad. A few minutes before four o'clock in the afternoon on an autumn day in 1917 a New Zealand troop train stopped at Bere Alston station in the Tamar valley. The train had eighteen carriages and was far longer than the country platform. In error, a number of men jumped out onto the track, but not on the platform side, thinking it was the afternoon refreshment stop. Within a few seconds nine were killed and three more injured, of whom one later died, when they were struck by a passing train.

During this later period of the war many medal awards took place locally in formal military ceremonies, usually with civic dignitaries and many families in attendance. The vast battles witnessed many acts of bravery, and as the soldiers themselves said, many acts of supreme bravery went unrecorded. In June 1917 Major-General W.G.B. Western of Southern Command presented Distinguished Conduct Medals and Military Medals to men of various regiments in a parade in Northernhay, Exeter. In September 1917 Field Marshal Lord French presented similar awards to men of the Devonshire and Worcestershire Regiments in Plymouth, and a few months later Lieutenant-General Sir Henry Sclater, General Officer Commander-in-Chief, Southern Command, made more awards to the Devons and Royal Engineers in Plymouth. In May 1918 Sclater presented several dozen medals at Exeter. Some were presented to grieving wives or mothers, and he pinned the Distinguished Conduct Medal awarded posthumously to Company Sergeant Major Salter of Ottery St Mary to his seven-year-old son's chest. The boy was wearing his father's South Africa and Sudan campaign medals. When Sclater returned in early October for a similar ceremony, he recalled the already famous last stand of the 2nd Devons at Bois de Butte on the Aisne on 28 May 1918. They had bought time with the lives of 551 officers and men, so that the British front line could be stabilised and strengthened after heavy German attacks. 'Surrounded by overwhelming odds, they refused to surrender', said the emotive report. It was ordered to be read in all Devon schools. A few weeks after the general's visit, at eleven o'clock in the morning on 11 November 1918, the fighting stopped.

CONCLUSION

The early voluntary and later compulsory recruitment ensured that tens of thousands of men across Devon willingly or unwillingly experienced the trials and tribulations of active service. Many died, and many ended the war scarred physically or mentally, or both. Their letters reveal their capacity to endure hardship, suffer wounds and the deaths of colleagues without losing their underlying conviction that the country was right to go to war, and a general assumption that the decision had divine sanction. Many letters spoke about the horrors of war, especially when optimism about British advances turned into depression associated with retreats, but understandably few soldiers appreciated their part in the larger battles swirling around them. Many soldiers seem to have ignored religion in their letters, but a substantial minority accepted, and perhaps drew comfort from, a belief that God's will would be done whether they lived or died. It should not be assumed that such noble sentiments which permeated a number of letters were merely trite phrases to please or impress friends and relatives at home.

Certainly the clergy of all denominations went to great pains to try to explain the war in terms of steadfast Christian Britain standing up to barbarian Germany, which now represented the Anti-Christ. They asserted that the onset of war owed much to a British failure to live fully Christian lives, and they put their energies into preaching the gospel of personal and national redemption. An idealised version of the noble Christian soldier quickly emerged. Despite all the criticisms of the nation's attitudes and behaviour, there remained a conviction that Britain was fundamentally a model of civilisation at its most elevated extent. The assumption of superior British virtues was perhaps epitomised by the preacher at the Annual General Meeting of the Devon Federation of Free Churches who declared in July 1916 that God's purpose was increasingly clear, as Egypt had been wrestled from Turkish domination and would become a Christian province within the empire, and one day soon Germany's African colonies would fall under beneficent British rule. In the same month the Wesleyan minister at South Molton confirmed that the British Empire 'is the greatest, richest and happiest of all empires ever established', and 'if England ruled the world, the world would be free'. He gave this eulogy despite his admission of an alarming range of domestic evils. 'Despite our unjust social order, the tyranny in our villages, the misery in our towns, the squalor in our cities, our national sins of drink and profligacy, the heart of England still responds to the call of the highest and noblest.'

To the civilian population the presence of thousands of men in uniform, many from distant parts of the country, was either welcome or fearful depending upon whether the hope of an enhanced income or anxiety regarding female safety was uppermost in mind. Low views of soldiers' inclinations were as common as praise of their patriotism and bravery. Understandably great publicity was given to local men awarded medals, and the early volunteers were enthusiastically cheered, even venerated. Nevertheless Devon was among the lowest counties recorded for voluntary enlistment, alongside a few other rural southern counties. The aggravation caused by the recruiting parties touring villages across each part of Devon revealed only too clearly the hostility to military service within many families. The prolonged absences, loss of loved ones and fears of impoverished dependents were no doubt constant worries, but perhaps too the self-contained nature of rural communities made the war seem less relevant. Thousands sought exemption when conscription was introduced, and although the applicants were sometimes treated cavalierly by particularly hostile tribunal members, and certainly so by the military representatives, there is substantial evidence to show that family businesses, the local economy and indeed families in their entirety would have suffered very badly if some applicants had been refused at least temporary exemption. It seems that practices varied widely, thereby causing lingering discontent, but at least some tribunals acted humanely to ease the suffering feared by universal conscription. Nevertheless, it was almost impossible for civilians of military age to shake off, however sound their reasons, the taint of inadequacy at a time of national crisis.

CHAPTER THREE

ALIENS, SPIES AND OUTSIDERS

Spies, refugees and conscientious objectors

This chapter examines three groups of people who, largely unwittingly, helped maintain the determination of the British people to see the war with Germany through to final victory.

The fear that numerous German spies and potential saboteurs had infiltrated British society before and during the war served to keep people constantly alert to suspicious activities in their neighbourhoods, and in doing so accentuated the general belief that Germany would stop at nothing, however underhand and deceitful, to bring about the collapse of Britain and its empire.

Britain's ready welcome to thousands of Belgian refugees who fled, often destitute, in the face of the rapid and highly destructive advance of the Kaiser's armies represented a further condemnation of Germany's treacherous behaviour. It was yet another nail in the coffin of Germany's claim to be a civilised country.

Finally, the resolute refusal of a small minority of British men to take up arms against this particularly despicable enemy aroused in many people across the social hierarchy a deep emotional hostility that often erupted into bitter confrontation, and sometimes actual violence. Far from accepting that conscientious objectors had inalienable rights in a supposedly liberal and democratic society, most people viewed and abused them as shirkers, cowards and, at worst, traitors. Their refusal to fight and the doubts they cast upon the moral worth of the war tended to reinforce rather than diminish their opponents' belief in the value of the sacrifices servicemen were making. The nation's cause became even more honourable: families could not bear to think that the death of their menfolk might be worthless.

SPIES

As we saw in Chapter One the presence of German spies in Britain was public knowledge as early as 1911. In that year Ober-Leutnant Max Shultz of the 13th Hussars was sentenced to twenty-one months' imprisonment at Exeter Assize. He had hired a houseboat on the river Yealm and, posing as a German newspaper representative, he had entertained lavishly in order to elicit information on fleet preparations during a colonial crisis between Germany and Britain centred on Morocco. Two guests became suspicious, however, and the police trapped him after he told his dockyard contacts to send information to his press office via a known German agent's address in Walthamstow, London. In the same year another spy, this time a German merchant ship captain, was caught in Portsmouth, complete with cipher. These were convicted enemy agents, but attitudes towards Germany were also fuelled by the spate of pre-war novels by William Le Queux, whose British agent Gerry Sant was not only the suave and bold precursor of Ian Fleming's James Bond but also foiled one dastardly German plot after another. His *Invasion of 1910* published in 1906 was a bestseller. John Buchan's *The Thirty Nine Steps*, in which the hero John Hannay outwits the German agents and exposes a British traitor in high places, was published in 1915 and intensified the spy fever of the early war years. The nation was led to believe that the Germans would stoop to anything to secure European domination. In another book published in 1914, this time claiming to be factual, Armguard Carl Graves told of his many exploits as a German spy until he was arrested by the British in 1912 and, after prolonged questioning and a brief prison sentence, agreed to become a British double agent.

When war broke out Lord Fortescue took no chances. At a combined meeting of Devon County Council and Exeter City Council a few days later he urged those living near 'vulnerable points to take a stroll to those places at any time, day or night, and if they took a shot-gun and a dog who disliked strangers it would do no harm, and let them take any steps, up to shooting, to keep at a distance any evilly-disposed person'. The immediate need was watchfulness for the presence of spies and saboteurs who would undoubtedly target troop movements and do their best to disrupt them by blowing up railway bridges and tunnels. He cited as particularly vulnerable the GWR's White Ball tunnel, Cockwood viaduct, the Teignmouth to Dawlish tunnels, Dart bridge at Totnes, Ivybridge viaduct and Paignton tunnel, and the LSWR's Meldon viaduct, Wallabrook viaduct, Brentor and Tavistock viaducts, and the viaduct and tunnel between Tavistock and Bere Alston. In his memoirs Fortescue wrote that he enrolled special constables to patrol these points. The remote metal viaduct at Meldon was his greatest worry. 'Accordingly I motored to Okehampton,' he recalled, 'and sought the assistance of the Police Sergeant there. He undertook to collect some sturdy men in the course of the next hour or so, and in due course reported he had got them waiting for me, I think, in the Town Hall. I gathered that they were not all very good characters, and the man recommended for the charge of the party was a poacher.' Nevertheless they were all sworn in as special constables, but, Fortescue said, 'I had omitted to bring a copy of the regulation oath from Exeter and the Police Sergeant had not got one so I had to invent one on the spur of the moment.' Adding further fuel for thought, an ominous incident occurred in October when two sentries guarding Laira Bridge (connecting Plymouth and Plymstock) were shot in the legs. The cause was never established, but a train was believed to have been passing at the time. In due course the railway companies increased the number of railwaymen guards along vulnerable stretches of their lines, and they were joined by local police.

Within a few days of war being declared Germans living and working in Britain were sought out and arrested. Twenty, mainly musicians, hairdressers and waiters, were arrested in Torquay, handcuffed and sent to Exeter's Higher Barracks. Forty-six were caught in Plymouth and lodged under guard in Exeter's St Sidwell's School before being transported to Dorchester Gaol. A German waiter in Westward Ho! and 'Yuma', a music hall contortionist in Bideford, were also detained, and so were eleven others in Bideford, eleven in Lynton, seven in Dartmouth, six in Exmouth, six in Ilfracombe, and one each in Topsham, Budleigh Salterton, Paignton, and Kingsbridge. Many, though, had already escaped the country, including the skilled lignite miners near Bovey Tracey, probably forewarned.

A spate of articles about spies kept anti-German emotions running high. One was convinced that most German waiters and hawkers had gone into hiding, and noted that many East End criminals were German. It was sure that all of them were spies and saboteurs with easy access to arms, wireless telegraphs, carrier pigeons and cars. It added that many Germans owned shops suspiciously near to vulnerable communication points such as railway bridges. The only reassuring note was that however hard Germans tried to disguise themselves they would always look arrogantly Teutonic. On Southdown Hill above Brixham a factory converted fish refuse into manure using machinery installed some years earlier by Germans, and a rumour spread that the large concrete platform there had been constructed in readiness for an invasion force's large gun, to be used to terrorise Torbay. The army inspected it but failed to unearth anything suspicious.

There was dismay that the Kaiser's brother, Prince Henry of Prussia, had visited south Devon in the summer of 1914, no doubt spying for an invasion route and recording Britain's defences. The *Sidmouth Chronicle* was convinced that Princess Leopold, sister-in-law of the Kaiser, had been the centre of a spy ring when she stayed in the resort as Mrs Sherenstein, and it claimed that German musicians in the resort were often to be seen noting the geography of the coast and installations along it. In 1916 Edith Keen caused a stir when she published her inflammatory memoirs. As a pre-war companion to Princess Viktoria of Prussia, the Kaiser's sister, she painted an unflattering picture of the Kaiser's foul temper, the royal family's arrogance and their brutality towards their servants, and she made much of their habit of deliberately spying on Britain during their state and private visits – something she was sure no English gentleman would do abroad.

In September 1914 a spy scare in Brixham was caused, understandably perhaps, by six locals taking a dip in the sea, climbing the rocks under the coastguard station and firing a revolver across the beach. Sea Scouts camping nearby on coast-watching duties reported them to the police, and wild rumours of German spies signalling to an offshore cruiser and attacking local inhabitants spread through the town, causing armed police to mount a hurried search. The miscreants were identified, questioned and eventually released, and the Sea Scouts were praised for their alertness.

In September 1914 a spy was reported drawing the railway viaduct at Filleigh overlooking Castle Hill park. Feelings ran high in nearby South Molton, 'and had the police returned with a German there would probably have been lively scenes', but it was merely a thoughtless holidaymaker. In May 1915 three equally thoughtless Okehampton teachers were detained by a soldier for photographing Meldon viaduct.

The previous autumn an angry crowd gathered in front of Plymouth's Globe Hotel, seeking the German spy they had heard was there. Police arrived, and a group of men in army and naval uniforms were bundled into taxi cabs which then immediately drove away, with several men from the crowd hanging on to them. Once again there was an innocent explanation: the officers had been overheard wondering about the identity of one of their number staying there. Nevertheless such incidents were widely reported, and did nothing to allay people's disquiet about what might be happening around them.

In October the *Teignmouth Post* stoked the fires, conspiratorially claiming that 'it is said on excellent authority that during the past few weeks, in fact since the outbreak of the war, a number of wealthy Germans and Austrians have acquired lonely and seemingly insignificant properties in Devonshire, a county which, thanks to its vast stretches of moor and coast, is peculiarly adapted to such operations as they may contemplate'. Some small substance was given to these suspicions by the disappearance of Count Conrad Hochberg from Croydon Hall near Washford in Somerset, who had integrated with local gentry, hunted with the Devon and Somerset Staghounds, played polo and supported local events. As no-one, not even his servants, knew where he was, the wildest rumours flourished. In May 1915 the sudden disappearance of 'a foreigner' arriving by car in Exmouth with 'an unholy curiosity' about army and navy matters caused an equal furore.

In the autumn of 1914, 2,000 people gathered in Torquay Pavilion for a meeting on 'Enemy Aliens in our Midst' chaired by Lord Clifford of Chudleigh, with the support of Lord Leith of Fyvie, Admiral Sir William Acland and many other local dignitaries and clergy. Clifford emphasised the nation's longstanding habit of welcoming foreigners and the shock of realising that some of them were proving to be our sworn enemies. In a highly emotional and provocative speech Leith proposed that all enemy aliens should be interned whether naturalised or not, and the navy should stop and search supposedly neutral ships – as he was sure many were minelaying around the coast at night. He asserted that many wealthy Germans and Austrians believed themselves to be secure as naturalised Britons while they spied upon troop and naval movements, and in due course sabotaged railways, factories and defences. 'They might have 200 Germans among them, 199 of which were honest and loyal, but there might be one – who he was no-one might know – who, if he remained at liberty might by means of his preparations and tactics by one foul treacherous blow, destroy many precious lives.' Everyone must be vigilant. Around the same time the Chief Constable of Devon aroused grave suspicions about a popular pastime by giving notice that no-one could keep carrier or homing pigeons without a police permit.

In 1915 William Le Queux visited Torquay with Lord Leith of Fyvie to give a public address that picked up the threads of his famous novel *Invasion 1910*. Spies were everywhere, he said. They were skilled in photography, geography and the means of recording and transmitting information. Well trained in English language, manners and culture, they could easily pass as natives. He suspected some were English army and naval officers, and in positions of sufficient authority to secure state secrets as well as details of troop and shipping movements. As a friend of Lord Northcliffe, the domineering press magnate, Le Queux was in a powerful position to get his voice heard and words read. In July 1918 another well-attended public meeting in Torquay called for the nation's future security to be protected by the final hounding out of all clandestine German business interests in Britain and the total isolation of Germany after the war. Making Germany pay dearly for its aggression became a key shibboleth for the future, and in due course the harsh peace terms contributed much to that country's long-lasting sense of humiliation and bitterness.

There was no let-up in incidents, not least because of the zeal of the police and the public. Lionel Norman, a visitor of independent means, was arrested in Newton Abbot in February 1915 on suspicion of questioning soldiers in public houses about the strength of local units stationed there. A visitor from Hull, he was found to be naive but not dangerous. When 'a well-known Plymouth postman' was arrested while rather foolishly walking near the seaplane base at Mount Batten carrying a telescope crowds gathered and wild rumours circulated. A German-born hairdresser and tobacconist by the name of Wolff in St Marychurch near Torquay was less fortunate. As he had been naturalised, he had not been interned at the outbreak of war despite local antipathies, but the outrage that followed the torpedoing of the liner *Lusitania* re-aroused hostility against him. A crowd of over 200 gathered in the streets, threats were uttered and his windows were smashed before the police moved everyone on. Whispering campaigns were also not unknown. In autumn 1914 two foreign lecturers at the University College in Exeter were viewed with grave suspicion, but one was able to prove his Russian ancestry and the other, although born in Germany, had lived in England for fifty years and was a British citizen. As late as December 1917 a solicitor's notice appeared in the *Torquay Times* threatening with formal prosecution any future perpetrators of malicious accusations that Charles Price, the manager of the Pavilion, was not of British birth.

Even the monks of Buckfast Abbey were not above suspicion – far from it. A small group of émigré French Benedictine monks had been living at the pre-Reformation monastic site since 1882. They had set about rebuilding the monastic church, a task that was to take several decades. By 1914 two-thirds of the monks were German, and in total forty monks of foreign birth had had to be registered as aliens. Their movements were severely limited, but nevertheless their presence aroused local suspicions.

It did not help that Dom Anscar Vonier, Abbot of Buckfast, was in Austria when the war broke out. A German by birth, he was naturalised in Britain, but there were stories, totally unjustified, that he had joined the German army. As the war dragged on and stories of German atrocities abounded, the German monks became the ongoing target of pent-up local hostility. In July 1916 members of Buckfastleigh Urban District Council (UDC) met the abbey authorities to discuss a memorandum that the UDC intended to send to the home secretary. The original agreement had been that no 'enemy alien' monks would leave the abbey grounds without being escorted by British subjects, and that all incoming and outgoing mail would be censored. Since then the UDC claimed that three young monks had returned to Germany without permission but with much local information, the abbot himself was the postal censor, anyone could visit on the pretext of attending services in the abbey church, and a pillar box and public telephone box were easily accessible to the monks at the abbey gates. The monks also worked in fields some distance from the abbey itself with little supervision. Asserting that spies had probably infiltrated the adjacent textile factory, the UDC complained that the failure to enforce adequate restrictions on the monks was a gift to enemy agents. The abbot was conciliatory, promising to do his best to ensure that all regulations were obeyed, but did respond wryly to the threat of formal internment with the remark that it would probably be less severe than routine life within his monastic order. He added that three monks were serving with Allied troops in France, and that the abbey was under French and papal authority, not German. It was also noted that Lord Clifford of Chudleigh, a prominent Roman Catholic benefactor of the abbey, had the greatest confidence in the community's integrity, and, as the abbot quietly but firmly suggested, nothing untoward had occurred in the last two years to cause upset 'even to the most nervous of the public'.

The UDC's memorandum led to a visit by a parliamentary commission, which backfired on the local protestors by recommending that tighter controls could best be introduced by local magistrates liaising with the chief constable to employ a rota of special constables to provide round-the-clock observation. The chief constable was willing but the magistrates found it impossible to find the men, and local councils refused to pay the costs. The War Office refused any assistance. The magistrates persisted in urging the government to send the German and Austrian monks to an internment camp, but Sir George Cave, the home secretary, was unmoved. At Question Time in the House of Commons in March 1917 he regretted the local refusal to act in accordance with the commissioners' recommendations, and reiterated that the monks were exempt from formal internment as part of the original agreement. Despite much lobbying of MPS, a request a few months later to deport the monks met a blunt refusal from William Brace, the under secretary, who drily added that forced repatriation would merely give Germany more war workers. Members of the Devon Joint Standing Committee were equally pragmatic. The chief constable believed that the seven French priests at the abbey 'will take jolly good care that they do not forget the conditions you ask them to fulfil' regarding watching their German colleagues, and the Honourable John Wallop noted that the monks were busy building the abbey itself, which 'should keep them out of mischief'.

As we have seen, though, not every arrest stemmed from paranoia. In June 1915 Abdon Jappe, a Dane, appeared before Plymouth magistrates' court charged with attempting to elicit information about the movements of warships and being in possession of electrical apparatus capable of sending messages to the enemy. He had been trapped by one of the plain-clothed Metropolitan policemen who kept constant watch over the dockyard during the war and had posed as a gullible civilian. In a high profile court case at the Exeter Assize Jappe was found guilty and sentenced to three years' imprisonment for trying to persuade two dockyard workers to transmit information to him in Denmark. In October 1915 Charles Keilm, a German merchant seaman landing from a Norwegian vessel, was arrested at Plymouth for masquerading as a Dutchman. He would have been lucky to escape the death penalty if he had possessed incriminating information to take back to Germany. From time to time Russians, Norwegians and Swedes were arrested in Plymouth as they tried to board trains or were found drunk without alien permits after they landed at the docks. All were fined £2 and repatriated. Plymouth police were also hot on the trail of lodging house keepers who failed to ensure foreign lodgers had the necessary alien permits or failed to register them as guests with the civil authorities. Fines could be steep, up to £10.

The possibility of raids by sea and air on southern Devon towns caused alarm when war broke out and never entirely went away. German warships shelled East Coast towns, German airships and Gotha bombers raided London and the eastern Home Counties and clear evidence existed that German submarines roamed the English Channel. In January 1915 some Totnes town councillors thought public lighting should be extinguished at night, while others mocked the alarmists, but nevertheless the motion that Totnes should be in darkness from 11 p.m. onwards was carried. Interestingly the ban did not apply to household lights, presumably because they were deemed not bright enough to help enemy pilots.

Although some doubted whether the ban was really needed, Captain Vyvyan, the Chief Constable of Devon, ordered all lights visible from the sea to be screened at night. His concern for absolute security proved a difficult decision for affected householders to uphold, but there were many citizens only too ready to catch them out. In November 1915 the manager of the Fortfield Hotel in Sidmouth was fined 7gns for not ensuring that guests obscured all seaward-facing lights. Earlier in the year a Royal Navy commander in Woolacombe was fined £2 for showing a light and a further £5 for assaulting the policeman who arrested him. He admitted that the strain of commanding a North Sea gunboat was affecting his health. In October 1916 magistrates fined two Exe estuary tradesmen 10s and 15s for showing lights, and in Exmouth the following month thirteen more cases were brought to court. In March 1915 a wealthy Paignton invalid was fined 10s because either her servants or companion left lights blinking intermittently when curtains moved by an open window. Her patriotism was not doubted, the court said, but the sergeant major who spotted the offence claimed she could have been signalling to an enemy boat in the bay. Certainly a U-boat was seen off Torbay the following month.

Fines later in the war could be heavy, perhaps because war weariness and frayed nerves were affecting the police and magistrates. In February 1917 Francis Lancey was prosecuted for lighting a fire on Holdstone Common in Combe Martin. He asserted he was a market gardener trying to improve the quality of his grazing land, but the police asserted he could have been signalling a submarine. His offence was taken seriously, and he was fined 20s. In May Edith Charles from London was also fined £1 for sketching without a permit in a restricted area near Mortehoe, and her pictures were confiscated. In August 1917 Leonard Thomas, a holidaymaker in Plymouth, was arrested for taking photographs likely to be of use to the enemy, and was fined the large sum of £5. The threat of spies was perceived as so great that in 1917 all schools received an Army Council pamphlet alarmingly headed 'The Inadvertent Disclosure of Military Information', and henceforth Devon's children had the heady mix of excitement and fear that came from being directed to take great care to whom they spoke and what they said.

Access to the coast by those not well known locally was severely restricted, and cars travelling at night were liable to be stopped and searched. As a tragic result, an army officer and a naval officer were killed on the night of 24 January 1914. Driving along Torbay Road in Torquay, they were halted by an armed sentry who, acting on orders, wanted their car's number and wished to search it. Angered by the hold-up, the officers said they were driving on, but the sentry threatened to shoot if they moved. The officers got out and faced the sentry's levelled rifle. Suddenly a shot rang out. The bullet passed through one officer, who died instantly, and struck the other one, who died later that night. Fortunately there was a witness who explained that the officers had deeply resented taking orders, and the formal inquiry eventually exonerated the sentry.

BELGIAN REFUGEES

In August 1914 Germany recognised that it faced a war on two fronts: Russia to the east and France to the west. As a result the German army planned to push through Belgium as quickly as possible to ensure the capture of Paris and the speedy defeat of France before Russia could finish mobilising its massive, if ill-equipped, forces. Nothing could be allowed to hold up the westward advance, and certainly not the towns and villages of Belgium however much that country's small army tried to stem the onslaught. The result was pitiful trails of refugees, many fleeing in haste with few if any possessions.

Less than a month after the declaration of war Miss Clara Andrew of Exeter was organising the collection of clothing to aid the hundreds of refugees who were beginning to descend upon Britain. As Britain had finally gone to war because of the attack on Belgium, its now desperate citizens were well received across the country. Exeter's *Express & Echo* epitomised the mood of the moment, saying, 'Homeless, yes, but not without a home where they will be warmly welcomed; destitute, perhaps, but not without friends who count it a joy and privilege to do something for those who have done so much for us, but for whose gallantry it is possible we might now all be in arms to repel the invader from our shores.'

The energetic Miss Andrew quickly persuaded the central refugee authorities in London to send families to Exeter, where she and a few other volunteers worked from hand to mouth collecting two sets of extra clothing for each of the refugees and securing some sort of temporary accommodation for them, all through the generosity of local well-wishers. The city council soon added its assistance, but the pressure for places grew acute. Even so, social class was not forgotten. For example, some refugees from the 'Official, Mercantile and Professional Classes' were allocated to the Judges Lodgings in Rougemont Castle, while families of 'other classes' were placed in its vacant stable and coach-houses. Others were housed in the St Thomas workhouse, but they 'were loath to come into the institution' because they had heard off-putting stories from unfortunate compatriots who had been dispatched to the cells of another local workhouse.

By the end of October 1914, 700 refugees had arrived in Exeter to be temporarily housed and fed, and to receive extra clothing, and then to be moved on to more permanent accommodation across Devon. They arrived at any time of the day or night, often 'poorly clad, wan and in some cases half-starved', said Miss Andrew. On Friday 30 October, for example, seventy arrived at three o'clock in the morning, and were duly met by Miss Andrew and her team to be taken, in pouring rain, to various sympathetic hotels and lodging houses. On another occasion a welcoming party waited at Queen Street station, but the promised train failed to arrive, and seems to have been misdirected to the north of England. As the war progressed the trains sometimes deposited more than 200 people at a time, and a line of cars, charabancs and trams gathered to take the anxious and exhausted refugees to a host of temporary addresses.

The towns and villages of Devon quickly rallied round, and accepted Miss Andrew and her rapidly evolving organisation as the centre of county operations. A large house in West Southernhay in Exeter had been lent to the committee as its administrative headquarters for receiving, equipping and homing refugees, and as the centre for the reception of new clothing. Other rooms in Queen Street received and sorted second-hand clothing for dispatch to distressed families still in Belgium; by the third week of September a ton and a half had been sent. Various fundraising events were organised, and that autumn several collections and sales across the city of Plymouth raised an impressive £486 5s 8d. A dance in Chagford raised £2 9s 0d. A South Brent concert by local musicians and singers raised £10. At Chelston women and children made 200 'useful' items of clothing for the refugees. At Bovey Tracey a vigorous branch of the Young Patriotic League gave 15gns from a jumble sale and bazaar. By May 1915 Crediton's total, through fundraising events and donations from individuals, schools and factories, reached £500. In due course Belgian singers and musicians began to contribute to major concerts for refugee funds. One in Exeter in February 1915 raised £100, and another in Kingsbridge raised £39 19s 3d. Events in Ilfracombe included a Belgian Food Fair alongside concerts by Belgian children and adults.

As the distribution of refugees from Exeter widened across Devon, local railway stations became the stages for formal reception committees. In December 1914 a deputation waited for the first Belgian families to arrive at the small station in

Staff and wounded Belgian soldiers in hospital in Ilfracombe, October 1914. (Ilfracombe Museum)

Loddiswell, from where they were dispersed to houses in the village and nearby South Milton. The energetic Belgian Relief Council in Ilfracombe arranged for rooms to be found in Watermouth Castle and Clyffe Hydro, and beds were reserved for wounded soldiers in the town hospital and the emergency one at Westwell Hall. Watched by large crowds, the first soldiers were met at the railway station in October 1914 by civic dignitaries, clergy and medical staff, and then taken by cars to the hospitals. Fires were lit in the wards, hot water bottles were put in the beds, and hot milk and beef tea were ready to be served. The arrangements were a little haphazard as all these welcoming activities had been undertaken a day or so earlier, but the soldiers had failed to arrive.

Enthusiasm spread through many communities. Cullompton, for example, welcomed its first refugee families in October 1914. The schoolchildren tidied the garden of the empty house, furniture and coal were donated, and crowds watched as cars drove the newcomers from the station to their new home. In the same month two houses were given rent-free in Crediton, and once again donations furnished and equipped them. 'A gratifying feature', announced the press, 'has been the support of the working classes, many of the poorest offering their mites.' Sidmouth housed fifty-three refugees in several private houses and converted empty properties, and some went to the Convent of the Assumption. Mayor Gregory of Tiverton recalled the variety of families accommodated in the borough: his memoirs list a doctor, teacher, postmaster, fisherman, and many labourers. He worked in close cooperation with the Heathcoat-Amorys, the Walronds and other wealthy families to provide accommodation, furniture, fuel and funds for sixty refugees.

The refugees had harrowing stories to tell, which were eagerly sought by the newspapers. Verification was impossible, and in the heightened emotions of wartime it was almost certainly considered unnecessary. One soldier said that Germans drove up in a car with a white flag and then opened fire with a hidden machine gun, a second claimed that the Germans gouged the eyes out of six civilians when Belgian soldiers held up their advance at a bridge over the Escant, and a third said that the Germans wantonly destroyed Termonde and desecrated its graveyard. The capture and sacking of the historic city of Louvain was frequently mentioned. One refugee blamed the destruction on drunken German troops, who were after loot from churches, museums and wealthy private houses. The Germans had then blamed the havoc on the foolish action of a few citizens who had fired upon the occupying forces. Another thought that the Germans deliberately adopted a policy of brutality to frighten and subdue everyone in their way, and asserted that they found this easy and enjoyable as cruelty was part of their nature.

In March 1915 things changed. Local newspapers suddenly published the decision that all Belgian refugee work outside Exeter would be the responsibility of an executive committee appointed by the Lord Lieutenant, Earl Fortescue, to be known as the Devon County War Refugee Committee. This would be a local agency of the Central Committee in London, and most of Miss Andrew's responsibilities, and authority, would be handed over to it. Lord Fortescue became its chairman, and, as his memoirs and correspondence intimate, much of his time was spent pacifying ruffled feelings and ensuring effective appointments were made.

Relations between the Exeter Committee and the Devon Committee, which became the Devon & Cornwall War Refugee Committee a few months later, were not harmonious. Trouble occurred over decision-making processes, finance and documentation when refugees initially lodged in Exeter and paid for by the city's committee subsequently decided to move into the county committee's geographical and bureaucratic territory. For example, when an Exeter-based refugee turned up in Newton Abbot in an attempt to secure work as a tailor, the question of his clothing and accommodation costs led to numerous letters and meetings. Every detail was exposed in a full column in the *Western Times*, including the mutual suspicions of uncharitable behaviour and unwarranted intransigence.

By July 1915 there were about 4,000 Belgian refugees in Devon and Cornwall, and the London Committee requested accommodation for another 2,000. Currently between thirty and sixty were coming each week, and this was expected to rise to 100 a week. Miss Andrew organised a week's tour of Cornwall for herself so that she could meet individuals and groups willing to accommodate refugees. She signed herself vice-chairman of the Devon and Cornwall Committee, although effective authority lay more in the hands of the new honorary secretary, Miss Bannatyne. By January 1916, 5,090 refugees were accommodated across the two counties, all of them coordinated through the city and county committees, both of which were based in West Southernhay.

Miss Andrew had not taken kindly to the changes. In his memoirs Lord Fortescue summed her up as 'energetic and kind-hearted, though lacking ballast', remarking that the changes were prompted by a 'considerable element of local jealousy and personal self-importance to be dealt with not least among the Andrews family'. Here he is referring not only to Clara but also to her brother and sister, who were key figures in the original city committee. Certainly Miss Andrew was the leading spirit initially, and her initiative had led Exeter to be the first provincial centre to receive and house Belgian refugees.

However, files at the Devon Record Office reveal her capacity to antagonise not only colleagues but also civic dignitaries, and certainly the rather *ad hoc* arrangements that suited the initial reception of refugees needed formalising, even though everything continued to be managed by teams of volunteers in Exeter and in the district and town committees across Devon and Cornwall. Indeed, local donations flowed in so well that most of the government grant subsequently introduced to support the maintenance of refugees was returned to the Treasury at the end of the war. The original Exeter Committee stayed aloof from the Devon and Cornwall Committee for a year, but eventually its work was subsumed within the dual county committee.

Gradually Miss Andrew was marginalised, and her copious correspondence with Lord Fortescue reveals her anger at the consistently hostile gossip about her centre's integrity and efficiency, much of which she thought, with justification, was targeted at her. Indeed, in one unpleasant incident her expenses claim for the week's tour of Cornwall was attacked as excessive, even though, as Fortescue himself stated in her defence, she was able to report a large number of new accommodation addresses. Fortescue's skill lay in his patient but determined attempts to create a more efficient and harmonious organisation without upsetting Miss Andrew too much or restoring her to a permanent key role. For a time she worked for the Exeter Committee and then the Devon and Cornwall Committee, but by the autumn of 1916 she had resigned to take up alternative voluntary employment in London. She did, though, receive her own well-earned Medaille de la Reine Elisabeth, awarded by the King of the Belgians, and now held by Topsham Museum. In 1918 Miss Bannatyne, the new honorary secretary, was made an MBE. She was the sister of Mrs Ludovic Amory, and highly regarded by Lord Fortescue.

In January 1916 Lord Fortescue reported that the West Southernhay centre had received and placed 7,700 refugees. For various reasons, though, a few hundred had been transferred from their original localities. In his report Fortescue hinted that not all refugees had settled congenially into their new communities, but in his memoirs he was far more forthright, lamenting that 'the refugees were not a nice lot; they were exacting and tiresome, and a proportion were (*sic*) criminal and immoral'. Even the final published report of the Devon & Cornwall War Refugees Committee recorded its surprise at the continuing goodwill shown by most local people, 'when it is remembered that the Refugees were not selected specimens; indeed, sometimes they were not very desirable visitors, and more often than not they were persons with a different standard of living and observances to those who housed them'.

Indeed, as early as November 1914 a leader in *Trewman's Flying Post* disparaged the tendency to 'spoil' the refugees, especially as so many of them were only 'peasants'. The north Devon village of Fremington welcomed several refugee families, and as everywhere else donations of money, clothing and fuel were readily forthcoming, and the doctor gave his services free. However, visitors can outstay their welcome, and two years later some residents were complaining that the Belgians were living in far too much 'luxury' compared with ordinary Devon working families. By 1917 families in Ilfracombe, a town that had made so many refugees welcome in 1914, were voicing similar grudges.

Medaille de la Reine Elisabeth awarded to Miss Clara Andrew. (Topsham Museum)

In Newton Abbot several refugee families were housed in the Highweek Church Institute but, the *Mid Devon Advertiser* recorded, 'with such an assembly it was only to be expected that there would be friction and unpleasantness at times'. Nevertheless the 'disagreeable happenings' were resolved by the local committee, and it seems that extra houses were rented and the relevant families dispersed. Similar disagreements, including physical violence between families, erupted in Teignmouth. When Count Goblet d'Alviella, the vice-president of the Belgian senate, attended a reception for Belgian refugees in Newton Abbot in February 1915, he emphasised the need not only for gratitude but also for good behaviour. Unfortunately he added to his listeners' misery with the news that the Germans were levying high taxes on all Belgian families, and had ordered that the remaining property of refugees could be seized and sold to pay them.

On occasion the law was invoked. In June 1915 a Belgian man was given the choice of three months' hard labour or internment in Earls Court concentration camp for wilfully evading the order to notify a change of address from Tiverton to Exeter. Exeter's chief constable bemoaned that 'the police not only in Exeter, but throughout the country, had had the utmost difficulty in securing compliance with the order. Belgian refugees had given the police everywhere needless trouble, and in some cases had wilfully evaded the order.' The Home Office had urged great strictness in enforcing notification, as it suspected German spies were entering the country masquerading as Belgian refugees. In May 1916 two Belgians from Wadebridge were sentenced to two months' hard labour for defying police orders that barred them from travelling to Brixham. A refugee employed as a cook in a doctor's household in Alphington, just outside Exeter, was fined during the food crisis of 1917 for wasting bread by throwing dry bits to the birds. The way the case was written up, though, hinted that this mean-spirited conviction stemmed from the doctor's wife's dislike of the female refugee.

Not surprisingly, Belgian and English children were little different. In September 1916 two Belgian and two English boys were fined in Tiverton for damaging fences and throwing the wood into the river. That December another Belgian boy and two English boys were birched in Exeter, for theft from several shops. And there was at least one inquest into the death of a neglected Belgian infant.

The spy scare meant that no foreigners were allowed to work on British fishing boats, despite the shortage of British hands and the willingness of some Belgian fisherman to earn their keep on Brixham boats. Some, though, took jobs at the quarries near Christow, some secured menial work at Seale-Hayne Agricultural College and others worked as labourers on farms around Crediton. The editor of *Trewman's Flying Post* remarked, 'Imagine the tangle a Devonshire farmer would get into giving a day's instruction to a labourer from Flanders.' By February 1915, 500 male refugees were known to be employed. In South Molton their wages were between 15s and 18s a week as labourers, and it seems that 50 per cent of this was deducted for their maintenance, 25 per cent kept aside for when they returned to Belgium and 25 per cent allowed as pocket money.

At a meeting in Exeter to discuss employment prospects, some local representatives asserted that fit men should be sent back to Belgium to fight, as the King of the Belgians wished. Some did return before the end of the war, but the British put no pressure on them to do so. In Sidmouth a group of soldiers returned in May 1915 under Commandant d'Affnay, a distinguished soldier who had been much feted locally. The soldiers received parcels of provisions when they left, and later the effusive d'Affnay wrote: 'I will not repeat all the exclamations of admiration, of astonishment, which were heard during the distribution: eatables, sweets, clothes and many other good things coming from Sidmouth are so beautiful, so good.'

In Combe Martin, Exmouth, Great Torrington, Moretonhampstead, Seaton, Shaldon, Tiverton and Ugborough, Belgian children attended the local elementary schools; and probably other schools accepted them too. In Exeter, and it is likely elsewhere, English classes were provided for the refugees, but no further evidence has emerged regarding how the children fared in the schools. Some, though, went to special schools, such as those in Teignmouth and Ilfracombe established solely for refugee children and staffed by Roman Catholic teachers and priests, largely drawn from within the Belgian community.

Notwithstanding the irritations and misunderstandings, local communities tried to make the Christmas and New Year period particularly memorable for refugee families. In 1917 in Exeter 200 refugees were entertained in Barnfield Hall. A tree was decorated with electric lights, oranges, crackers and tinsel, each refugee received a present and the children got extra clothing as well. Everything had been donated.

There is copious evidence that the Belgians were grateful for the hospitality. In July 1917 the Belgian refugees in Teignmouth presented the town with a publicly displayed Devonshire pottery vase on a brick column surrounded by an ornamental rockery, with the inscription 'A tribute of gratitude from the Belgian refugees 1914–1917'. In July 1918 the refugees in Newton Abbot entertained the local Relief Committee when the Medaille de la Reine Elisabeth was bestowed on Miss Froude, the town's honorary secretary. Similarly inscribed medals were awarded to several other secretaries, and, as we have seen, to Miss Clara Andrew.

At last, in January 1919, amid much mutual admiration and expressions of friendship, Lord Fortescue took formal leave of the last 200 Belgian refugees in Exeter. His memoirs, though, acidly state that the office was 'finally closed, to the great relief of all connected with it'.

CONSCIENTIOUS OBJECTORS

The issue of conscientious objectors sprang up in 1916 as conscription replaced volunteering, and those with a deep-seated objection to war service were forced to justify their convictions to the tribunals. Amid some controversy, the law introducing conscription also allowed exemptions on grounds of personal conscience, as well as those where the applicant was in a war-related occupation, the sole family breadwinner or in a business liable to collapse if he was taken away. There were numerous applications by conscientious objectors across Devon, and tribunals had great difficulty in identifying genuine cases from those whom they suspected were using this process because no other avenue for avoiding active service remained open to them. Applicants could argue for one of three categories of exemption, but of course with no guarantee they would get any. Some were prepared to serve in the Non Combatant Corps, in uniform but not fighting, some were 'alternativists', prepared to undertake war-related civilian work but free from military control, while some were 'absolutists', who eschewed all work connected with the war.

A *Western Evening Herald* reporter visited a Non Combatant Corps working on railway construction and maintenance in France and concluded that 'any slacker who succeeded in getting into the NCC in the belief that he would have an easy time would soon have cause to change his opinion'. The men came from all walks of life – tradesmen, teachers, bank clerks and farmers, and most professed religious scruples against serving in the front line. They received the same rations, pay and uniforms, although devoid of any insignia except a NCC shoulder badge, as ordinary soldiers. They had no complaints, said the reporter.

As many local reports intimate, applicants experienced great difficulty in persuading tribunals of the strength of their cases. Some tribunals seemed a little more sympathetic than others and tried to weigh the evidence even-handedly, but others were clearly guilty of harassing the applicants. The military representatives on the tribunals were invariably hostile, and more often than not immediately appealed against what they took to be an adverse decision. Public opinion was equally hostile, and the tortuous tribunal and appeal procedures took place against a background of aggressive newspaper articles and correspondence, and also local council and other meetings deploring the presence of conscientious objectors on the streets. Physical violence against them was not unknown in Devon. Liberty of conscience was to some extent enshrined in law, but its manifestation in ardent pacifists was perceived by most people as culpable selfishness and rank cowardice. These men were the widely hated 'shirkers'.

At Barnstaple in March 1916 the tribunal dealt sharply with Arthur Chilcott from Shapland & Petter's Raleigh Cabinet Works, who claimed absolute exemption 'as a preacher of the Gospel of Jesus Christ' and objected as a member of the Plymouth Brethren to being engaged in anything connected with the war. The mayor cut short Chilcott's defending statement, and at his refusal to join the NCC cried out, 'What! Call yourself an Englishman. It makes my blood boil. I am surprised to think we have such a man in the town.' The tribunal poured scorn on Chilcott's acknowledgement that he had shot rabbits – 'They cannot kill back', retorted one tribunal member

– and amid applause the exemption was refused. In August this tribunal sent the pastor of the local branch of the International Bible Students' Association to the NCC after he failed to identify that the New Testament quotation 'I have not found so great faith, no, not in Israel' came from the miracle of the centurion's servant. The alleged aptness of the military analogy was laboriously emphasised by the tribunal. On occasion the scoring of points over applicants went to extreme lengths, with one north Devon conscientious objector mocked for buying anything on which purchase tax had been paid, as the tax went to pay for the war.

Although the anti-conscientious objector stance of the local newspapers means that the tribunal reports cannot be fully trusted, they do suggest that clear proof of relevant and long-held religious convictions before the war could work in applicants' favour, while a recent conversion, however powerfully defended, would not. In general, although not invariably, those sects with a clear record of genuine pacifism such as the Quakers and Plymouth Brethren were accepted as a foundation for exemption and non-combatant service. In April 1916 in Torquay two applicants were allowed into the NCC on these criteria, while another who merely claimed membership of the Anglican Church was told he would have to do what most adherents of the Church of England were doing – fight for their country. At Crediton Sir Ian Amory scorned a young man's argument that 'the Spirit of Christ' entered him at the age of sixteen and since then he had eschewed all violence. 'The lad,' he stated, 'was a very stupid one,' and merely got hold of views that might exempt him; but in the end he was allocated farm work rather than military service.

Many churchmen had little time for conscientious objectors. In March 1916 the Revd Captain W. Leighton MC spoke on the heroism at Gallipoli, saying that 'if they came across any "conscientious objectors" who quoted the Bible to support their case, he would recommend that they should be used as sandbags'. That May the Congregational minister in Braunton devoted a sermon to asserting that if the conscientious objectors were right than everybody else was not only wrong but stood 'condemned before the judgement seat of God'. This was ridiculous, he argued. Jesus had said in the parable of the good shepherd, 'there were wolves to be destroyed, and men like chaff were to be burned with fire'. Confident in his congregation's answer, he asked, 'Do you think Christ would stand by carelessly while a coward attacked a pure innocent maiden or ill-used the helpless?'

In March 1916 the *South Molton Gazette* published an article firmly condemning conscientious objectors. It picked up many of the points made from pulpits. If their theories were to prevail 'we should have a nation of shirkers and skulkers, keen only on saving themselves'; the British Empire would fall, the small nations of Europe would be crushed and Germany would be triumphant. That cannot be God's will, the *Gazette* asserted triumphantly. A particularly sneering leader in *Trewman's Flying Post* said that conscientious objectors should be put to work erecting barbed wire fences in front of the trenches, as that does not involve actually killing the enemy.

Plymouth Education Committee was extremely pleased that a teacher who admitted being a conscientious objector resigned from his post at the High School. The borough council was incensed, though, that it could do nothing to remove a finance officer who had secured the rare success of complete exemption as a conscientious objector. 'This man,' one member thundered, 'has been a wretched blot upon the Corporation employees.' However, the very vehemence of some members' comments caused a few others to demur at what they perceived to be the excessive persecution of genuine pacifists.

Exeter City Council had little patience with Alfred Chandler, an anti-conscription activist and member of the Union for Democratic Control, who was successfully prosecuted and imprisoned for distributing pamphlets that asked 'What are we fighting for?' The town clerk said that 'this appalling pamphlet' claimed Britain was motivated by a 'gratification of hatred' and a 'lust for vengeance'. The incident led to questions in the House of Commons regarding the suppression of the Union.

At a high-profile court case in Newton Abbot in May 1916 William Hamlyn, secretary of the local branch of the Shop Assistants Union, and Charles Baker, chairman of Newton Abbot's No-Conscription Fellowship and district secretary of the Trades & Labour Council, were fined £2 each as absentees under the Military Service Act and handed over to the military authorities. All their applications and appeals for exemption had failed. Many in court applauded the decision, but many too applauded Hamlyn and Baker. A week later Charles Baker, now termed Private, was court martialled and imprisoned for six months for refusing to obey army orders or to undergo a medical examination. He said he was an Internationalist and Socialist, and did not believe in resorting to wars to resolve disputes. He was joined in prison by three others from Devonport, Holsworthy and Parracombe. A year later in June 1917, Hamlyn, also called Private, was brought before his second court martial for refusing to obey military orders. This was immediately after his release from a first court martial's prison sentence for the same offence. Once again he refused all war-related employment, and this time received a two-year sentence.

Several others from Newton Abbot were placed in the NCC even though some were dedicated Plymouth Brethren. The reports suggest that the cases were rushed through, with applicants having little time to make their cases. Other applicants failed totally, and two more Newton Abbot pacifists, Harry Bearne and Owen Smith, found themselves faced with active service. With appeals having failed, in June 1916 Bearne and Smith were called up and formally refused to obey army orders. At Exeter barracks soldiers formed up on three sides of a square, the two men were marched into the middle, their crimes were read out and prison sentences of six months imposed.

Most newspapers relished such humiliations. Arthur Chilcott from Barnstaple, together with two other conscientious objectors from Devonport, also endured ritual humiliations at Exeter barracks. A vigorously hostile editorial in *Trewman's Flying Post* condemned their utter selfishness, especially in refusing farming and feeding the nation. The trouble they caused, it thundered, was 'the result not of abnormally developed conscience, but of exceptionally self-opinionated quibbling. The objectors may be sorry to know (I hope they are) that short of pro-Germans and rebels and peace cranks they are doing more than anybody else in Britain to help the other side.'

Abusing the appeal tribunal was counter-productive. In October 1917 Sidney Linscott, a Newton Abbot market gardener, claimed conscientious objector status but failed to attend his appeal. Instead he sent an angry letter scorning the tribunal's integrity, asserting it to be the tool of the military authorities and stating that it was incapable of giving an impartial and unbiased judgement. He wrote that he was cultivating an extra acre of rough ground, but the tribunal was unmoved by this and by a supporting letter from the local branch of the ILP. 'They knew all about this sort of thing in Newton Abbot,' said the military representative, and the appeal was quickly dismissed.

In a particularly celebrated case Henry Hyams, a Paignton architect, received absolute exemption as a conscientious objector in March 1916. He was a founding member of the No-Conscription Fellowship, and would not aid the war in any capacity. The report records the tribunal's standard questions and Hyams' skilful answers avoiding the traps set to get him to acknowledge he would support the war or engage in pre-meditated violence:

Q – Do you object to any service of a military nature?

A – Yes.

Q – Would you help a wounded man on the field of battle?

A – I would never be near the field as I would never be a soldier.

Q – Supposing someone did your sister a wrong?

A – I might commit private murder in the heat of the moment, but I refuse to take part in this war, in cold blood.

The tribunal reluctantly agreed with a confident Hyams that the law obliged them to grant him absolute exemption. Success eluded him, however, as the military representative lodged a successful appeal, and Hyams' resort to a mix of Christian and International Marxist arguments in his defence fell on completely deaf ears. He refused to don a uniform and was imprisoned.

The tribunal appeal of Howard Evans, a single man aged twenty-one, who worked in HM Dockyard in Devonport as an electrical engineer, portrays the impatient and unsympathetic flavour of many reported exchanges. In July 1918 Evans appealed as a Baptist conscientious objector, and the *Western Times* reported:

> The Chairman: Do you object to the Navy? Evans: Yes.
>
> Mr Kekewich: Don't you realise that the electrical work you are engaged in is for the purposes of this war? – Yes, I do.
>
> And you prefer to fight from a safe distance? – That is so, but I have the Scripture to justify me.
>
> You say you are justified in creating weapons of war, but not in fighting in the field. Your work in the Dockyard rather tends, indirectly, to knock the conscientious objection on the head.
>
> Capt. Stirling: Not indirectly, but directly.
>
> Evans: I entered the Dockyard without any religious convictions whatever, but since then I have had personal experiences …
>
> Capt. Stirling: For goodness' sake, let us get down to common sense. We don't want speeches or sermons, but cold-blooded facts. What are you doing in the Dockyard?
>
> Mr Kekewich: Are you helping to make bombs etc.?
>
> Evans: I have to make anything according to instructions.
>
> Applicant was proceeding with a speech when Capt. Stirling interposed with: 'Do speak in common or garden plain English. The whole thing is absolute hypocrisy.'
>
> Applicant, quoting from Scripture, said: 'He that is bound seek not to be free, and he that is free seek not to be bound.'
>
> The Revd E.M. Bacon (Baptist minister): May I say a word or two?
>
> The Chairman: No, no: we have already heard a good deal. The appeal is dismissed.

Some did discriminate between the genuine conscientious objector they professed to admire and the shirkers and anarchists they thought made up the rest of the non-combatants. In November 1917 Crediton's Congregational minister wrote that 'your true conscientious objector (for whom I hold the greatest respect) has been made to suffer great hardship, in that he cannot for very shame group himself with these sprigs of Anarchy and is therefore impelled to decline to avail himself of the privileges of the conscience clause, but, instead, gets into khaki and eats his heart out in the trenches, unless he is fortunate enough to get into the Red Cross or Army Service Corps'. He came dangerously close to saying that all formal applications for exemption by those claiming to be conscientious objectors were, by his definition, false.

On 1 March 1917 the 250 inmates of Dartmoor Prison were transferred to other prisons, and nearly 900 conscientious objectors were moved into the complex, which was redesignated as a Works Settlement. Cell doors were not locked, routines were supposed to be less severe than prison, and the warders were to be instructors in various useful trades in which the inmates could earn money if they so desired. The decision caused a furore across the county that persisted until the end of the war.

Some months later the Right Revd Lord William Cecil, Bishop of Exeter, visited the Settlement and was appalled by what he saw there. He wrote a public letter to *The Times* under the heading 'Anarchic Dartmoor: A Hotbed of Malcontents', asserting that 'If the Government desire a revolution after the war they could hardly have proceeded in a more efficient manner.' Outraged, he argued that all these men with 'fancied or real' grievances against society have ample opportunity to organise resistance, 'armed or passive, against the existing order of things'. He claimed that meetings ended with singing the Red Flag, not the National Anthem, and that sacks of post went in and out 'no doubt conveying instructions for those plans of bloodshed which may at some time bring according to their view, liberty, and, to our view, ruin, to England'. Only a minority held religious convictions, he believed; three-quarters were politically motivated revo-lutionaries who angered ordinary citizens by refusing to help the farmers but eating their generous rations, all the while enjoying the beauties and safety of Dartmoor with considerable freedom, being allowed to come and go from the prison as they pleased. In reply, the Home Office explained that the men were allowed to send and receive letters without restriction, but the only outside meetings they could attend were religious services. The workload was a difficult issue, it acknowledged, as many men were not fit for physical labour and all work had to be supervised, but each man had to do whatever work was allotted to him – mostly clearing waste ground and making up a Dartmoor road – or else risk being returned to the army. Soon afterwards a *Daily Mail* reporter watching Dartmoor claimed the men gleefully performed a play in which they ridiculed the Bishop of Exeter, alongside 'a typical soldier'.

Some were less convinced about the subversive activities pervading the Settlement. At the South Devon Congregational Union meeting in October 1917, one minister moved a resolution condemning 'the brutal outrages' and repeated sentences inflicted upon so many conscientious objectors, and urged the government to give these men the absolute exemption to which they were

The Right Revd Lord William Cecil, Lord Bishop of Exeter, 1916–36. (West Country Studies Library)

entitled. Several others agreed, but in the end the meeting recognised the power of a counter-argument that the Union as a whole would only incur public obloquy if it was perceived, however erroneously, to oppose the war effort. Members feared being tainted by association. The East Devon Congregational Union was bolder, and although some disapproved of conscientious objectors the annual meeting passed a resolution objecting to any ill-treatment of them and praising their overall integrity – despite acknowledging the likely presence of a few 'black sheep'.

A *Daily Chronicle* reporter had a modicum of sympathy for the conscientious objectors. He appreciated they lived among a consistently hostile population outside the Settlement, and he was convinced that the men found living together amid so many different sects and ideologies stressful. He acknowledged that many found the Dartmoor weather daunting and the clothing issue inadequate, while the work of clearing acres of boggy scrubland and building a firm road were tasks that had defeated convicts for the past century. He found that the manager and instructors – they were no longer governor and wardens – exercised great tact in very delicate circumstances.

Nevertheless, persistent rumours circulated regarding the appalling treatment routinely meted out to the incarcerated men. One story claimed they were put in painful restraining suits, and leg and arm irons, and another said they were stripped and locked in a sentry-like box into which scalding and freezing water could be poured through the top at any time, until the victim collapsed. When questions were asked in the House of Commons, William Brace, the under secretary at the Home Office, admitted these instruments existed at Dartmoor but were not used on conscientious objectors; he thought they were mischievous stories put about by the conscientious objectors themselves, and that it was possibly the showers which had been portrayed as torture chambers. However, in May 1917 Brace admitted that fifteen troublesome Dartmoor conscientious objectors had been punished under civil law and sixty-two lesser offenders dealt with by the manager.

On 8 February 1918 the men at the Settlement refused to work all day in protest at a colleague's death from, they asserted, grossly inadequate treatment by the medical staff. H.W. Firth had previously endured imprisonment in Wormwood Scrubs and Maidstone Prison before coming to quarrying work, although already ill, on Dartmoor. The strikers claimed that he was 'a mere bundle of skin and bone' when admitted to Princetown Hospital. The incident reached the House of Commons, where Sir George Cave, the Home Secretary, bluntly overrode the accusations in a statement that the doctors at Maidstone had certified that Firth was fit for travel and work, his duties at the quarry were light, and he had died from diabetes and not ill-treatment.

The activities of the Dartmoor conscientious objectors were forever newsworthy and always cast in the worst possible light. One hefty man was due to be returned to the army for bad behaviour, but sat down in Princetown High Street and refused to move. As a jeering crowd gathered he was dumped in a farm cart and sent to Exeter. Constable Screech of Yelverton claimed in court that when he tried to arrest a conscientious objector he was 'hustled and obstructed' by the suspect's colleagues. The *Western Times* primly asserted that it had always suspected the validity of their pacifist views. Eleven conscientious objectors arrived late one night at Yelverton station only to find the last train for Princetown, 5½ miles away, had left. Two had bicycles and set off, but the others refused to walk, and none of the local residents would give them food or shelter; they had to wait for a wagon to come from Princetown early the following morning. Thirty conscientious objectors were 'hooted' through North Molton when they arrived on a large brake for logging work. When their luggage followed, a large crowd threatened to overturn the cart. The newspaper added, 'Considering that nearly a hundred of North Molton boys are risking their lives daily at the Front, the residents greatly resent the coming to their midst of these men whom they rightly regard as shirkers.'

The creation of the Dartmoor Settlement led to numerous Commons questions. The controversies never went away, but the government never admitted anything wrong was happening. In April 1917 Sir Clement Kinlock-Cooke, Unionist MP for Devonport, asked how many conscientious objectors had been given leave at Easter together with free travel passes, adding that thousands of soldiers and sailors had had no leave for months, some even for a year or more. The answer was that 274 of the 856 men had had leave and 166 of these had had free passes. Another MP inquired after allegations of gross indiscipline at Dartmoor. The Home Office conceded that problems had existed, and threats of close confinement or transfer to the army had had to be used. Other issues raised were the food rations, the leave to wander around Princetown and other nearby towns, the mocking and omission of the National Anthem, and the numbers engaged in paid work. William Brace had to admit that the rations were better than those received by ordinary prisoners, the men had considerable liberty at weekends, the National Anthem was omitted at some meetings and services, and not all the men were able to work; but the law was not being broken in any of these instances. The alleged violence of some conscientious objectors was often referred to by MPs. Two of them were supposed to have sneered at a soldier who had lost a foot, and when his colleague punched one of them the other conscientious objector struck the soldier over the head and face with his stick. William Brace admitted he had heard this story, but 'it had … been impossible to identify any of the parties'. In answer to another question regarding the possibility of shipping the whole Settlement to the Western Front, ideally as a forced labour corps, Sir George Cave said that the Allies would not take kindly to these extreme pacifists being shipped to France.

Local towns vigorously objected to the large numbers of conscientious objectors appearing in their midst. In April 1917 a crowd surrounded a group of conscientious objectors in Tavistock, words were exchanged, one was struck by a wounded soldier and eventually the police broke up the fracas. In May Tavistock's UDC formally thanked the Home Office for banning, at least temporarily, all Dartmoor's conscientious objectors from the town. Moretonhamstead Parish Council, too, condemned the 'loathsome and pretentious humbugs' at Princetown. South Molton Town Council grew incensed at the behaviour of conscientious objectors in the town. One member sneered, 'Their influence was pernicious. When he saw the Objectors swank and swerve (*sic*) how he restrained himself he did not know. While they bounced around the town with kid gloves and walking sticks, businessmen were being made to give up their businesses.' Stories were recounted by the councillors that the conscientious objectors corrupted the young with pacifist and Socialist ideologies, and, worse, drank the German emperor's health. A resolution barring them from the town was sent to the local MP.

Resolutions calling for more severe treatment were common, although in vain. Totnes Borough Tribunal showed its colours by passing a resolution condemning 'the liberties and privileges allowed a number of so-called conscientious objectors now at Princetown Prison who have refused to do their duty to the King and country'. The mayor called them traitors, and castigated their leisured existence in comparison with the ordeals suffered by so many men from Totnes serving in the army and navy. A second resolution was quickly agreed, calling for work 'of national importance' at home or abroad to be imposed upon them. Dartmouth Town Council passed a similar one against the 'nice holiday at Princetown', and so did a mass meeting at Plymouth's Guildhall called by the mayor. The Guildhall meeting, in common with many others, tarred the conscientious objectors with both subversion and immorality. They were 'poisoning the minds of the youngsters with disloyal sentiments' and, equally appallingly, rendering it impossible for young women to go out without an escort.

CONCLUSION

All in all, the fear of real and imagined spies, the sympathy for the refugees and the heated controversies surrounding the conscientious objectors, played their part in accentuating antipathies, heightening tensions and strengthening the nation's resolve to win the war. There is no evidence of a concerted German effort to flood the United Kingdom with a well-trained spy network, but people did not know that – and there were enough alarms and reports for them to think that a huge anti-British German conspiracy was well under way. The government played its part in heightening the tension by placing so many coastal areas as well as naval ports out of bounds to ordinary citizens, issuing leaflets about the dangers of talking to strangers, arresting many foreign sailors who walked upon British soil without permission, and ensuring that all those it termed aliens were subject to strict controls on their movements. Indeed, the notion that German spies were hidden among the thousands of Belgian refugees never entirely disappeared, and there were enough highly placed agitators such as Lord Leith and William Le Queux to ensure that everyone remained on their guard for long-term secret agents masquerading as British officers and gentlemen, and perhaps society ladies. With so many German submarines known to be prowling around the English Channel, the thought of agents being landed and signals being transmitted at night were, perhaps, not so ludicrous as they seem now.

The German armies storming through Belgium in 1914 might not have been guilty of all the atrocities attributed to them by British newspapers, but certainly the collateral damage they caused in Belgium was immense. Thousands of civilian lives were lost and many thousands more were forced to flee the country when their homes and livelihoods were destroyed. The flood of tales of German brutality told by both refugees and Allied soldiers was so overwhelming that it created an immense and lasting tidal wave of emotionally charged anger. The terrible fate of tiny Belgium grasped firmly in the claws of a rapacious and barbarian Germany was too good a piece of propaganda to miss in the nation's efforts to justify its headlong slide into a major European war. There was an immediate and lasting outpouring of sympathy for the refugees within Devon's towns and villages, and the hopeless but determined resistance of the Belgian army and people evoked great admiration, not least because Belgium itself was perceived as the innocent victim of Germany's greater aggression towards France and its ally Britain.

Before August 1914 the British nation was well aware of Germany's attempts to rival its empire, navy and trading network. Germany's conquest of Belgium, and its alleged subversion of Britain's fighting ability through a web of secret agents, stoked the fires of the national resolve to defeat its assailant, not least because it was widely assumed that for all its faults Britain and its empire represented all that was morally good in the world while Germany had revealed itself to be comprehensively corrupted by evil ambitions and passions.

Set against this emotive background, the small number of conscientious objectors who refused to play any part in the war found themselves abused as shirkers, cowards and traitors even when their convictions led them to stand up to the district tribunals, appeal tribunals and military courts, whose members largely loathed them. The right of legal protest that was supposed to be enshrined in the United Kingdom's concept of constitutional government fell foul of the powerful forces at work to secure enough men to fight a world war of appalling attrition, while also ensuring that the nation stood firm behind the war effort. With most families anxiously hoping their relations and friends would survive the war, and with an increasing number of them mourning their losses, the arguments of conscientious objectors sounded particularly hollow and, worse still, implied that the sacrifices the families were making were wrong and without worth. Few wanted to think such thoughts. With many clergy publicly denying the assertions of conscientious objectors that Jesus Christ forbade the use of arms, and with little popular support for the international Socialist and Marxist creeds that some objectors professed, it was not surprising that the Dartmoor Settlement seemed to comprise an obnoxious alien breed whose greatest success, somewhat ironically, was to polarise local opinion in favour of the war.

CHAPTER FOUR

CASUALTIES, CHARITIES AND CAUSES

Caring for the wounded, supporting the troops, campaigning for a better society

In March 1917 a contributor to the *Crediton Chronicle* reflected that, 'The war has brought to Devonshire, not tumult, but, on the whole, a deeper silence. Her sons, very many of them, are no longer about the house, and her daughters, too, are quiet with the quietness of those whose hearts are far away.' It is an evocative portrayal of the constant anxiety and sense of isolation and helplessness endured by so many mothers, sisters, wives, daughters and girlfriends. With so many men risking their lives, women of all social classes feared the arrival of telegrams with the worst possible news. Nevertheless they, too, found significant roles to play from the moment war broke out. Not only were there households, great or small, to run, but many women were caught up in the numerous calls for voluntary and paid war service, and in the diverse campaigns to remedy what was widely perceived as the declining sobriety, morality, and parental responsibility of the nation.

This chapter looks at a number of domestic campaigns fought within the county. Some were devoted to the greater care of thousands of sick and wounded servicemen, some to raising large sums of money for the many charities supporting victims of the war at home and abroad, and some to tackling grievous social problems, such as drunkenness, prostitution and child neglect, which many believed had been heightened by the wartime dislocation of family life. Both men and women were involved in all the campaigns, but the most unusual feature was the rush of so many women to involve themselves at all levels in the work of the military and voluntary hospitals, refugee associations, working parties, charity collections, and feeding stations. Their work soon caught the public imagination, not least because local newspapers recognised the commercial as well as the patriotic value of listing the names, charitable deeds and donations of significant families and societies within their area. Women's support for the war, encouragement of the troops, and active involvement in relief work were recognised as important contributions to the war effort both in terms of psychological motivation and material benefit. This high profile may well have stimulated the greater attention paid to working-class women during the war as the all-too-often victims of social deprivation, especially as so many of them were struggling to hold families together while their men were absent. Just as many women were perceived as capable and dedicated ministering angels so their poorer and more vulnerable sisters were frequently viewed, usually by middle class commentators, as fragile vessels liable to disintegrate under the combined stresses of poverty and isolation. During a war that quickly became one of relentless attrition, the cause of supporting working-class women to care for the next generation of workers and defenders of the nation soared in significance.

THE GENESIS OF THE EMERGENCY HOSPITALS

When Queen Alexandra, the wife of King Edward VII, reconstituted the British Red Cross Society on 17 July 1905, she said, 'I appeal to all the women of the Empire to assist me in carrying out this great scheme, which is essentially a woman's work, and which is the one and only way in which we can assist our brave and gallant Army and Navy to perform their arduous duties in time of war.' In 1909, as we saw earlier, the Secretary of State for War inaugurated the Voluntary Aid Detachments to supplement the Medical Service of the Territorial Force in case of invasion, and Devon was in the forefront of the movement. These became, in effect, the principal arm of the Devonshire branch of the British Red Cross Society. Under Countess Fortescue, the Red Cross president, eight divisional committees were chaired by female vice-presidents drawn from the upper echelons of county society. The county director was J.S.C. Davis, an ex-Indian administrator, whom Earl Fortescue described as 'methodical and business like, but a little slow and precise'. He added, however, that 'though a very dry and undemonstrative man he was beloved of his staff who would do anything for him', and he gives Davis the credit for encouraging and coordinating the thirty-seven local VADs as well as ensuring that all personnel, whether cooks, clerks, attendants, stretcher-bearers, drivers or nurses, were thoroughly trained for a national emergency. Each of the eight divisions within the county had an assistant county director who was responsible to Davis, and the county education committee was sympathetic enough to the VAD movement to provide many of the training classes for its members. By 1914 the young but capable Miss Georgiana Buller, daughter of General Sir Redvers Buller, had become Davis's assistant director in Exeter, and effectively his deputy.

When the army mobilised in August 1914 Davis was called upon to provide hundreds of beds in VAD-supported hospitals in Exeter, Torquay and elsewhere for the expected sick and wounded men from the British Expeditionary Force. Within a few weeks First Line Hospitals were established at Exeter in the West of England Eye Infirmary and Episcopal Modern School for Girls, and at Torquay in the Town Hall. Soon afterwards a First Line Hospital was set up in Newton Abbot by the Order of St John, which worked closely and harmoniously with the Red Cross. In Plymouth and Devonport there were large and well-established naval and military hospitals, but it was feared their capacity would soon be exceeded in any European war, and the War Office immediately requisitioned several Plymouth schools.

A reporter from the *Western Times* toured the Eye Infirmary after its conversion but before the first patients arrived. 'With the ladies of the Voluntary Aid Detachment in attendance,' he wrote, 'all necessary details had been attended to … One passes though wards fitted out perfectly commanding beautiful views, and absolutely flawless from the hygienic and sanitary point of view, with their cross ventilation and fine light. Take, for instance, the three rooms on the top floor which have been fitted out as wards for officers. They command fine views of the Haldon Hills and are the last word in comfort and light and air.' He noted, too, the central Red Cross on each neatly folded counterpane, the personal locker by

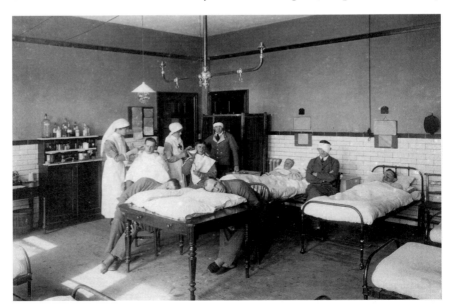

A posed photograph of soldiers undergoing treatment at No. 1 Military Hospital, Exeter. (Devon Record Office)

each bed, the wheelchairs stored nearby and arrangements made for the patients 'to sit out in the grounds for a chat and smoke, while in wet weather there will be other rooms set aside for them'. A year later, in August 1915, the number of war hospitals in Exeter had grown to five, all of them coordinated under the direction of Georgiana Buller. The hospital termed No. 1 was in the Eye Infirmary, No. 2 in the Episcopal Girls' School, No. 3 in the Children's Home in Heavitree, lent by the Board of Guardians, No. 4 in a storehouse in Topsham Barracks, and No. 5 in the College Hostel for Women and Congregational Church School near the Castle. Well-wishers had given Exeter VAD a motor ambulance, and also a large house for the extra nurses employed across the city.

The *Devon & Exeter Gazette* affirmed that 'the success has been in large measure due to the foresight which led Devon women to organise in peace'. This was largely true, but although most VADs comprised women a few men's detachments were formed to provide orderlies and run an efficient transport system, especially for stretcher cases. The local VADs were coordinated by a mixed male and female headquarters staff in Exeter, and, said the *Western Times*, 'when the war broke out the machinery was ready and all that was necessary as far as headquarters work was concerned was to enlist more women workers'. In the event it was not that simple. Certainly the VADs were prepared for war, but not for the prolonged worldwide

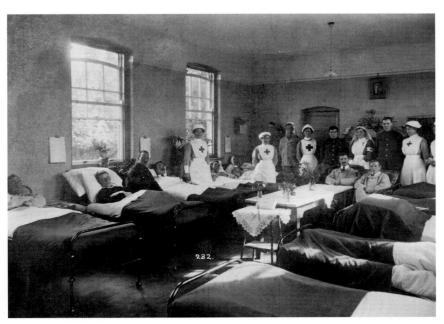

Staff and patients in a ward at No. 1 Military Hospital, Exeter. (Devon Record Office)

The kitchen at No. 1 Military Hospital, Exeter. (Devon Record Office)

The dining room at No. 1 Military Hospital, Exeter. (Devon Record Office)

conflict that actually erupted. The chart below lists all the Red Cross and VAD hospitals established in Devon during the course of the war; many were set up in 1914 but more were added each year as one campaign of attrition followed another. Many hospitals were housed in mansions loaned by wealthy local families for the duration of the war, with their indoor staff taking on some of the duties such as laundry, cooking and cleaning, and often the lady of the house assumed domestic charge as its commandant. In due course most properties had huts or marquees erected in their grounds to provide extra beds.

Red Cross and Voluntary Aid Hospitals in Devon and the number of beds provided

First Line Voluntary Aid Hospitals

Exeter (became a Military Central Hospital in 1916)	1,170
Torquay	370
Newton Abbot	150
Sidmouth	100
Uplyme	100

Second Line Voluntary Aid Hospitals

Barnstaple	60
Buckfastleigh (Officers)	50
Budleigh Salterton	20
Chudleigh	53
Crediton	90
Dawlish	15
Exmouth	73
Honiton	50
Ilfracombe	45
Instow	20
Ivybridge	50
Kingsbridge	24
Northam	65
Okehampton	22
Okehampton (Artillery Camp)	14
Paignton	50

Plymouth	286
Plympton	50
Salcombe	40
Seaton	100
Sidmouth (The Beacon)	12
Sidmouth (Officers' Treatment Centre)	25
Tavistock	23
Tiverton	130
Topsham	30
Torrington	100
Totnes	75
Yealmpton	16
Additional emergency beds at some hospitals	44

Civil Hospitals taking military patients

First Line

Torquay, Torbay Hospital	76
Torquay, Western Hospital	115

Second Line

Axminster Cottage Hospital	10
Barnstaple, North Devon Infirmary	36
Brixham Cottage Hospital	10
Dartmouth Cottage Hospital	15
Exmouth, St Luke's	10
Newton Abbot, The Infirmary	44
Teignmouth Civil Hospital	20

Private Hospitals

First Line

Stoodley Knowle Officers' Hospital, Torquay (The Hon. Mrs Burn)	33

Second Line

Barrington Officers' Hospital, Paignton	14
Bicton, East Budleigh (Lady Clinton)	60
Bystock, near Exmouth (Frederick C. Hunter, Esq.)	6

Castle Hill, South Molton (Countess Fortescue)	4
Chagford Convalescent Hospital (The Hon. Mrs Trefusis)	11
Cliff Hydro Officers' Hospital, Ilfracombe	50
Everest Officers' Hospital, Teignmouth (Lady Cable)	22
Flete, Ivybridge (Mrs Mildmay)	10
Froyle House Officers' Hospital, Torquay	18
Keyberry House, Newton Abbot (Miss Tindal)	8
Lyncourt and Branstead, Torquay (The Hon. Helen Cubitt)	7
Mazonet Officers' Hospital, Stoke Gabriel (T.E. Studdy, Esq.)	16
Manor House Officers' Hospital, Moretonhampstead (Viscountess Hambledon)	20
Manor House Officers' Hospital, Torquay (Lady Layland-Barratt)	26
Mount Tavy Auxiliary Hospital, Tavistock (Annexe 4th Southern General Hospital, Plymouth)	60
Peamore, Exeter (T. Kekewich, Esq.)	6
Upottery, Manor Convalescent Hospital (Dowager Viscountess Sidmouth)	9
Watermouth Castle Officers' Hospital, Ilfracombe (Mrs Penn Curzon)	40
Winsford Cottage Hospital, Beaworthy (Mrs George Webb Medley)	10

Total

At its peak Devon provided 4,287 beds – comprising 3,522 in the Voluntary Aid Hospitals, 335 in civil hospitals and 430 in private hospitals.

ORGANISING THE HOSPITALS

Each VAD hospital was responsible to the VAD headquarters in Exeter, which in turn was responsible to the army's Assistant Director of Medical Services in Plymouth. The Exeter headquarters acted as a clearing house for casualties coming into Devon from ports of disembarkation, and for allotting men leaving hospitals to convalescent homes. The headquarters kept the records of all staff, and all stores and appliances were supplied through it. The bureaucracy was staggering in its complexity, involving arranging and recording each patient's admission, treatment, transfers and discharge, the supply and distribution of thousands of items of clothing, the supply, storing and usage of dressings and drugs, the organisation of transport to and from the numerous hospitals, and accounting for every penny spent. Great pride was taken in providing effective care of the wounded for the lowest possible cost. Up to the end of 1915 Devon hospitals had cared for 9,061 patients, and was fourth in the national league table behind Kent (23,370), East Lancashire (10,690) and Hampshire (9,921) but was second lowest in cost at £1 0s 9d per patient, just behind Gloucestershire at £1.

On arrival in Devon casualties went to the fully equipped First Line hospitals and were passed on to the Second Line hospitals only when they were deemed suitable for convalescent care. The First Line hospitals were managed on military lines, and the War Office paid for equipment and staff, giving a capitation allowance for the patients to cover running costs. In the other hospitals equipment was provided from private sources, and the great majority of staff, whether doctors, nurses, orderlies, cooks and cleaners, gave their services free of charge. The government grant only covered the keep of the patients, heavy laundry and staff meals. The hospitals relied upon the generosity of the public to ensure that meals and recreational facilities were improved beyond a basic level, together with the maintenance and replacement of furniture and equipment.

Each hospital, whether First or Second Line, had devoted groups of fundraisers who arranged concerts, fetes, sales and special collections throughout the war to cover extra monthly expenditure and to ensure a 'comforts fund' was always at hand. In Newton Abbot two families provided additional wards, in Torquay collections and private gifts provided five extremely hard-worked ambulances for home and overseas use, in Sidmouth hairdressers waived charges for hospital patients, and well-wishers subsidised the massage and heat treatment given in Sidmouth Baths for stiff joints, while in Crediton local farmers provided a fully equipped war emergency ward. In most localities motor car services for the casualties were given free of charge. Most wealthy owners of the private hospitals waived all rent, and some completely or substantially subsidised the conversion of their properties and operational costs.

In December 1914 a *Totnes Times* reporter visited the large house recently converted into Totnes VAD Hospital, to find that the men had just had a Devonshire cream tea, 'a cheery fire was burning, a gramophone was playing and the men were either reading or being taught how to play Patience'. The article said that Totnes VAD had been prepared for the emergency for the past three years: the house had been promised by the Chaloner family, necessary alterations had been agreed, and a host of equipment had been identified 'so they could call for the loan of the articles when they were needed'. The list included milk cans, water jugs, wheelchairs, meat choppers, corkscrews, bedsteads, blankets, pie dishes, knives, forks and spoons of various sizes, soup ladles, paraffin lamps, lockers, mincing machines, bread cutting machines, mattresses, household pails, bedsheets, slippers, pyjamas, small tables, large teapots, trays, pastry boards and rolling pins, hot water bottles, looking glasses, enamelled jugs, mugs, plates and saucepans, stew-pans, washing-up bowls and towels, and kitchen and floor cloths. The reporter added, 'The members of the Voluntary Aid Detachment have been on the *qui vive* for some time, and they are naturally pleased that they are to be allowed to render some service.'

In similar vein, in May 1915 the VAD hospital at Plympton opened in a spacious house lent by Major and Mrs A. T. Tolcher, with donations covering everything it needed. The *North Devon Journal* noted that the same foresight had enabled Bideford VAD to be formed and trained, with a property carefully earmarked to become the Northam VAD Hospital in the event of war. Nevertheless, on occasion emergency hospitals could be created quickly. In 1917 Sir Henry Lopes, Brigadier Lord St Levan and the Earl of Mount Edgcumbe, helped by several specialist firms and a collection organised by local newspapers, ensured that a fully equipped VAD hospital opened with minimal delay in Plymouth Millbay's Territorial Drill Hall in 1917.

Funds were always needed. Mrs Mildmay, the energetic VAD vice-president and wife of the MP for Totnes, together with the local VAD secretary, constantly encouraged local village groups to drum up funds through flag days, sales, concerts and garden parties for the four hospitals in her husband's constituency at Plympton, Salcombe, Yealmpton and Totnes itself. In December 1916 the Totnes hospital celebrated its second anniversary with an evening's entertainment for the local VAD, including musical numbers staged by several of the convalescing soldiers. The county director, hospital commandant, mayor and Mrs Mildmay were lavish in their praise of the local volunteers: 450 soldiers had passed though the hospital. Significantly, the mayor 'in a few well-chosen words, reminded his hearers that it was the work done for many years before the war in the face of ridicule and opposition which made it possible to open and manage a Hospital at Totnes'.

Reports survive of some emergency hospitals' facilities and domestic arrangements. In November 1915 Knightshayes, the Heathcoat-Amory family's Victorian mansion overlooking Tiverton, was fully equipped as a six-ward VAD hospital largely through local donations of money and equipment. Then, and later, the *Crediton Chronicle* reported how well it was supplied with gifts of cakes, eggs, fruit and vegetables, chocolates and sweets, tea and cream, honey and jam, pheasants, chickens, hares, rabbits and venison, cigars, cigarettes

Wounded soldiers and staff at Torrington VAD Hospital. (*Western Times*, 5 July 1918)

and tobacco, eau de cologne, magazines and books, and pyjamas, pillows and cushions. In 1917 Enderley, a large mansion in Torrington, became a VAD hospital for sixty-five and eventually a hundred patients. It had a consulting room, bathrooms with hot and cold running water, a dining room and all necessary kitchens and service rooms, a billiards room and a hall with a piano and gramophone, a spacious veranda and large garden, and a cottage for the staff. All the necessary furniture and equipment had been donated, volunteers cared for the gardens, cars were made freely available by local residents, and local produce and extra funds were regularly forthcoming.

Raising funds for the hospitals

Newspapers and school logbooks are full of hospital fundraising events. Before the war many voluntary hospitals relied on the proceeds of the annual 'Our Day' collections, but the war intensified local efforts on behalf of all hospitals. Our Day was usually, although not invariably, linked to Trafalgar Day, and the activities associated with it were many and varied. Often teams of street sellers offered customers a range of souvenirs costing from a penny to a shilling, such as paper flags, silk flags, postcards illustrated with Nelson's final signal, and trinkets such as medallion anchors, battleship lanterns and naval sword tie pins. Our Day concerts often included musical and comic items from convalescing soldiers as well as local artistes, and invariably loud applause greeted the patriotic tableaux of costumed adults and children, suitably accompanied by stirring songs and poems. At Torquay in 1917 they posed as Angels of Mercy, Heroic Belgium, La France Roses, The Dawn of Victory and allegorical portrayals of the Dominions and Home Countries; and at Paignton in 1918 as St Olga of Russia, Joan of Arc, Queen Elizabeth and Sir Walter Raleigh and Britannia.

In Torquay the annual Strawberry and Cream fetes in the Princess Gardens proved immensely popular fundraisers. In June 1915 sports events, swimming races and a high-diving show were additional attractions, and it was estimated that 4,000 people attended. Indeed, the lady helpers were overwhelmed, and securing one of the shilling teas involved a lengthy wait. In October 1915 Newton Abbot raised £239 19s 9d during a Red Cross flag day, with women and wounded soldiers collecting on every street corner alongside displays put on by the Boy Scouts and Girl Guides, Sea and Army Cadets and the St John's Ambulance Brigade; there was also an evening concert at the Electric Theatre. In the same month the ladies of Brixham raised £80 4s 9d by hawking Our Day Red Cross badges at the railway station, fish market and street corners, as well as organising auctions of boxes of fish and sales of cakes and flowers. The town also raised over £650 to purchase and maintain a Red Cross motor ambulance for work in France.

The decorated tram used to raise funds in Torquay for wounded soldiers' hospital comforts and trips. (Torquay Library)

An outdoor tea for wounded soldiers in Torquay. (Devon Record Office)

In January 1917 Ilfracombe VAD Hospital publicly thanked the town for its generous weekly gifts of produce, magazines and tobacco, especially over Christmas when the Girl Guides had collected eggs each Wednesday and Friday in the market, the Boy Scouts had given up their weekends to do a host of jobs, including chopping wood and running errands, and families had continued to donate festive food, drinks, decorations and presents despite the growing shortages. In the summer of 1917 the proceeds of a huge rummage sale in Exeter were devoted to the city's war hospitals, and later in the year an exhibition and sale of the work by wounded soldiers, including cushions, smocking, rugs, tablecloths, basketwork, fretwork, etchings, watercolours and needlework pictures raised £105.

The 1917 financial statements for Chudleigh VAD Hospital have survived and show the extent of its reliance on voluntary contributions. In that year it received £1,939 7s 10d in government allowances, which was supplemented by £277 13s 2d in county Red Cross grants and £528 8s 8d from local fundraising. The end of year balance was just £28 3s 1d. In addition, it was local support that enabled the hospital to expand from twenty-four beds in 1914 to thirty in 1916 and fifty in 1917, and add three emergency beds in 1918. The Red Cross and VAD Our Day collections were crucial. Across Devon they totalled £8,590 7s 4d in 1915, £7,755 16s 5d in 1916, £12,299 7s 10d in 1917 and £19,843 0s 3d in 1918. They were 'singularly successful', said the Red Cross after the war.

PATIENTS AND NURSES

Initially the arrival of lengthy trains containing the walking wounded in ordinary carriages and the stretcher cases in specially designed ambulance carriages was a significant local event, as well as a major logistical exercise for the Red Cross, VADs and police. In October 1914 a hundred wounded soldiers arrived at Queen Street station in Exeter from Southampton Docks. Many were still in dirty and bloodstained uniforms, and most were tired. They were welcomed by a large crowd, which gathered outside and on the road bridge over the track, although the platform was reserved for doctors, ambulance staff and nurses. Forty stretcher cases were carefully loaded onto ambulances and taken to the Eye Infirmary, and others went by car to the Episcopal School. Some of the wounded waved, but others were too badly injured to respond to the repeated cheers.

The crowds, though, were soon seen as a hindrance. When a subsequent ambulance train arrived at Queen Street on a freezing cold December day in 1914, onlookers were kept well away from the station precincts, and just doctors and nurses and a stream of forty private cars were awaiting the casualties. The preparations were meticulous, but nevertheless a 'none too cheerful' reception was the reporter's view of the cold, silent and empty station as the wounded men disembarked. In Plymouth, too, exuberant crowds were soon kept at arm's length after they caused delays when the first ambulance train arrived at Friary station. The *Western Morning News* described the more orderly scene when the second train arrived with 125 men. For some time before the train arrived:

> the ladies of the Devon Voluntary Aid Detachment, in their picturesque uniform, were preparing comforts for the wounded in the way of soup, tea, coffee, cigarettes, sandwiches, etc, while the men of the 4th Southern General Hospital, Salisbury Road, under Lieutenant-Colonel H.W. Webber and other officers, got ready stretchers and other necessaries for transporting the wounded ... The police under Inspector Cooms were assisted in their task by a strong force of military.

A major hospital not managed by the Red Cross and VAD was Oldway in Paignton, a grand mansion recently built by the Singer family of sewing machine fame in the style of the Palace of Versailles. Paris Singer paid for Oldway to be converted into the American Women's War Hospital, thereby allowing American women in the United Kingdom, including several married to English aristocrats, to contribute to the war effort. The president

The American war hospital at Oldway Mansion, Paignton, 1914. (Torquay Library)

was Lady Arthur Paget, the chairman was the Duchess of Marlborough and the committee members included Viscountess Harcourt, Lady Lowther, Lady Randolph Churchill and Mrs J. Astor – all well known in the United States. Oldway's gilded banqueting hall, exotic ballroom, grand reception rooms, numerous stately bedrooms and the domed riding school adjacent to the main house became wards, accommodating between twelve and twenty patients each, and other rooms were turned into an operating theatre, X-ray room and dispensary. The nurses lodged in the servants' quarters at the top of the house and in other properties owned by the Singer family nearby.

The first contingent of 150 wounded soldiers arrived at Paignton station from Southampton on Sunday 27 September 1914. The cot cases were carried to wagons and ambulances, and the walking wounded, with their heads, arms or legs in bandages, boarded the cars that took them to the new hospital. Among the welcoming party of civic dignitaries and medical staff was Paris Singer himself. The *Totnes Times* recorded, 'It is a far cry from barrack room to a palatial mansion, and the "Tommies" who are "in residence" at Oldway can scarcely understand their new surroundings, with which, nevertheless, they are delighted.' Many were in a filthy state on arrival, with uniforms caked in mud and blood. At Oldway 'thick, dark lavender dressing gowns and pyjamas, made by American women, have been provided for the convalescents, who sit or limp around the terrace in the sun'. 'Gramophones, books and newspapers are provided, those able to sit up play cards or do jig-saw puzzles, there are bed-rests and desks for the disabled, and smoking is allowed at all times, to the great relief of those who cannot sleep.' The soldiers, mainly British initially, were full of stories about their experiences, largely at the Battle of Mons, but the clear propaganda message was that the German artillery was grossly inaccurate, their cavalry 'not up to our standard' and their infantry 'a soft thing and funk the bayonet'. However, rather more darkly, it was reported that 'many of the men cannot realise their safety, and suddenly start up out of a feverish sleep under the belief that they have been caught by the enemy "off their guard"'.

In June 1915 Oldway's first thousand patients were analysed. The great majority had been admitted with shrapnel, shell and grenade wounds. The average stay was twenty-three days, and all except thirty-five who were invalided out of the army were eventually furloughed. There was a relentless stream of convoys to the hospital: twelve were recorded between 20 December 1915 and 19 August 1916, containing a total of 1,202 men. By October 1916 the third set of 1,000 patients was being analysed, and their condition was more serious. Now the average stay was over thirty-three days, and of this group 4 died, 58 were invalided out and 104 were transferred to specialist hospitals. When the United States entered the war in 1917 Oldway was devoted exclusively to American casualties, and the American hospital

Crowds gather to watch wounded soldiers arriving at Paignton station, 1914. (Torquay Library)

also took over Paignton's Redcliffe and Esplanade hotels. 'Some shack,' a lad from Ohio was reported as saying when he first saw Oldway. A dark shadow, though, fell over the hospital as the war neared its end. In October 1918 over 500 American soldiers arrived in Paignton in several heavily loaded trains. Many of the men were seriously ill. Over the next month a hundred were to die, most of complications arising from the epidemic of so-called Spanish influenza that swept through their ranks. They were buried in Paignton cemetery, where they lay until transferred to the United States for reburial nearer home after the war.

Various sources give further glimpses into the lives of the staff and patients in these wartime hospitals. At the convalescent hospital at Stover Park, near Newton Abbot, the men were up at 6.30 a.m., with breakfast at 7.45 a.m., dinner at 12 noon, tea at 4 p.m., supper at 7 p.m. and lights out at 9 p.m. After breakfast they went for a healthy 'march', then the medical staff examined and dressed their wounds, while the afternoons were devoted to walks around the gardens, fishing and motor car trips, and the evenings to billiards, whist and reading. In 1914 Ruth Whitaker, daughter of the vicar of Broadclyst, helped organise the Linen Room Centre in Exeter, which largely involved equipping the hurriedly established war hospitals with an array of bedding, clothing and towelling donated by local shops. Then she became a VAD probationer nurse at No.1 Hospital. Decades later she wrote, 'Looking back, it seems to me that Matron did a wonderful job, turning that assembly of untrained nurses, many of whom three weeks earlier had hardly made a bed or washed-up a tea-cup, with a scratch collection of Sisters, into an efficient and smoothly-running hospital highly-esteemed by the patients. Her chief apparent qualities were her imperturbability and her immaculate neatness.' One of Ruth's first patients was a soldier whose leg had been blown off. The stump went septic, smelt terrible, and every change of bandages and draining by syringe was painful. 'But', she marvelled, 'his weedy little body had astonishing toughness, and he fought, and the doctors fought, and I fought, and the last enemy was defeated, that time.' Ruth had only admiration for the soldiers, whom she found invariably polite, always grateful and, when they were able, assiduously helpful in sweeping, dusting and polishing.

Just as Ruth, the clergyman's daughter, thought of becoming a wartime nurse, so did many ex-pupils of the largely middle-class Maynard Girls' School in Exeter. One of them described her twelve-hour daily routine – a never-ending round of sweeping and dusting wards, disinfecting and cleaning bathrooms, 'carbolising' and making beds, changing dressings and washing bandages, making up and administering medicines, giving out and clearing away meals, and at two hours' notice rearranging the wards and moving reasonably fit patients to convalescent beds ready for the next convoy of patients.

Nurse Braithwaite served in Exeter's No. 5 Hospital, and the soldiers' entries in her 'common book' reveal not only their gratitude but also the grieving, and the grudges, they brought with them. Private William Logue wrote about the loss of two close comrades during his time at the Front. Lance-Corporal Wright drew a graphic picture of a small figure trembling in the hand of a grim-faced uniformed soldier who is saying, 'So you are one of those "wot-yer-ma-call-its" wot wouldn't kill a man if he was trying to kill you, but would let someone else do it even if that somebody else got killed in the attempt.' Private Rogers noted down his views of the rights of men, and managed to fit in his thanks, in a short poem:

> The right to work for daily bread
> The right to fashion countries' laws
> The right to march the measured tread
> Of those who fight for righteous cause.
>
> The right to live – the right to die
> The right mock charity to defy
> To love a woman with a will
> To love good nursing better still

Tittle-Tattle was the magazine of No. 1 Hospital, and contains a mix of humorous and reflective entries. The food was gently mocked, as two slightly amended versions of a well-known verse and saying reveal:

> Mary had a little lamb
> And very little too
> Since lamb is eighteen pence a pound
> What else could Mary do
>
> Patients may come and patients may go
> But rhubarb goes on for ever.

The Germans and their underhand ways were mocked less gently:

> I'm a German, a spy and a waiter
> And proud to be liar and traitor

In the dear Fatherland
We are made to understand
No civilian career can be greater

A longer poem tries to portray a soldier's fears of lovers torn apart by death:

To A Letter Returned From The Front

If thou could'st not find him,
Why return to me?
Why return, to lie there
So pathetically

Think'st thou art of value
To anyone but him?
(Nay!) Useless unto all men
Priceless unto him

Darling, priceless treasure
He'd have hugged thee tight
Hugged thee, yet thou leavest him
Lonely in the fight

Useless little ghost thing
Why return to me?
Just to say I'll see him
In Eternity.

Not surprisingly marriages occurred between soldiers and nurses. Charles Chapman was wounded at the Battle of the Somme in July 1916, and met Nurse Gladys Izdebski while in hospital in Newton Abbot. Subsequently discharged from the army, Chapman courted Gladys and they married surrounded by their families in the summer of 1918. Far less happily, in 1917 Private Bertie Rose was found guilty of marrying Mary Rusk, his hospital nurse in Plymouth, while he still had a wife and two children in Burnley. Perhaps not surprisingly in the turmoil of war with its transient populations and prolonged separations, bigamy was a risk taken by a number of married men – and indeed some married women. Among the well-publicised cases, Elizabeth Barras was a nurse in a Sunderland war hospital where she met and married Sergeant Frank Mitchell, although a year earlier he had married and subsequently deserted a widow with two children in Plymouth.

Not only nurses were misled. A Miss Congdon of Plymouth found herself pregnant by Private Thomas Gribben and went through a marriage service with him, only for his first wife to find the marriage certificate in his pocket when he visited her in Salford. 'I must have been in drink,' he was reported as saying to her. Sometimes women were the adulterous partners. Beatrice Williams lived in Plymouth and was unhappily married, so she decided to marry James Newbold, an unsuspecting seaman, as well. The Assize court advised him 'to separate from the woman and get to sea as soon as he could'. Vera Foster was sentenced to twelve months' imprisonment for bigamously marrying Lance-Corporal Windward in Newton Abbot under a false name while her husband was serving abroad. Occasionally both partners were guilty. Private Albert White married Elizabeth Horsham of Teignmouth while he was stationed there, but she found out he was already married – and then he found out she was too.

CONVALESCING

The hospitals did their best to restore wounded soldiers to sound physical health and, while doing so, to raise their confidence and morale before their return to active service. Royal visits occasionally punctuated routines. The aristocratically supported Oldway Hospital was visited by Queen Mary as early as 12 November 1914. Accompanied by Lady Fortescue, she was met at Paignton station by Mr and Mrs Singer, and then spoke to each of the 158 patients in the thirteen wards. In September 1915 King George V and Queen Mary went by Royal Train first to Exeter and then to Plymouth and Torquay. In each place they processed slowly by car from the stations through cheering crowds to meet staff and patients at various war hospitals. Schoolchildren were given a holiday, and taken by teachers to wave flags along the routes. At a VAD-funded reception in Victoria Hall in Exeter for 900 wounded soldiers from across south-east Devon, the king singled out Georgiana Buller for praise for running the five war hospitals in the city, which by then possessed 600 beds and 250 staff. In Plymouth many patients were wearing the bed gowns presented to the hospital by Her Majesty, each one adorned with the inscription 'Good Luck from the Queen'. In February 1918 parties of wounded soldiers assembled at Exeter St David's station and on the Hoe in Plymouth to meet the Prince of Wales on his visit to the Duchy of Cornwall.

Christmas was made special for the soldiers, and indeed for patients in all hospitals, and as always the quality of the festivities relied almost totally on the generosity of local people. In 1916, for example, carol singing, trees and

King George V and Queen Mary visit Exeter War Hospitals, 8 September 1915.
(*Devon & Exeter Gazette*, 9 September 1915)

decorations, full Christmas dinners and teas, and individual gifts were reported
in detail at the hospitals in Exeter, Paignton, Newton Abbot and Knightshayes,
and probably other war hospitals enjoyed much the same. Alcohol, though, was
barred to all servicemen undergoing hospital treatment. Over the course of the
war there were several court cases arising from well-wishers and publicans buying
and serving drinks to wounded men. In 1918, for example, a Buckfastleigh
publican was fined a hefty £20. The soldiers' status was made obvious to the
public, publicans and police by the red ties and bright blue, not khaki, uniforms
they had to wear at all times. They remained under army discipline.

Many other entertainments and outings were arranged for soldiers by local
well-wishers, and paid for by sales, collections and concerts, or wealthy donors.
Regular trips were organised for the wounded in Exeter. In May 1915 a fleet
of sixty cars organised by the VAD and Automobile Association took 200 men
to Sidmouth for tea and a musical entertainment. The following month 300
soldiers, most with bandages, some on crutches and a few with 'armless sleeves'
or 'distorted faces,' attended by fifty nurses and orderlies, travelled in 110 cars to
Torquay at the invitation of the mayor for a sea trip, a tea and entertainment by

Wounded soldiers on an outing in Ilfracombe. (Ilfracombe Museum)

Wounded soldiers arrive at Torquay Pavilion for a concert, June 1915. (Torquay Library)

the Municipal Orchestra and the Zyps concert party at the Pavilion. The village of Bradninch raised money through local flag days to put on several activities a year for parties from nearby Exeter: in January 1918, for example, it was a whist drive, tea and dance. Nearby Broadclyst did the same, with the village being decorated with flags and bunting, welcome signs straddling the road, a marquee for tea erected in the school grounds, and sports or concerts taking place as the seasons dictated. In 1915 a Shilling Fund was organised in Newton Abbot to raise money for regular outings in trains, cars and charabancs to Dartmoor and local seaside resorts. In 1918 two wealthy families in Teignmouth arranged a series of seventeen outings to tea, competitions and concerts on the pier for wounded soldiers, not only from Teignmouth but also from Exeter and Newton Abbot.

A HIDDEN CONTROVERSY

With justification, the ability of Devon's Red Cross and VAD to establish, staff and maintain a host of emergency hospitals was widely praised in the press. After the war the Red Cross calculated that 58,200 patients had been admitted and cared for by 2,600 staff, of whom the great majority were VAD members working as nurses and ancillaries. It acknowledged the vital role that medical officers and fully qualified nurses played in ensuring that the numerous VAD probationers were trained.

These figures, though, do not include patients and staff at the five Exeter hospitals after they were transferred to direct military control in 1916. This transfer did not attract much attention at the time, and it was only after the war that the deep divisions between the Devon Red Cross and the military authorities were made public, largely at the instigation of the Red Cross in its post-war report of its work. It seems that Sir Alfred Keogh, Director General of the Army Medical Services, acted unilaterally in suddenly withdrawing the Exeter hospitals from the county director's control, then transforming them into military hospitals and finally, in a unique and highly controversial appointment, making Miss Georgiana Buller their overall military adminis-trator. Despite Red Cross complaints, the deep resentment of army medical staff forced to serve under a female civilian, and the resignation of several senior doctors who protested that they had been unfairly treated by Miss Buller, the new arrangement remained unchanged, even though reconsideration was hinted at by the War Office on several occasions.

The reason for this unique wartime decision was never made clear, although it turns out that Keogh had been a longstanding friend of Sir Redvers Buller, and certainly his daughter saw no need to challenge the change in her working circumstances. Earl Fortescue's memoirs note that 'she was masterful and aspired to the role of Florence Nightingale, and there was endless friction between her and Mr. Davis – sometimes pin pricking, sometimes serious, and I got more than my share of confidences and complaints from both'. But he also records that 'she was exceedingly efficient and made good, working her staff unsparingly and herself so remorselessly that in 1919 her health completely broke down'. After the Armistice Davis, the county director, was made a Commander of the Order of the British Empire (CBE), but Miss Buller became the far more illustrious Dame Commander (DBE).

The popular novelist E.M. Delafield served in the VAD in Exeter during the war, and perhaps gives us a further insight into what went on there. In 1918 she wrote *The War Workers*, setting it in the fictitious Midland Supply Depot whose director, Miss Charmain Vivian, the daughter of Sir Piers and Lady Vivian, ran it as a virtual dictator, using a mix of superior social status, personal charisma, emotional blackmail and sharp rejoinders to get her way. People often became anxious in her presence. For example, she ensured her staff worked consistently hard, often to the point of feeling guilty and missing their breaks, by making sure she was seen to be endlessly busy herself; and she was always on the watch for developments linked to the Depot, such as a new canteen, over which she could exert control. If Miss Vivian was based upon Miss Buller, then she comes across as a determined and successful organiser but also disconcerting, manipulative and lacking in genuine warmth. An obituary was more charitable, noting not only her remarkable efficiency and demanding standards but also her fairness in dealing with 'co-workers and juniors', and how her strength of character and mastery of procedure – described as 'a forensic ability' – combined to overcome 'prejudiced opposition'.

The Red Cross's post-war report complains bitterly about being continually 'harassed and thwarted' by the War Department 'for whose benefit it had for years laboured strenuously and unceasingly.' It lists broken promises, gross insensitivity, 'vacillation and indecision' by senior army officers in Southern Command, and repeated and unnecessary inspections among the issues that threatened the efficiency of hospitals. In one example Southern Command refused to pay a small remuneration to several particularly poor but devoted VAD volunteers who worked unpaid in the Second Line hospitals, and brusquely instructed Davis to 'abstain absolutely from contemplating the acceptance of service of poor women in humble circumstances'. Outraged, the Red Cross declared that it could not have carried on without 'the personal exertions and sacrifice of women of small means', and found some money itself. The Red Cross believed that Southern Command sought to control all Devon's voluntary hospitals, and in 1917 Davis and all nine assistant county directors were only just kept from resigning at a formal inquiry into the consistently bad feeling by pleas not to jeopardise their essential work. It was a sorry conflict that undoubtedly eroded morale and threatened the effectiveness of the hospitals.

THE MAYORESS OF EXETER'S DEPOT

Supporting the hospitals and also many other wartime relief activities was the celebrated Mayoress of Exeter's Depot, which opened on 10 August 1914, primarily to send extra clothing and food to men serving abroad. By December it operated several funds. These included clothing for Belgian refugees, a Comforts Fund to send regular parcels to soldiers at the Front, a Hospitality Fund, primarily to provide all the men on troop trains stopping at Exeter with refreshments, a Prisoners of War Fund, and also a Linen League, which was linked to a Clothing and Emergency Fund to help local hospitals and respond to requests from naval units around the south-western coast and county battalions in India, the Middle East and the Western Front. In 1915 the Depot established workrooms where women and a few male carpenters made surgical bandages, swabs, shell dressings, sphagnum moss bags and

The Mayoress of Exeter's Depot at work. (West Country Studies Library)

The Exeter Committee for Comforts and Hospitality, at an Exeter railway station, with churn, jugs and funnels. Sir James and Lady Owen, mayor and mayoress of Exeter, are third and fourth from the right in the front row. (Devon & Exeter Institution)

other hospital 'necessaries', such as crutches, splints and stretchers. Dozens of schools and women's working parties raised funds and made articles for the Depot, and the local newspapers regularly listed these gifts alongside the individual monetary donations made by the Depot's wealthy patrons.

The Crediton Ladies Patriotic Working Party was one of many across the county, and the list of products it produced between September 1915 and August 1916 typifies the significant output and variety. The ladies produced, to order, 220 pairs of socks, 92 shirts, 67 mufflers, 305 sandbags, 279 bandages, 913 treasure bags, 24 belts, 180 flytraps, 78 vests, 86 kitchen cloths, 11 helmet veils and 4 rifle cases. The Tiverton Working Party met every Thursday in the Town Hall, and the *South Molton Gazette* concluded that 'many find it a comfort in this time of national strain to talk over hopes and fears about the khaki-clad dear ones either in England or abroad'. These working parties had strict guidelines from the War Office. For example, mufflers had to be made from fleeced wool, in drab shades, and be 58in long and 10in wide, while mittens needed to be 8in long, also in drab shades, with short thumbs and no fingers.

In 1916, when funds were low, the well-organised Totnes women's group held a garden party that raised £112 for raw materials to continue their vast output of assorted clothing. It was an elegant occasion, reminiscent of pre-war social events in aid of fashionable causes. Stalls selling flowers, vegetables, cakes and other produce, together with competitions and sideshows, were arranged

Primrose sellers in Ilfracombe, 19 April 1915. (Author's collection)

decorously around the lawns and tennis court of the large house of a wealthy committee member. Particular attractions, it was reported, were fortune-telling, rifle-shooting, a raspberry and cream tea, and musical entertainment in the summer house. Food shortages were not yet obvious.

Money to buy raw materials and finished goods was always in demand. In Ilfracombe children gathered primroses to help raise £15 16s 0d for the Red Cross and the Depot on Primrose Day in April 1915. In other places that year forget-me-nots were picked and arranged in bunches to supplement the paper flowers offered for sale on Forget-Me-Not Day. The town of Bideford, for example, raised £42, and the villages of Bradninch and Spreyton raised £9 and £8 respectively, far from insignificant amounts bearing in mind all the other wartime charities competing for attention. In 1916 the Forget-Me-Not Day raised £3,000 across the county, a major boost to funds. It was calculated that the Depot administered, 'in cash and in kind', at least £100,000 during the course of the war.

In November 1914 the Depot collected £300 and numerous gifts to send Christmas parcels of tobacco, cigarettes, chocolates and warm clothing to 2,200 men of the Devon Regiment serving at the Front. After sending thousands of cigarettes to the troops in France, in 1915 Devon units in the Dardenelles requested that some were sent there too, so yet another appeal was launched. It was found that the soldiers welcomed gifts of cakes, and after some early disasters packaging and sealing were greatly improved and they

"MOTHERING" TOMMY ATKINS.

Lady Owen and soldiers with refreshments at Exeter St David's, 1915. (Devon & Exeter Institution)

began to arrive whole and edible. Units also requested gramophones and records, books and magazines, small musical instruments such as harmonicas, and games equipment such as dominos, draughts, footballs, and cricket bats and balls. As one regimental sergeant major explained on a visit to the Depot, a semblance of normality was all-important during brief periods of relaxation.

From June 1915 regular parcels were sent to Devon Regiment men who had been identified as prisoners of war in Germany and Turkey. Considerable difficulties were experienced in securing up-to-date information about the men and their prison camps, and also ensuring that every parcel only contained permitted goods, mainly easily preserved food, toiletries and clothing repair kits. A vast correspondence grew between the Depot, the War Office and the Admiralty, and also between the Depot and local families of prisoners of war. By the end of the war 22,341 food and clothing parcels had been sent to Germany and 804 to Turkey. Ninety per cent of the parcels to Germany were acknowledged, but far more went astray – it was assumed purloined – on their tortuous way to the Turkish camps. Eventually the Depot decided to send redeemable money orders to the prisoners in Turkish camps so they could purchase not only goods but also better treatment from their guards. Lord Fortescue was probably correct in assuming that the Turkish army treated its own men badly and was therefore unlikely to treat its prisoners any better.

By December 1914 groups of Depot volunteers had handed out 11,564 lunchboxes costing 6d each to men in the troop trains arriving in Exeter. A soldier's letter records, 'They gave each man a milk loaf, and butter, with ham, an orange, piece of cake, packet of cigarettes and a water bottle of tea.' Military secrecy demanded that details of troop movements could not be publicised in advance, but in October 1914 Lord Kitchener himself gave permission for the Mayoress of Exeter to be informed by telegram of troop trains passing through Exeter in time for working parties to be organised. The drain on resources was relentless, but it seems that every troop train, whatever time of day or night, was met by men and women who handed out packed meals and mugs of tea. Often the mayoress, Mrs Kendall-King, and her successor, Mrs (later Lady) Owen, were there.

During three days in March 1915 over 1,500 bags of refreshments were handed to soldiers at Queen Street station, and this hectic period was followed by yet more appeals to city traders and the public for gifts of produce and money. In January 1916, however, the Hospitality Fund was stretched too far to continue the 6d meals. Well over half a million had been given out, and recently 12,000 had been distributed in just one week as troop movements intensified in preparation for a major campaign. The volunteers had been up night after night. Reluctantly in that year handouts were limited to 2½d – usually a large bun and a mug of tea.

The Depot also undertook one-off collections when the need arose. During the 1914 mobilisation it supplied the under-equipped 3rd Battalion of the Devon Regiment with numerous blankets. Later on it gave several field ambulances to various Devon battalions, and when the Germans started to mount gas attacks the Depot dispatched thousands of gas masks.

The Depot received numerous cards and letters from men grateful for the station refreshments, or the parcels received overseas. As important as the gifts themselves was the fact that people were thinking of them and wishing them well. A typical letter was from the crew of the minesweeper HMS *Gossamer*: 'You may be assured that the articles are very welcome and full use can and will be made of them during the cold days and nights which are experienced up here.' No doubt the men were referring to the parcels of warm under-clothing the Depot often sent to ships, especially Devon's requisitioned trawlers, drifters and paddle-steamers. Such vessels offered their crew little protection in rough weather. Another letter said how grateful a group of soldiers had been to receive tea and sandwiches on the platform in Exeter at six o'clock in the morning, as they had had nothing since leaving their camp at eleven o'clock the previous evening. A trooper from Exeter wrote with pride, 'I am constantly being told by men of different regiments out here of the generosity they met with from the Mayoress of our old city and her band of helpers when passing through Exeter Station.' Another soldier described how he was woken up by a colleague as their train drew in to Exeter, and 'seizing my mug I made my way to where a most charming lady was issuing tea as fast as men could drink it … Then before I could notice what had happened someone pushed a packet in my hand. I opened it and promptly ate the contents and then found the little card – and it was the sweetest gift of all, because it supplied the one thing everyone wanted – a message of good luck.'

Never-ending fundraising

The Red Cross and the Mayoress of Exeter's Depot did not, of course, have the monopoly on fundraising. Among many flag days devoted to Allied Relief Funds in 1915, Russia's Day in Plymouth raised £164 and France's Day in Torquay £366. In July 1915 Barnstaple raised £50 for France's Day, then £106 in September for Russia's Day, and finally £250 on Our Day in October for War Hospital Funds. Women and convalescing soldiers were the most conspicuous flag and souvenir sellers on all these occasions. Belgium was not forgotten. As we have seen, money, clothing, accommodation and practical help enabled thousands of refugees to settle reasonably comfortably in Devon. In July 1915 a particularly grand fete was held in the gardens of the Bishop's Palace in Exeter, which raised £1,271 on behalf of a Belgian soldiers' hospital in the south of France. Princess Clementine of Belgium arrived in the Royal Train, and Lady Clinton, Lady Poltimore and the Mayoresses of Exeter, Plymouth and Barnstaple ran stalls.

The demands were never-ending. In October 1918 the *Teignmouth Post* listed the flag days and other fundraising events held in the town that year: a total of £2,647 had been collected. The beneficiaries included St Dunstan's Hostel, YMCA Hut Fund, Church Army Huts, Hospital Saturday Fund, Waterman's Collection for the Hospital, Merchant Service Guild, Dr Stephenson's Homes, Comrades of the Great War, West Teignmouth Parish Hall Fund, King George's Fund for Sailors, Lifeboat Day, Dr Barnado's Homes and France's Day, as well as the Red Cross, War Hospital Hut Fund, Prisoners of War Fund, War Hospital Supply Depot and the Women's War Work Depot. In addition the *Teignmouth Post* noted that the town's churches had sent £130 that year to the Mayoress of Exeter's Prisoners of War Fund.

The most prominent wartime charity – but also the most ineffectual – was the Devon Patriotic Fund. It was launched by Lord Fortescue at the start of the war to relieve the widespread distress feared among poorer families because of the anticipated dislocation to industry and commerce, and to offset the loss of income when men left home to serve in the armed forces. The fund grew fast, with several large donations from wealthy families, numerous house-to-house collections, a newspaper fund and an array of local events. At a formal general meeting in Exeter at the end of November 1914 Sir Ian Amory was able to report that the fund totalled an impressive £38,803, but as widespread social distress had not occurred very little had been spent. Modest grants made to servicemen's needy dependants – up to 7s 6d to wives and 1s 6d for each child – totalled £2,286 15s 0d, and had involved over 1,000 wives with nearly 2,400 children. Another £1,024 13s 0d had been spent helping equip Devon hospitals and purchasing materials to be made into clothing for the troops abroad, and other small amounts had financed numerous letters supporting servicemen's families making claims for war allowances. As Lord Fortescue explained, the dependants' grants were usually in the form of loans, and most were paid back by families when their war allowances were eventually received.

The report of the meeting hints at its awkwardness, for no-one knew what to do with the money. As Fortescue said, the government had introduced generally satisfactory levels of war and separation allowances, and other funds, notably the nationwide Prince of Wales Fund, were targeting the needs of impoverished servicemen's families. The meeting ended with the face-saving agreement that it was wise to keep in hand as large a balance as possible, for although the expected social distress had not yet materialised it would surely come. In addition, Fortescue explained, many more married men were joining up, and their families might need assistance in due course. Yet the meeting remained fearful of widening the Fund's remit, and refused to sanction any permanent payments to widows and their children on the grounds that the war might last a long time yet, precedents might be set and too many cases would rapidly deplete the fund.

In November 1917 Fortescue finally had to admit that the Devon Patriotic Fund had not been needed. For the year ended 8 August 1917 it had spent just £2,038 11s 1d, and received £559 0s 3d in donations and £1,209 19s 7d in interest on the vast sum invested. Few operational details survive, but if Newton Abbot's relief committee was typical it was extraordinarily difficult to squeeze money from the fund. When an unemployed widow in poor health with a daughter at home and a son in the army applied for aid the meeting dissolved into confusion and acrimony, with some members asserting and others denying that she had a call upon them. She received nothing, and the same mean-spiritedness dominated a second case, when a renewal of 5s a week aid was reluctantly made to another widow unable to work and with a son in the forces. Lord Clifford of Chudleigh in the chair certainly took the pessimistic view that funds had to be conserved for the inevitable economic crisis. Parsimony reigned supreme, and the meetings always contained a discernible whiff of suspicion that applicants were not as impoverished or deserving as they made out. Indeed, in 1915 a woman was sentenced to three months' imprisonment for defrauding the fund of £3 15s 0d.

Throughout 1918 the government was particularly aggressive in marketing its War Bonds scheme, offering good rates of interest as well as a comforting sense of patriotism. Towns and boroughs across the country were set targets based on their populations, and local committees devised a range of publicity stunts linked to the two major pushes for funds – first the Business Men's Week and then, some months later, the Women's War Weapons Week. In Plymouth displays including mock tanks, fighter planes, naval cutters and dug-outs advertised the Business Men's Week and across the borough £460,000 was invested, much of it by local firms, comfortably exceeding

Exeter's War Bond advertisement. (*Western Times*, 6 March 1918)

Business Men's Week in Ilfracombe: selling War Bonds from the lifeboat. (Ilfracombe Museum)

Dawlish children celebrate the first anniversary of their school's War Savings club. (*Western Times*, 22 February 1918)

the £400,000 target. In Exeter a huge barometer recorded the ever-growing total until it reached £250,000, well above the £150,000 target, and enough to pay for a destroyer and 'a big squadron of aeroplanes'. With the cost of an aeroplane set at £2,500, Dawlish's £13,211 paid for five, not the four it targeted, and Ilfracombe's £27,500 was enough for eleven, not the nine it anticipated. Even the village of Woodbury raised £3,800, far more than was needed for its single fighter. The Women's War Weapons Week was equally publicity-conscious. In Torquay the all-female organising committee launched the event with a huge eye-catching procession involving the Volunteer, Silver and Salvation Army bands, contingents of police, firemen, convalescing soldiers and naval personnel from the harbour, and also members of the Women's Auxiliary Army Corps, VADs, Nursing Associations, St John's Ambulance Brigade, Women's Land Army and War Hospital Supply Depot. Included, too, were 200 local children who had invested in the government's 15s 6d War Savings Certificates. Torquay's total for the week was £42,400. Among many other towns doing well, Axminster raised £17,579, Tavistock £28,476 and Barnstaple £31,346.

DOUBLE STANDARDS

Women were highly praised for the role they played in strengthening the nation's determination to win the war whatever the cost, in maintaining their households despite the uncertainties of the economy and in filling the gaps left by men in the labour market. They were also recognised as the devoted preservers of family well-being and morale at a time of great stress, and as the key figures in numerous charities that contributed so much to the overall war effort. No doubt comforting to many families, the League of Honour established local branches for young women, who solemnly promised a life of temperance, chastity and prayer amid wartime temptations and pressures. Although the vicar of Sidmouth believed the League's extremism, even in wartime, was something of a slur upon the fundamentally good character of both men and women, the small town produced a hundred members. There was also relief that most suffragettes supported the war, and had relaxed their vigorous, and often violent, pre-war campaigns for the female vote.

Yet at the same time, women, especially those from the working classes, were at the centre of widespread concern regarding their capacity to cope satisfactorily with the strains of wartime living without their menfolk nearby. As we have seen, their encouragement of recruiting was welcomed, but they were also suspected of persuading many men to stay at home. 'Women of England do your duty! Send your men <u>to-day</u> to join our glorious Army' was a common advertisement that recognised the power of the female voice, but as early as September 1914 a female dignitary complained at an emotionally charged recruiting rally in Torquay that 'it is not the wives but the mothers who are keeping the men back'.

Women were perceived as frail vessels as well as guardian angels. In November 1914 an open letter was published from the wives of several diocesan bishops that drew upon both themes, and sought to emphasise the moral influence a woman of good character could exert upon a man. 'Many a man has been kept good,' they asserted, 'by thinking of the good straight girl he knows at home who expects him to be good and straight,' and a man who may be going to his death should not carry to war 'as his last remembrance of the women and girls of England anything but what is pure and gentle and straight and true.'

War saw a significant enhancement of various middle-class campaigns to reduce the allegedly soaring incidence of working-class women's drunkenness, sexual immorality and child neglect, and these campaigns were fuelled by the readiness of local newspapers to devote many columns to court cases, meetings and correspondence on the subject of female irresponsibility and fecklessness. The campaigns were not, of course, new. Mountains of evidence produced by public and private surveys since Victorian times had revealed only too clearly the debilitating effect of poverty upon family life and individual self-respect, and as a result the enduring battle to supplement the vagaries of local charitable relief with some small degree of state welfare provision had got under way. The workhouses gave those who were desperate enough to seek admission free medical care and their children free schooling; and legislation was passed giving support to institutions caring for the mentally and physically handicapped. Angry debates raged in Parliament and the press about the merits of state and rate subsidies supplementing the *ad hoc* but deeply venerated voluntary provision of basic meals and medical care for necessitous children by local charities. It was the war, though, with its slaughter of a generation of young men and its alarming threat to the security of the empire, which was to provide a remarkable stimulus to the state's provision of care for mothers and their unborn and newly born children. With the nation facing an uncertain future, it was part of a far more sympathetic attitude towards the hardships of working-class lives.

COPING WITH SHORTAGES

In the summer of 1915 the Devon Education Committee debated the Board of Education's memorandum urging the establishment of classes for housewives in economical cookery, especially regarding meat. It was not, it seems, taken very seriously. The committee members, entirely male, doubted the value of such classes, some believing that all working-class women were well versed in the subject, some cynically asserting that the enhanced war allowances meant women no longer cared about absolute economy, and some convinced that upper-class households would never set an example and forgo their choicest cuts of meat.

This casual attitude did not last, and within a few months growing fears about national survival ensured that far more determined efforts were made to publicise the numerous ways in which households could economise. In 1916 the Plymouth War Economies Exhibition showed off the results of special lessons in schools. A variety of cheap meals were displayed 'to show how scraps may be used in a tasty way, what to do with stale bread, and the variety one may have in potato dishes'. Other stalls showed how remnants could be turned into serviceable clothes, and included jerseys made from stockings, slippers from felt hats and a girl's cloak from a man's overcoat. In March 1917 Barnstaple War Canteen and School of Cookery opened to provide 'cheap sustaining meals' and to show women how to make them at home. The county council's domestic science staff lectured housewives here and elsewhere on the use of bones and vegetable skins for soup, boiling potatoes in their skins, boiling rather than frying meat, using ground rice and flaked maize instead of flour, mixing sweet and sour fruits such as dates and rhubarb, using dry bread in milk puddings, and avoiding the use of sugar as it was in such short supply. In the summer of 1917 Exeter Food Control Campaign Committee opened a bureau in the High Street with the banner 'The Kitchen is the Key to Victory', and an exhibition of cheap ingredients and meals complete with domestic science demonstrations and numerous free leaflets and recipes. The themes changed daily with, for example, demonstrations of ironing without starch, using fir cones and cotton reels instead of coal and using old pickling bottles to bottle fruit. Leaflets and articles often took on a moral and quasi-religious tone, and rammed home the sinfulness as well as the unpatriotic implications of waste – even, one said, of crumbs of bread dropped by children not sitting close enough to the table. The newspapers said the lectures and exhibitions were well attended. In one example over 600 women attended the county council's cookery courses in and around North Tawton, and certainly school cookery lessons took a distinctly economical turn, showing that perhaps these initiatives had some success in helping households cope better.

THE FRAILER SEX?

In November 1915 a female speaker gave an address on 'Women and The War' to Torquay Debating Society, in which she asserted that 'women had proved they were ready to serve, work and drudge, so that the men of the nation might be free to do their duty'. She praised the wartime jobs they held, the voluntary work they undertook and the strains they endured at home, and went on to argue that they deserved the vote and better maternity care. She lamented the problem of female drunkenness, child neglect and the waste of family war allowances, but challenged the prevailing assumption that these evils were soaring. Afterwards critics, largely male, in her audience gave full vent to their deeply entrenched perceptions of female weaknesses, and largely ignored her plea for reforms. In this context it is significant that Tavistock UDC condemned women, not men, as the main cause of drunkenness and immorality at the annual Goose Fair held that November. People, especially visitors, 'were amazed and disgusted at a spectacle of such coarse and shameless profligacy', said one aggrieved councillor to general agreement. The desire to look alluring was attacked by the *Torquay Times* in an article that criticised the lurid make-up used by many young women. 'Why, oh why,' it lamented, 'do they all paint and powder their faces and stain their lips until the artificial colouring on their fresh skins vies with the vivid hues on their coats? And they do it so badly.'

In similar vein it was prostitutes rather than their clients who were targeted by Plymouth's police. As early as September 1914 the military authorities asked the chief constable to deal severely with women importuning servicemen, and he agreed. Correspondents railed against prostitutes passing on venereal diseases to troops badly needed at the Front, but rarely sullied the good name of the troops with similar careless acts. The ex-chairman of Plymouth Sanitary Committee first expressed disgust at the 'scenes in broad daylight which made me furiously jealous for the credit of Plymouth', and then anger at the 143 men laid up in a service hospital with sexually transmitted diseases. A few such as Major Soper of the Salvation Army saw things differently. She pinpointed the willingness of troops to evade the orders not to frequent particular streets. 'War,' she said, 'discovered their weak places, it did not make them.'

Not surprisingly a series of salacious court cases hit the Plymouth press, most regarding suspected brothels, and alongside them were lengthy reports of meetings of moral welfare groups dedicated to the cleansing of the borough's life. In 1917 the annual report of Devonport Town Mission expressed disappoint-ment that despite full wartime employment 'there was no improvement in the moral and spiritual condition of the town. Immorality among young women, and especially married women whose husbands were away, was rampant.' At another meeting in Plymouth, Mrs Astor accepted this prevailing view and rather despondently declared, 'If the girls lived straight, clean lives, they would have a decent town and decent men.' Magistrates despaired of cases where young women refused charitable help, failed to stay in Homes of Refuge or the workhouse, and ended up being regularly arrested.

Newspapers regularly reported child neglect cases that reached the courts. Many involved young mothers who had become habitual drunkards, and compounded this state by using profane language and regularly consorting with groups of men, often soldiers billeted in the area. Some were single parents but others had husbands away in the forces. In November 1914 'a painful scene' was described in Exeter Police Court when three children were removed from the care of their regularly drunken mother. In Torquay a young mother was fined and lost her six-year-old daughter, for leaving her alone while she went drinking. In Devonport the NSPCC deemed the wife of a man absent on war service to be totally incapable of caring for their four young children, aged six, three, nineteen months, and nineteen days, with the result that the older two were sent to the workhouse.

Imprisonment was far from unknown for repeated offences. The wife of a ship's cook in Plymouth was given three months for repeated drunkenness, cohabiting with other men and leaving her seven-year-old daughter covered in sores and vermin. The court bemoaned that too many women were like her; while their husbands were serving their country they wasted their 'generous' war allowances and neglected their children. On occasions both parents were found to be incorrigible, and the courts were at a loss regarding how to proceed. In Newton Abbot five children and their parents lived in persistently filthy conditions despite warnings, fines and short spells in prison. In court again, the father was told he should have made his wife do 'his duty', but it was the mother who was held to have 'had a disgraceful record, both as a wife and mother' and received a further six weeks' sentence. In two similar cases in Plymouth it was the women's neglect that was deemed the most unnatural, a witness in one emphasising that she 'left the children for hours on end crying their eyes out', and the police in the other asserting the woman, often drunk, 'was lazy and worthless'. When a Tiverton couple were found guilty of gross neglect of their three ragged, verminous and sore-covered children, the father was fined but the mother was sent to prison, together with her baby, for a month. The great publicity and harsh sentences given to the few cases of women convicted of falsifying claims for relief and family war allowances contributed to the general feeling that culpable irresponsibility was widespread. And the court raged and despaired over the mother at Dolton who wasted her war allowances, and left her three children without shoes and underwear and barely fed. Their bedding was rotten, the windows broken and the fire without fuel.

It was female as much as male drunkenness that drove the strong temperance movement. 'When the mother drinks her children are often born drunk,' asserted one campaigner, 'and afterwards they imbibe alcohol through the mother's milk.' 'Drink threatened the deterioration of the race,' thundered a celebrated temperance lecturer, F. Eardley-Wilmot, in Paignton, and, he warned, it was 'accelerated by the alarming increase in drunkenness among women.' In Plymouth in 1917 the chief constable, with the garrison and naval commanders' support, reinstated an earlier wartime order to all licensed victuallers not to supply women with drinks for consumption on their premises, except those with meals, after six o'clock in the evening. If the order was disobeyed the military authorities would bar the premises to all servicemen. It might have worked, as prosecutions for drunken behaviour there dropped from 281 in 1916 to 157 in 1917—71 women and 86 men.

Just possibly, too, the situation in Plymouth was relieved a little by the establishment of regular street patrols by teams of female volunteers who were linked to the League of Honour and to several women's recreational rooms established by the National Union of Women Workers. Their work in talking to and perhaps befriending girls they encountered, and persuading at least some of them to enjoy the facilities of the recreational rooms, was praised by the chief of police and supported by the provost marshal. The praise, though, had a backlash, as the chief of police thought their work precluded any idea of introducing female police officers into the borough. In Newton Abbot, Sister Bertha Harmstan was singled out for praise at the Church Army's annual meeting for her wartime rescue work with vulnerable young women. The vicar of Wolborough admitted that he had opposed her appointment but now rather sadly acknowledged the need for it.

SINGLE MOTHERS

Some young women had particularly unhappy lives. In 1917 St Olave's Home in Exeter was particularly busy, admitting 107 girls and caring for 74 babies until they were boarded out. Most fathers made no contributions to the costs of baby care, and through fear or alienation most of the mothers sought no contact with them. Although the Bishop of Exeter said that homes such as St Olave's could give some girls 'a fresh start in life', he suspected, as did many at the time, that a significant proportion of them would show a 'definite deficiency of moral sense'. If so, they should remain 'permanently under some humane form of segregation'. Usually this meant incarceration in a mental asylum.

One girl admitted to St Olave's at the behest of Newton Abbot's magistrates was Rose Hammacroft, a young domestic servant from Parke, the naturalist Baron Bouck's mansion near Bovey Tracey. Other servants had noticed that she had become depressed, and then found a bottle of lethal 'salts of lemon' by her bed. When challenged, she admitted she wished to kill herself after she had become pregnant by a soldier in the town. Another was Elsie Roberts, also a domestic servant. When Henry Hooper, a railway worker in Exeter, returned home one evening he found a baby on his doorstep; Elsie had left it there. The father was a soldier, now serving abroad. When Elsie realised she was pregnant she had fled to London, and then back to Newton Abbot to see if friends would take the new-born baby. When this failed she travelled to Exeter, and in desperation deserted her baby; she was observed standing in the road near Hooper's house. A third was Beatrice Hill from Barnstaple, aged just fifteen, who had become besotted with a wounded but married soldier, and then insisted on following him to Manchester and Salisbury even though he had rejected her. She was eventually convicted of theft and admitted to St Olave's, like the other two, as an alternative to prison. Hilda Barnes, aged sixteen, met a different fate. Her body was found cut in two on the main railway line at Stoke Canon. She had fallen under the influence of Private Edward Woodward, who was billeted in Exeter. In court he admitted that she had been too scared to face her parents after staying out with him until 2 a.m., but he had not thought of accompanying her home. An open verdict was recorded.

There were a number of cases of unmarried young women, predominantly named as domestic servants, who hid the birth of their babies, and indeed hid the bodies of their dead babies. One was found buried in a garden, one in a box under a bed, one wrapped as a parcel, one tied up in a tablecloth, one hidden in a cook's room and one floating in a shallow pool by a river. Their mothers were found, but not those of other babies, whose bodies were left under a park bench in Torquay, in the ashes of a bonfire near Tiverton or in the river at Exeter. However suspicious police and magistrates might have been, in court doctors were not usually prepared to say with absolute certainty that the babies had died violent deaths, and 'natural causes' or 'still-born' were duly recorded, although concealing the birth was a crime in itself. One domestic servant sent to Exeter Assizes on the charge of poisoning her baby girl through excessive medication because her husband, who was abroad, was not the father, was released because expert witnesses could not say whether it was an illness or the medication that caused the death. A second young mother sent to Assizes for drowning her baby in the river Exe was judged to be mentally and morally incapable of understanding the seriousness of what she had done. Such appallingly sad cases were far from unknown before the war, but the tone of the reports and the comments made in court suggest that most people thought immoral behaviour was on the increase.

Yet some evidence exists that the illegitimate birthrate did not rise during the war. Although it was undertaken as early as the middle of 1915, an NSPCC survey based upon the rescue and preventive work of fifty-seven branches of the National Union of Women Workers and fourteen Women's Patrol Committees across Britain, including Exeter, Plymouth and Devonport, asserted that there was no substance in the claims that large numbers of illegitimate 'war babies' were being born. It admitted there was always a higher illegitimate rate in garrison towns, but alarmist accusations, it said, 'are without foundation and reflect unfairly on the character of our soldiers and our girls'. However, the report did not doubt that there existed 'grave cause for anxiety on account of the prevailing low moral standard as well as on account of intemperance, often the result of thoughtless treating; nor that there has been much giddiness and foolish excitability among the young girls, leading often to most undesirable conduct'.

CHANGING ATTITUDES AND NEW INITIATIVES

The war saw a marked increase in popular support for greater state intervention in the lives of mothers and children. Punitive approaches, the workhouse safety net and charitable efforts at rescue and care were increasingly perceived as insufficient to ensure the nation's mothers and their babies acquired and maintained a satisfactory state of physical and mental health. In July 1914, just before the war broke out, the Local Government Board offered grants to local authorities and voluntary organisations for the implementation of approved schemes of maternity and infant care. Other than desultory exchanges of correspondence between Devon County Council and the Board on a cheap scheme of health visiting limited to the urban areas, nothing happened until 1916, when greater pressure from within the county as well as from the Board brought the issue to the surface again.

With firm prompting from Earl and Countess Fortescue, in February 1916 Devon Education Committee agreed a coordinated county-wide scheme for health visiting and maternity centres with the county's Public Health Committee and the voluntary Devon Nursing Association. The Fortescues had sent a striking joint memorandum to the education committee in which they stated that 161 out of the 346 practising midwives were untrained, 110,000 people in 200 parishes had no nurse, and Devon was the county with the highest puerperal mortality rate between the Wash and the Severn. They offered a solution, which the county council accepted. The Nursing Association, in which Lady Fortescue exercised considerable influence, provided a team of skilled health visitors who would work within an overall scheme built reassuringly on the successful partnership already existing for inspecting and treating elementary schoolchildren. The county council agreed to pay for fourteen health visitors who would offer pre-natal and post-natal support, give child-care classes and act as school nurses, and would pay for trained midwives, doctors and hospital care when the health visitors thought they were needed. The county would also pay for new midwives to be trained in districts currently without them. District and borough councils supporting the scheme would provide maternity and infant welfare clinics, with volunteer groups providing administrative support. The government grants – those offered initially in 1914 – would cover half the costs.

Scott's Emulsion advertisement.
(*Western Evening Herald*, 6 October 1916)

It was significant that by 1916 patent medicine manufacturers had seen the way the winds of welfare reform were changing direction, and sought to take full advantage. Just as companies such as Oxo and Phospherine had used pictures of servicemen in the front lines and personal recommendations from them to promote the revitalising aspects of their products, so Scott's Emulsion began to promote its body-building qualities through advertisements showing frightening comparisons between the mounting deaths of men in battle and the far greater mortality rate of British babies and infants. 'FOUR ARMY CORPS of BRITISH children are carried away by weakness and disease every year', thundered one advertisement, and another asserted that in the first fifteen months of war more British children died than British soldiers on the world's

Scott's Emulsion advertisement.
(*Western Evening Herald*, 5 September 1916)

battlefields. In confirmation, the NSPCC calculated that in the first thirteen months of the war 109,725 British men had been killed but 140,370 babies had died.

Sensing the mood of the moment, in March 1916 the *Western Evening Herald* published a grimly worded article on Plymouth's infant mortality rate. Out of 5,037 babies born in 1914, 553 had died within a year, and the article argued that at least half the deaths had been caused by the town's insanitary conditions or parental ignorance or both, and were therefore avoidable. It cited the medical officer of health's belief that the greatest child-killer was diarrhoea, which stemmed from filthy, fly-ridden conditions and careless, unhygienic baby care. It followed this with a second article asking why two years had passed with nothing done since the government had offered grants for infant welfare schemes, and then a third article praised Mrs Astor's offer of a year's salary for a trained nurse if a baby clinic could be opened in the town. 'Her idea,' the paper added disingenuously, 'was that it would be an example to the municipality in the saving of children.' Soon afterwards the 1915 figures showed a similar death rate: 4,255 babies had been born and 506 died.

In July 1916 Plymouth Borough Council finally accepted a comprehensive scheme drawing upon medical officers, midwives, voluntary association nurses, health visitors and voluntary helpers to provide home visits for expectant mothers, a consultation centre for them, a post-natal clinic offering advice and cheap patent foods, home visits to children under school age and skilled treatment for complicated births and post-natal problems. The first infant welfare centre opened in the Town Hall, Stonehouse, in April 1917, and three others followed, together with three voluntarily funded hostels for older children to stay in, if their circumstances warranted it, while their mothers had their babies. A vigorous campaign was launched to preach the benefits of the new scheme, and to reassure suspicious families that it had nothing to do with the humiliating Poor Law.

Each Christmas during the war the *Western Evening Herald* promoted a successful Shilling Fund to ensure that a voluntarily funded Plymouth Day Nursery could continue to care for the children of mothers 'who must go out to earn a living'. By 1917 three other nurseries in the city were funded by wealthy families – the Astors, Sir John and Lady Jackson (a local MP and his wife), Lady Bethell and Lady Pole-Carew. Each nursery was open from 7.30 a.m. until 7.30 p.m., and most of the children were under three years of age. They were washed and changed on arrival, fed three times during the day and encouraged to have an afternoon sleep. A much-praised feature was the opportunity they provided for classes of older schoolgirls to work in them as part of their Mothercraft courses. Infant welfare had fast become a fashionable cause to support.

The 1917 Baby Week in Plymouth was a big event. Every mother and baby born within the last twelve months was invited to a Babies At Home reception, and a rally and demonstration was held during which Mrs Astor proposed a resolution that everyone should promise to promote maternity and infant care within the town. There was also an Infant Welfare Exhibition, with a Wrong Room and a Right Room, and a series of lectures. A key speaker was Sir George Newman, the Board of Education's chief medical officer, who in traditional vein pointed the finger of blame firmly at the 'neglectful, careless or ignorant mothers' and asserted that they must become 'well-informed, skilful and experienced'. The campaign continued into 1918, with the *Western Evening Herald* proclaiming that 'the future of the world may depend on the number of strong and vigorous English men and women there are in the world fifty years hence'. Speakers elsewhere repeated these messages. When Sir James Owen, the Mayor of Exeter, attended Sidmouth Baby Show in July 1917 as the guest of honour, he stated that parental ignorance was the greatest threat to babies' lives, and added that 'Babies were a sacred charge to the mother because they belonged to the Nation and were the nation's wealth.'

In February 1916 Exeter City Council agreed to fund three maternity and infant welfare centres based on the areas served by the three health visitors. Two had been established by April 1916. A year later Dr Stirk, the city's medical officer, praised the well-attended Infant Welfare Centre held in an old school building on Exe Island. It had more than 100 members and a very active health visitor; usually thirty mothers attended when the doctor was there and twenty on the weekly sewing days. Many poor families lived in the neighbourhood, and donations were constantly being sought to subsidise the provision of cheap or free milk and baby food. In 1918 a new maternity home was opened in Dix's Field by Lady Owen as a joint venture by Exeter Nursing Association, the city council and the city's Lying-In Charity.

Other districts followed suit – Barnstaple, Bideford, Brixham, Dartmouth, Exmouth, Ilfracombe, Newton Abbot, Northam, Paignton, South Molton, Teignmouth, Tiverton and Torquay. 'They might say with truth,' one speaker admitted in Torquay, 'at the present time it was more dangerous to be born a baby than to go out to France to fight.' If this problem had been tackled successfully a generation ago, he asserted, the nation would have a million more men to put in arms. In 1917 Lady Florence Cecil, wife of the Bishop of Exeter, was guest of honour at Teignmouth's Baby Week Fete, and despite the success of the town's Infant Welfare Centre she chose to highlight the thousands of women who still abused 'the gift of motherhood' through 'ignorance, neglect, carelessness, and disease that could and ought to be prevented'. It fills us, she said, 'with shame and pity'. By the time of Baby Week in 1917 Tiverton's health visitor was a familiar figure. At its Baby Show eighty mothers were presented with badges, ribbons, tea and milk, and a letter from the mayoress saying, 'A great price has been paid for our freedom, and the life of every mother and child has doubled in value.' At the opening of Newton Abbot's Infant Welfare Centre, one speaker put developments in their place simply and aptly by acknowledging that 'we're now looking at things we neglected to see before'.

CONCLUSION

The honouring of women working in charitable enterprises and, conversely, the humiliations of women trapped in distressing circumstances filled numerous columns in numerous wartime newspapers. The two extremes suggest that editors shared the general surprise and gratification at the extent of female volunteering, and also found it particularly easy to adopt a puritanical attitude towards the weaknesses of a minority of the working classes at a time of national crisis. The vital role of women in encouraging their men to fight, maintaining stable homes while they were away and participating in charitable endeavours was widely acknowledged. Any less elevated behaviour during the war seemed particularly reprehensible.

However, no adverse publicity could take away the overwhelming importance of women, whatever their domestic circumstances, as bearers of children and their primary carers. In this respect the war brought in its train considerable state investment in the facilities thought necessary to ensure as many women as possible received readily accessible pre-natal and post-natal advice and care. Medical practitioners had contributed much to the agitation. This was partly because they had collected the statistics of the chronic ill-health and death of so many babies, and partly because most of them possessed a low view of the child-rearing abilities of poor working-class families. The war brought about a different perspective. Fears that the nation might crack under the almost intolerable strain, and fail to maintain its overall willingness to see the conflict through to victory, finally engendered greater sympathy, even admiration, for working-class women as wives and mothers capable of running family homes successfully by themselves on precariously small incomes. Rather than assuming, as had so many middle-class commentators, that poverty, fecklessness and immorality were the natural lot of a large proportion of the working classes, largely brought about by their own inadequacies, the war engendered greater hope that state-subsidised welfare schemes, based upon an elevated concept of motherhood, would assist working-class mothers to provide their children with the best possible domestic environment. Arguments about national and imperial security, rebuilding the population, regenerating the economy and the rewards due to millions of families at war eventually all came together – if only, as we shall see, for a perilously brief period of time.

CHAPTER FIVE

PERCEPTIONS OF CHILDHOOD

Skilled workers, ardent patriots, healthy parents

This chapter examines the impact of the war upon children. It reveals the immediate impact of the war upon their lives both within and beyond the classroom, and how attitudes towards young people changed as threats mounted to the security and prosperity of the nation and empire.

THE PROGRESS OF REFORM BY 1914

By 1914 some battles to secure the better health, education and working conditions of the nation's children had been won, but the war was far from over. Reformers consistently aroused the determined hostility of those convinced that state-subsidised elementary schools were already giving many children an education far exceeding their needs as domestic servants, farmworkers and factory hands, and more than enough to make them dissatisfied with those roles and turn them into social and political agitators. The plethora of advertisements in every local newspaper certainly reveals the never-ending demand for these traditional groups of lowly paid but utterly essential workers. Indeed, many reformers themselves were fearful of going too far down the road of state intervention in working-class lives, partly because of cost but also because the Victorian assumption of a divinely ordered social hierarchy, with its accompanying emphasis upon personal responsibility and the effectiveness of charitable giving, was still a potent force. And as we have seen already, there was always the nagging worry that many of the poor were in a deplorable condition because of their inherent fecklessness, and too much state intervention might encourage their helplessness rather than elevate them.

Although the grossest abuses of the past had been eradicated, most Devon by-laws allowed young children to work long hours before school opened and after it closed, and indeed many worked during the lengthy midday break. Children could leave school at fourteen, but many families chose to take advantage of other by-laws allowing them to leave at thirteen if their previous attendances and academic standards had been satisfactory. Old attitudes died hard, especially in the Devon countryside, and tacit agreements between parents, school managers, farmers and magistrates still meant that many children became farm labourers for several days at a time during the busy periods of hay, corn, potato and soft fruit harvesting. Indeed, the school manager, farmer and magistrate were often the same person.

Some beneficial, but typically circumscribed, legislation was passed in the early twentieth century, and was still thought novel, even radical, in 1914. In 1906 local authorities were allowed, but not compelled, to spend ratepayers' money on feeding carefully identified and strictly 'necessitous' children. The following year an Act of Parliament established a medical department at the Board of Education under Dr (later Sir) George Newman, and from 1909 local authorities were obliged to medically inspect all elementary schoolchildren, but state-subsidised treatment was not allowed until 1912 and was not made compulsory until 1918. Until then, if parents did not secure the recommended treatment, either through private practitioners or charities, they ran the risk of prosecution. In 1914 local authorities were required for the first time to identify all children who could be classed as displaying learning difficulties, but adequate provision for many of them either within ordinary schools or special institutions was still a long way off. Indeed, many classes of younger children often included a few older but slow-learning children, along with all their likely behavioural problems.

In Devon the county council was totally responsible for 226 county elementary schools and for the staff and some maintenance costs of 316 Anglican, non-conformist and Roman Catholic ones. The urban areas of Barnstaple, Exeter, Tiverton, Torquay and Plymouth/Devonport looked after their own elementary schools. The county council was also responsible for aiding the couple of dozen small secondary schools across Devon, and for building new secondary schools if it so desired. It displayed very different attitudes towards the two sectors.

SECONDARY SCHOOLS

During the war there was a modest increase in free secondary school scholarships for particularly able elementary school pupils, despite the consistent opposition on grounds of cost and the folly of trying to turn too many working-class pigs' ears into silk purses. In Exeter 25 per cent of places at Hele's, Maynard's and the Modern Schools were reserved for scholarship winners. They amounted to just forty-seven places offered by the city council and various charities each year.

Annual competition for these potentially life-changing awards, and for the 361 across the rest of Devon outside Plymouth, was fierce. Statistically, just one elementary school child out of every thirteen aged eleven had a chance of success. Headteachers recorded the rare cases of success with great pride, as ironically the greatest lustre for an elementary school came from a scholarship-winning pupil leaving early to go to one of the socially prestigious secondary schools. Indeed a public row broke out in Paignton in 1916, and cast grave doubts upon the quality of its elementary education, when no local children won scholarships, although several had been successful in neighbouring Torquay and Brixham.

Hardly any building work occurred during the war. Newton Abbot Mixed Secondary School, with 208 places, was completed in April 1916 only because it was too far advanced to stop. It brought the county's total places to just over 1,600. In that year the county council agreed new technical schools for Barnstaple and Torquay, but their construction was postponed until the end of the war. In 1918 a more ambitious programme was stimulated by enhanced government grants, and modestly sized mixed secondary schools were planned for Exmouth, Ilfracombe and the Teignmouth-Dawlish area, and girls' secondary schools in Dartmouth, Kingsbridge, Totnes and Tavistock. In the post-war economic turmoil these new schools were a long time coming.

In 1917, in an announcement that was as startling for its social implications as much as its educational innovation, Plymouth Education Committee declared that over 1,000 more elementary schoolchildren within its borders were deserving of a secondary school education. It also advocated the establishment of a West Country university with several campuses, one of which would be in Plymouth. Others would be Seale-Hayne Agricultural Institute near Newton Abbot, St Luke's Teacher Training College in Heavitree and the Royal Albert Memorial College already established in Exeter, which had aspirations of its own to become the centre of a fully fledged university. Again both visions were a long time coming – the first when the 1944 Education Act created the present universal primary-secondary school progression, and the second when the Universities of Exeter and Plymouth were created in the 1950s and 1990s respectively.

Elementary education at the outbreak of war

In the infinitely larger elementary sector the immediate pre-war years saw a concentration upon the vocational training side of children's schooling. The county council increased the number of domestic subject instructresses from five in 1902 to thirteen in 1913, thereby enabling more girls to attend the cookery and housewifery centres established around the county. Gardening classes for boys were encouraged with modest equipment grants, and for school leavers and young adults the county provided a scattering of vocational classes in milking, butter-making, cheese-making, poultry-keeping, sheep-shearing, thatching, ploughing, fence-making, hedging and ditching, and rope- and spar-making in village centres. Exeter, too, aided vocationally oriented continuation classes for school leavers, and also extend its cookery, laundry and housewifery courses for girls. A female committee member acknowledged 'it would fit the girls for domestic service', and the chairman, Alderman John Stocker added it would be popular with the public, 'who frequently complained that money was being spent in teaching children subjects that would be of little or no use to them in after life'. In a clear, if tacit, recognition of the crowded slums of the West Quarter, in 1913 the city instituted a successful summer holiday school 'to take some of the children out of the miserable squalid surroundings of a poor district into a playground or field where organised games and organised occupations could be arranged'.

The county council also wrestled with health issues. More school nurses were appointed so that more parents could be fully informed of the doctor's recommendations after the inspections, be given advice about effective treatment, and be followed up to ensure it had happened. Treatment for adenoids, ringworm, discharging ears, defective teeth and poor eyesight was arranged through hospitals, dentists and oculists, and necessitous cases were subsidised. However, Dr Adkins, Devon's school medical officer, added, 'I would remind the Committee that as long as the unsatisfactory conditions of the lighting, drinking water, ventilation, cloakrooms, feeding, clothing, housing and hygiene education exist, so long will many of the defects continue to be in evidence and demand treatment.'

Many county education meetings were devoted to the inadequacies of antiquated elementary school buildings, and remedying at least some of them if they were council schools and urging the managers of church schools to follow suit. Common failings were the use of closed stoves whose heat only warmed those near them, the absence of adequately opening windows and fresh air, the physical restrictions of fixed staged seating for infants, and also the ubiquitous middens and cesspits which were the breeding grounds for flyborne diseases. Many schools had no running water, and used local pumps and wells. 'It was monstrous', thundered the Honourable John Wallop, 'that children attending the schools should have to hawk about the village for drinking water.' In 1913 Holsworthy Wesleyan School was so bad that the Board of Education threatened to withdraw its grant if no repairs were undertaken, and at East Worlington Council School the narrow dirt approach track, the lack of any playground and the foul earth closets 'with a pile of dirt and used newspapers' were utterly condemned by the county surveyor. He recorded, too, that Farway School 'had a very neglected appearance. It is dark and dingy, and filled with obsolete desks. The surface of the playground is covered with sharp stones.' Kilmington desperately needed better lighting, heating and ventilation, new lavatory basins and a playground. Many school buildings in Plymouth were equally inadequate. Three boys' classes and four girls' classes were taught in single long rooms at St Peter's School, and the pupils endured poor lighting and inadequate heating. The worst, Grey Coat, was another school threatened with the loss of government grant.

EVACUATIONS, ENLISTMENTS AND ECONOMIES

The onset of war, however, gave the hundreds of elementary schools and their thousands of children a dramatic new purpose. They became an integral part of the war effort.

Initially, though, it seemed that nothing was too good for the soldiers, and anything was good enough for the children. Several school buildings were requisitioned by the military authorities and converted into hospitals or barracks, most for the duration of the war. Nearly 5,000 children in five large three-decker schools in Plymouth were displaced, and hurried arrangements had to be made before the autumn term to house some in Sunday school buildings and to crowd others into schools that the army had not seized. Often a double shift system operated, when classes from a dislodged school had to share the accommodation and facilities of a host school. One school used the building each morning and the second school each afternoon; if the weather and local facilities permitted, each school spent the other half-day in the open air for lessons, games or rambles. It was a far from perfect arrangement. The headteacher at Keppel Place Higher Elementary School for Boys complained that fewer subjects could be taught, the boys were 'fagged out' at the end of a four hour shift, and attendances were declining as families were attaching 'less importance to education'. In 1915 Hyde Park Girls School was also requisitioned. The pupils had to work a double shift with Laira Green, but attendances fell because of the considerable extra walking distance to school, and they plummeted in June 1916 when a twelve-year-old schoolgirl was murdered by a soldier in a nearby field. The soldier, subsequently sentenced to death, had been a lodger in her house.

By 1917 any sympathy with the military authorities had evaporated. Parents complained, and so did Plymouth's Education Committee and MPs, but to no avail. By then 6,000 children had been displaced, representing over 17 per cent of the school population, and another 5,500 in the 'host' schools had had their routines disrupted. To make matters worse, one committee member complained, Exeter had had no schools requisitioned. This was not quite true as the large Episcopal Modern School for Girls in Pennsylvania was taken over as a hospital in September 1914; the pupils were fortunate to find alternative accommodation in Summerlands and Rougemont House.

Across Devon many male teachers enlisted, and the policy of unrestricted volunteering caused difficulties. As early as 13 September 1914 the headmaster of Okehampton Council Boys' School bemoaned the loss of several colleagues, and the desperate resort to amalgamating classes made it 'almost impossible to carry on the work of the school'. By January 1915 his own class had more than fifty pupils covering four years of age. By July 1915 thirty-one Exeter teachers were in the armed forces and seven female teachers had joined the VAD. By July 1916 ninety-one of the 208 male teachers of military age within the county authority had gone, two were working in munitions and forty-four had attested. Exeter City Council became gravely concerned at the loss of male teachers, the shortage of female 'war supply' replacements and the costs. In 1915 it closed Exe Island Girls' School, saving four teaching posts, and distributed the ninety-nine pupils among neighbouring schools. All non-teaching head-teachers whose schools had less than 250 pupils were ordered to become class teachers. This experiment was tried in Teignmouth, but the schools' managing bodies strongly objected to classes being left unsupervised when visitors or deliveries arrived, or problems occurred elsewhere in the school. In March 1916 the county education committee admitted that some schools had had to close for brief periods as no teachers had been available to replace those enlisting.

Several headmasters of boys' schools in Plymouth and Exeter criticised the unreliability of some female temporary teachers, and blamed them for a decline in standards of work and behaviour. In October 1918 the exasperated headmaster of Charles Boys' School in Plymouth wrote a formal complaint that 'The frequent absences of Temporary Women Teachers is (*sic*) a serious and disturbing element. I think when the Authority staff the schools with women, it should have sufficient reserve to fill the vacancies when teachers are absent. At present the three male teachers have to bear the strain of the extra work thrown on them whenever a lady absents herself.'

Devon possessed numerous small village schools, and the presence of a single teacher for two dozen or fewer children rendered their *per capita* costs much higher than large urban schools with classes of forty or more. Wartime economies were sought everywhere, and inquiries, reports and meetings went on throughout the war regarding the financial and educational viability of at least thirty schools, causing much unrest in the villages and a great deal of anguish within the county council. In the end just the tiny schools at Luton, Nethway in Brixham, Travellers Rest in Swimbridge, North Huish, Cockwood, South Tawton and East Budleigh had to close. They had ten or fewer pupils who, it was asserted, could travel with relative ease to neighbouring schools that had vacant places. The decisions were made very reluctantly. Despite the financial cost, and the educational difficulties of one person trying to cater satisfactorily for the needs of children aged between three and fourteen often in a single room, the great majority of members believed, with some justification, that the loss of the village school would mean the locality becoming far less attractive to rural workers and their families. County councillors also believed that villages benefited from having a schoolteacher – 'a woman of education and refinement' – in their midst. And, of course, the local school tended to supply the local farmers, rectors and squires with their labourers and servants – as both the supporters and the critics of these small schools frequently observed. Sectarian issues rumbled around the council chamber too, with hints that some county councillors favoured closing the council schools, while others preferred to see the end of church ones.

CHILDREN MAKING GIFTS

Not surprisingly schools were keen to support the war effort, and many lessons and activities started to gain a new relevance to children's lives. Soon after the outbreak of war many girls, and a few boys, got to work knitting socks, mittens, scarves, balaclavas and jerseys, and making handkerchiefs and belts both within and outside school hours, for local servicemen and Belgian refugees. The demand was endless, with the wool being found at home, donated by school managers or charities, or purchased from the proceeds of school sales and concerts. At Wolborough in Newton Abbot the children sent socks, mittens and balaclavas to naval crews in the North Sea, among them the submarine C16, which had moored recently in Torquay harbour. (Sadly all the crew perished when the submarine sank off Harwich on 16 April 1917, after colliding with the destroyer HMS *Melampus*.) That Christmas pupils in Bovey Tracey sent several dozen parcels containing woollen clothes, chocolates and stationery to local servicemen. The following Christmas the parcels included, probably by request, cigarettes, socks, Vaseline, sweets, boracic powder, combs, belts, bootlaces and paper and envelopes. Tobacco and cigarettes were highly prized by servicemen, and children brought these items from home or purchased them out of pocket money to add to the parcels. The girls of Heathcoat School in Tiverton put a packet of cigarettes in the toe of each sock they knitted. Among the most active schools was Furzeham in Brixham. In November 1917 it celebrated sending its 240th weekly parcel to Old Boys on active service – each one containing packets of cigarettes, tins of cocoa, coffee, milk powder, sardines and meat, sweets and preserved fruits, and soap and candles. Often the children here, as elsewhere, attached letters to the parcels, telling the recipients their names, where they lived, how they had saved up their money, how grateful they were to the soldiers and how much they loved their country. The cards and letters of thanks the schools sometimes received in return were highly prized. Local newspapers often listed the totals of goods and money collected by schools for particular hospitals and other charities,

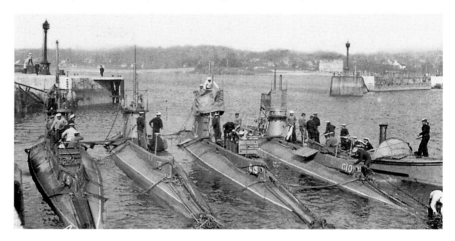

The submarine C16 (far left) in Torquay harbour. (Michael W. Pocock)

A class of girls at Ilfracombe Church of England School knitting for the soldiers, October/November 1914. (Ilfracombe Museum)

A class of boys at Ilfracombe Church of England School knitting for the soldiers, October/ November 1914. (Ilfracombe Museum)

and such publicity must have been viewed with mixed feelings by teachers, as inevitably it invited invidious comparisons as well as much-deserved praise.

The flow of gifts was not entirely one way. In late November 1914 an American navy collier, the *Jason*, steamed into Plymouth harbour escorted by torpedo boats and welcomed by dozens of ships' sirens and hundreds of cheering schoolchildren. It was laden with 1,200 tons of Christmas presents, the gifts of families in the United States to the children of British and French servicemen.

Children following the war

A number of logbooks record the amendments to geography, history and English syllabuses that were made so that children could understand the background to the war and follow its course. Additional lessons on illustrious British naval and military commanders, both past and present, were compiled at Christow. At Aveton Gifford the vicar lent the headteacher copies of the *Illustrated London News* to keep up to date with events, and to provide a few pictures and maps. The pupils of Grove Council Boys' School in Totnes had a series of lessons spanning 1914 and 1915 on the recent crises in the Balkans, the history of Belgian cities and the war in Belgium, the construction and use of Zeppelins and submarines, the founding and growth of British imperial possessions, the answer to the question 'Who were the Huns?' and the lives of British heroes, including Sir Walter Raleigh, Sir Phillip Sidney and Admiral Blake. Not surprisingly, drill and physical training also loomed larger in many schools.

'There was not enough of it,' said the chairman of the Teign and Dart Teachers' Association in 1915. 'They were only allowed an hour a week split up into quarter-hours and one could do nothing in that time.' A few schools considered themselves fortunate to secure the services of locally based army instructors.

Local soldiers and sailors gave children contact with the war beyond their own families when they wrote letters to their old teachers or visited schools on leave or while convalescing. A young Plymouth school-leaver, now a bugler in the Royal Marines, wrote to Grey Coat School about his experiences on the cruiser HMS *Cordelia* in the Grand Fleet. Great Torrington Council School got long letters from India, where a teacher was serving in the Territorials. The children at St Philip & St James School in Ilfracombe were regaled by a lengthy series of talks, including an early wartime pilot on his training and his aeroplane, a steward on a White Star liner, now a troopship, on his voyage to Australia and back via the Suez Canal, a Royal Naval Reserve seaman on his experiences in the White Sea and Archangel, including his adventures sealing and ice-breaking, and men who had taken part in the Battle of Loos, the Dardenelles landings, an anti-Zeppelin project on the East Coast, and served on HMS *Malaya* at Jutland. Possibly some talks were graphic. At Ilfracombe a soldier spoke about the Battle of Cambrai, where a bullet had passed through his chest, lung and back. At Tavistock an Old Boy 'gave a most interesting description of bombs and bomb throwing. The address was illustrated by showing actual bombs.'

Headteachers were proud to record visits by Old Boys and members of staff who had won medals for bravery or gained commissions, or both. Alfred Davey, an Old Boy of Great Torrington Council School, reached the rank of major and was heavily involved in the fighting around Gaza; and Highweek School in Newton Abbot was particularly proud of Captain Stanley Renton, who enlisted as a private, gained a commission, won the Military Cross and was killed in action in 1917. Grove Council School in Totnes recorded several Old Boys who were promoted to sergeant and warrant officer, and four who received commissions. Its Old Boys also won a Distinguished Service Order, a Distinguished Conduct Medal, a Meritorious Service Medal and four Military Medals, and one distinguished soldier received a Military Medal and two bars.

THE SIGHTS AND SOUNDS OF WAR

Children found the sights and sounds of war irresistible. In Honiton many children missed school on 22 October 1914 as 'the Canadian motor transport passed through the town this afternoon'. In common with many schools, the children in Kingskerswell were given leave to watch the local recruiting rallies in June and September 1915, and that summer many stayed away to watch the convoys of motor cars taking the wounded from Exeter to Torquay. Heathcoat Girls' School was situated by the entrance to the textile mills in Tiverton, and one afternoon was completely disrupted when 'A recruiting meeting was held this afternoon outside the Factory gates at ¼ to 2 with the result that the children got mixed up with the crowd and neither teachers or children could possibly get near the gates. The last speaker finished at 2.30 and it was close to ¼ to 3 before we got to school.'

Aeroplanes were a fascinating novelty. At Heasley Mill and Aveton Gifford the children were released from school to watch them fly over. The machines were so slow that there was no need to rush. 'It was in sight for about ten minutes,' said the head at Heasley Mill. Children at Beer flocked around a seaplane landing by the small harbour, and no doubt numerous children were entertained by the sight of the Short seaplanes on their anti-submarine patrols from Beacon Quay in Torquay and at Mount Batten in Plymouth. A headmaster in Tiverton had a rare experience: 'If anyone had told me as a boy that I should become the Headmaster of the Heathcoat Boys' School and to this had prophesised that in turn one of my own pupils would fly round the top of St Paul's Steeple like a bird I should have thought him to be a Romanticist equal to Jules Verne.' Equally rare were the British airships, probably from the RNAS base at Chelson Meadow just outside Plymouth, that enthralled the children of Ilfracombe and Loddiswell as they droned

The Heathcoat lace factory at Tiverton, with the Heathcoat Girls' School to the right of the entrance. (Author's collection)

slowly overhead. On 20 July 1916, the headteacher at Loddiswell noted ruefully that many children left the playground at midday to follow the airship and missed the afternoon registration.

Royal visits were equally entertaining. Schools in Exeter, Plymouth and Torquay closed on 8, 9 and 10 September 1915 respectively so the children could line the streets when King George V and Queen Mary visited the military hospitals, and decorated patients. On 25 February 1918 pupils from Eggbuckland, Crownhill, St Budeaux and Tamerton Foliot schools marched to Crownhill at 11.30 a.m. to salute the Prince of Wales on his way from Princetown to Plymouth. The boys in Princetown's Church Lads Brigade had even greater enjoyment as they formed part of the Guard of Honour for the prince's visit there, and had two days off school – one for the rehearsal and another for the visit.

The special days

King George V was Emperor of India and monarch of the dominions of Canada, South Africa, Australia and New Zealand, and dozens of West Indian, African and Asian colonies, and the most widely honoured wartime day in the school year was 24 May – Empire Day. The Earl of Meath had advocated such a celebration since 1901, and although some schools had marked the date before 1914 with teas or visits to the cinema to see a patriotic film, and by singing the National Anthem, it took the involvement of the empire in the war to turn it into an official day of commemoration in 1916. In 1917 the *Times Educational Supplement* eulogised the 70,000 schools marking Empire Day with due martial ceremony and special lessons on the watchwords 'Responsibility, Sympathy, Duty and Self-Sacrifice'. The goals of Empire Day were clear-cut, it asserted: 'It aims at preserving the proud memories of the past; it designs instruction in the facts of the present; it dreams of the realisation of great ideals in the future.' It recognised the changes that war had wrought, as before the war the empire 'seemed remote, unreal, too high for ordinary men and women. Before the war the message of Empire Day had somehow a savour of being only for so-called "upper classes", had a faint flavour of the academic about it … Now it is gradually being recognised as merely a statement of the common heritage.' The task of establishing 'a tradition of kinship' with the peoples of the Empire was thrust firmly on the schools, as 'in no place but the school can these traditions be adequately preserved and vitalised'.

By 1916 the *ad hoc* celebrations had been replaced by lengthy and deliberately emotional ceremonies recommended by the education authorities, with local councillors and clergy becoming fully engaged in giving talks on the significance of the empire and the duty of the rising generation to preserve it. Christian service and imperial responsibility became inextricably entwined, a process reinforced by the common elements of later Empire Day activities – the processions of local schoolchildren around playgrounds or through villages carrying flags and banners, the hymns of martial Christian glory, the Union Jack saluted as pupils marched by the flagpole, special talks on British pre-eminence and benevolence across the empire, prayers centred on the Empire Day watchwords, the singing of the National Anthem and a final blessing by the clergy. The patriotic recitations and songs heard across Devon included 'Drake's Drum', 'Land of Hope and Glory', 'Who Sails

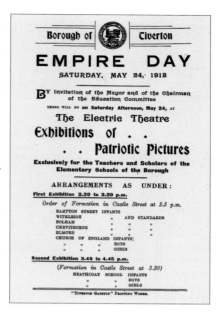

Borough of Tiverton Empire Day Programme, 1913. (County Record Office)

with Drake?', 'Where are the Boys of the Old Brigade?', 'At the Thought of Britain's Glory', 'Motherland', 'Song of the Banner', 'Mariners of England', 'The Reveille', 'Love of Country', 'Till the Boys come Home', 'Play up and Play the Game', 'Boys of Great and Greater Britain', 'The Daisy or the Empire's Emblem', 'Rule Britannia', and Kipling's 'The Children's Hymn' and 'Recessional'. The vast majority, rather ironically, tended to highlight purely British virtues and achievements. Not surprisingly, the most frequently chosen hymns were 'O God Our Help in Ages Past' and 'To Thee O God We Fly'.

Parents usually attended, and so did soldiers convalescing and on leave; often collections were taken for Red Cross hospitals and service charities. Often, too, classes of children put on plays, dialogues or tableaux featuring the dominions and colonies, which usually emphasised how important it was for their loyalty to be reciprocated by the mother country. At Great Torrington pupils recited Tennyson's 'India and the Colonies', with groups of children representing each part of the empire. The girls of Haywards School in Crediton performed a war masque entitled 'Empire's Honour', and those at Homelands School in Torquay performed the pageant 'Britannia Calls'. Both included a series of costumed tableaux highlighting the loyal responses of different dominions and colonies, and the four nations within the United Kingdom. Each year 1,000 Plymouth children marched to Charles Church, to attend a service where the

The Empire Day certificate awarded to Ralph Edds in 1915. (Topsham Museum)

vicar spoke on the glorious deeds and great suffering of overseas soldiers in the service of their king. At Okehampton and Barnstaple huge processions from all the schools marched through the towns to meet, along with parents, civic dignitaries and clergy, for mass services of remembrance and thanksgiving.

The Empire Day message was always made personal, and fundamentally became a clarion call for future Christian soldiers. To resounding, if possibly mystified, applause a minister in Barnstaple told the assembled children, 'Play the game, be fair, be kind, do your duty, fear God, honour the King, and love all men, and then God, who has made us mighty, will make us mightier yet, and the greatness of this great Empire shall not wane, but increase as the generations go on.' Equally typical was the talk by the headmaster of Furzeham School in Brixham in 1916: 'The British Empire stood for freedom, justice, liberty and righteousness, and if Britain fought for these principles, God would be sure to be on her side.' In Exeter the Revd Ivan Gregory kept things simpler, but no less awe-inspiring, telling the boys of Episcopal School that 'many of the boys who had sat in the desks were now serving their King and Country. Some had died, many were wounded, but they worthily maintained the high reputation of the School. As long as lads came forward, as had the old boys of the Episcopal School, the British Empire would never die.'

Trafalgar Day – 21 October – was important too. It provided the perfect opportunity for the glories of past victories at sea, ironically largely against Britain's current allies, the French, to be linked to the expected naval triumphs of the present war. Naturally Lord Nelson loomed large in the special lessons on Trafalgar Day, but so did Admiral Sir John Jellicoe, Commander-in-Chief of the Grand Fleet – at least until the less than glorious Battle of Jutland in the summer of 1916. No opportunity was lost to ensure that children appreciated the stark message that the Royal Navy's dominating presence across the seas and oceans of the world was the only guarantee that the empire would be politically and economically secure and Britain remain prosperous.

St George's Day, 23 April, was less prominent, but as a national saint's day it offered another opportunity to link the triumph of the Christian soldier over the dragon of evil to the justice of England's war against Germany. In 1917 the full force of the Church of England was mobilised when Exeter Cathedral filled with Boy Scouts, Girl Guides, Army Cadets and Sea Cadets, as well as nurses and convalescing soldiers, troops from the local barracks and civic dignitaries, for a celebratory service.

Many speakers at school events trusted that God supported the British war effort, and this assumption pervaded many children's weekends through the well-supported denominational Sunday schools. In Newton Abbot, for example, four Church of England schools provided 600 members of Sunday schools. One area of children's lives little affected by the war was the celebrated 'Treat', the traditional summer outing organised by all Sunday schools as a reward for regular attendance and for learning a great deal by heart. Often Treats were trips to the seaside or local beauty spots, and involved getting a hundred or more children onto trains or convoys of cars and charabancs, then providing them with plenty of sports and a glorious tea. Some schools lost several days' schooling if the Anglicans, Baptists, Congregationalists and Methodists had Sunday schools in their catchment areas. Most Treats continued throughout the war, although more often to local farms and big houses than to the seaside, and teas became more frugal as the food economy campaign took hold. Nevertheless 'it was a pretty sight', said the *Totnes Times* in July 1916, to see the children, teachers and parents of Buckfastleigh Wesleyan Sunday school 'sitting informally on the grass or in the more dignified chairs and doing justice to the good things provided, for this was a real picnic. After tea Mr Dyer and Mr Abbott were busy organising races and other games for the children. The fun waxed fast and furious until dewy eve had really come.' Sunday schools remained powerful institutions, and schools had to earmark an official day's holiday for each Treat or suffer the punishment of a much-diminished attendance. Even at the height of the food shortages in 1918 the Ministry of Food said that 'margarine or butter would be available as well as bread, if not used to excess, but no sugar,' for Sunday school Treats.

CHILDREN RAISING FUNDS

Early in the war schoolchildren were seen as a widespread source of cheap, enthusiastic and obedient labour. They were also seen as effective propaganda agents within their families and communities. Not surprisingly, therefore, they made significant contributions to a host of war charities through direct family giving, a host of concerts and numerous sales of work. Across Devon schools assisted Princess Mary's Fund for Christmas Gifts to the troops, Primrose Day and Our Day collections for the Red Cross, Sir Arthur Pearson's Fund for Blinded Soldiers' Children, St Dunstan's Home for blinded servicemen, Field-Marshal Lord Roberts Memorial Fund, Jack Cornwell Memorial Fund, the YMCA Hut Funds, and the RSPCA Sick and Wounded Horses Fund.

Overseas aid was not forgotten, with collections for the Belgian, French, Russian and Serbian Relief Funds. The girls in one Plymouth school helped sell penny flags for the 1915 French Flag Day. Some extracts from the essays they wrote beforehand appeared in the *Western Evening Herald*, and maybe give a glimpse into the lessons they received. One wrote, 'I am going to save every farthing I get till I get a penny and then buy one. I'll ask people in the street if they want any. I will tell them all about it.' Another said her aim was 'To sacrifice a penny to buy a flag instead of buying sweets, and then we can feel proud and say "I have done my bit in the great war of 1915."' A third wrote, 'Three cheers for the red, white and blue. I do not mean the Union Jack, but the pretty little red, white and blue little French flag which will be sold for a penny each on Saturday. The money will be given to the French soldiers who have done so much for us.' Anticipating every eventuality, a fourth wrote, 'Some hard-hearted folks may say "What have the French done that they should receive these tributes from us?" Of course we know this is very cruel because the French allies have helped us and stood by us a great deal. News came to us this morning informing us that there are more French victims to the poisonous gas, so there is more need than ever for the money now.'

Among many other examples, in 1915 the senior girls of Haywards School in Crediton supported the Red Cross by putting on the operetta *Princess Ju-Ju*, and the girls of Tavistock Church of England School gave several performances of the operettas *The Wishing Cup* in 1917 and *Mayday in Welladay* in 1918. At the other end of the scale the little school at Peter Tavy had only twenty-three children, but the staff and children proudly raised small sums of money for the Belgian Relief Fund, the Over Seas Club, the National Sailors' Society, the YMCA Hut Fund, the *Weekly Dispatch* Tobacco Fund, the Serbian Relief Fund and the Jack Cornwell Fund. In Torquay, though, a note of caution was sounded when the education committee heard criticisms that some head-teachers were subjecting the children to undue pressure to contribute to one

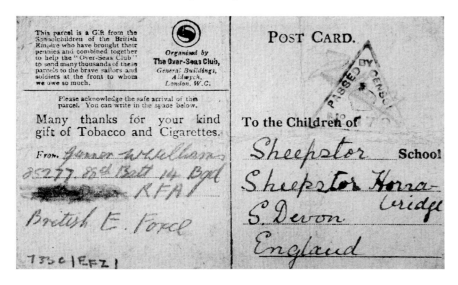

Gunner Williams's thank you card to Sheepstor School. (Devon Record Office)

charity after another, possibly, it was intimated, for the kudos it would bring to their school's reputation.

CHILDREN, SHORTAGES AND SAVINGS

The traditional virtues of thrift and economy, preached so often to children, assumed new significance in 1917. In that year, as food shortages grew acute, the government sent a pamphlet entitled *A Talk to School Children on Our Daily Bread* to every school. It highlighted the U-boats that were menacing merchant vessels bringing grain to Britain, and encouraged children to eat only when really hungry, to cut bread thinly and to eat every scrap of food. Shrewdly, it asked them to make sure they told everyone else this news. The strictures were taken seriously. One boy was prosecuted for being seen 'wasting a piece of bread, in weight 6 ozs'. His mother claimed the bread was bad, but the magistrate merely exclaimed, 'Stuff and nonsense; we all have to eat it,' and imposed a hefty 10s fine.

In similar vein, when the government sought to promote War Savings it sent local speakers armed with leaflets entitled *How Everybody Can Help to Win the War* to every school to drum up family enthusiasm for saving towards the 15s 6d certificates. Many headteachers became the honorary treasurers for the local War Savings Associations, and proudly recorded the rising total of certificates sold. No doubt many children flocked to the War Savings Exhibition in Exeter, attracted by the German biplane, field gun, machine gun, a sniper's gun and part of a Zeppelin that were displayed to remind

Lionel Heath's 1915 Overseas Club Christmas Day Gifts Certificate. (Devon Record Office)

everyone that the war still needed to be won, and that saving certificates would help Britain secure victory. As part of the government's later economy drive, troops of Devon Scouts and Guides collected huge quantities of waste paper for commercial recycling, and in doing so they raised sufficient money to purchase a Red Cross trailer for transporting wounded men.

Food became scarce in 1917, and at the behest of the Boards of Education and Agriculture many schools abandoned their ordinary gardening syllabuses and concentrated upon the mass production of potatoes. At Cotleigh pupils filled every square inch of soil around the school building with potatoes, and in October 1917 a Devonport headmaster proudly recorded his boys lifting 5st of them from newly broken ground. Sometimes additional scrubland was found to cultivate during the emergency, although the extra back-breaking work was not always welcomed. Despite the objections of the headmaster, the pupils at West Lawn School in Teignmouth were obliged by the managers and county horticulture instructor to try to remove tree roots from a manifestly unsuitable sloping and partly waterlogged area adjacent to the school. 'Very little progress was made', recorded the *Teignmouth Post*. At Tiverton the boys of Heathcoat School had to clear a large area of sloes and dig in a '100 loads' of road sweepings, ashes and leaves before planting. At Aveton Gifford the managers foisted a very weedy plot on the school, but the head insisted this intensive war work had to be undertaken out of school hours. To his chagrin, birds ate many of the young potato plants, the plot needed spraying twice with a mixture of copper sulphate and soda, and still much of the eventual crop was diseased. In Exeter some long-neglected nursery land earmarked for schools by the education committee proved beyond the efforts of children to cultivate, and had to be abandoned.

The shortage of food for children themselves was a worry to some school managers and local councillors, but as always the keenly contested questions of publicly funded intervention and the identification of genuine need loomed large when possible solutions were discussed. In January 1915 the county education committee resounded to a variety of views on the provision of 1*d* midday meals. Some members thought they should be generally available and not limited as at present to schools where voluntary groups provided them, while others spoke against such blanket interference with parental responsibility and local initiatives. A survey found that about 40 per cent of schools either provided some sort of hot milky drink or facilities to heat food at midday, although often only in the winter months; but the medical officers warned that food provided by parents was frequently 'neither sufficient nor suitable'. In the end a typical compromise was reached, whereby a circular was sent to all schools recommending the expansion of voluntary efforts where managers thought they were needed. The education committee voted to provide the basic equipment if requested, but not the labour or ingredients; they would need to be provided locally through voluntary effort or charges to parents, or a combination of both. A few schools, Hartland and Ivybridge for example, took advantage of the offer. In the autumn of 1914 Plymouth Education Committee decided that the city had little need of subsidised school meals as employment prospects were growing not diminishing, and it took no action to expand provision beyond the ninety-seven 'necessitous' children formally identified by teachers and medical officers.

Charities, though, were active. In Exeter one provided 'farthing dinners' to children and adults, and an average of 114 were receiving this very basic meal in January 1916. A winter soup kitchen in the city's Lower Market proved popular, and provided 1,400 gallons 'of steaming, nutritious, tasty soup' each week to 500 adults and children a day. So many children missed school to be early in the queue that they were issued with tickets that gave them priority places when they arrived. It was 'a splendid help to the poorest classes of the city', said the *Western Times* in February 1917. When food shortages grew more acute later that year a Civic Communal Kitchen opened in the city, providing what were termed 'patriotic' 2*d* meals without any taint of charity. Over 200 were served each weekday, and the menu varied to include soup and jam roly-poly pudding, soup and meat and vegetable pudding, and baked hot-pot and milk pudding. Similar schemes operated in Barnstaple and Cullompton.

CHILDREN AND THE COUNTRYSIDE COLLECTIONS

Another subject given a pragmatic wartime purpose was nature study. The girls from Plymouth's Hyde Park School collected chrysanthemums from families and friends to give to the local hospital for wounded soldiers. Schools in Exmouth and Tavistock made up large boxes of mixed vegetables for local warships and hospitals. Right across the county children brought eggs to school under the National Egg Collection scheme, to add to the weekly gifts by villages and towns to Red Cross hospitals. Between January and October 1916 Little Torrington School collected 3,000 eggs, and by then Chudleigh's wartime total had reached 9,098. By that summer a dozen or so villages centred on Newton Abbot had collected over 45,000. Sometimes children wrote their names and addresses on the eggs, and sometimes they received letters of thanks in reply, which often emphasised the servicemen's gratitude that people at home had not forgotten them. 'We are so glad', wrote one soldier, 'to see that little girls like you think of the wounded soldiers now resting in the hospitals of England, after fighting the beastly foe.' Less comforting would have been a message from another soldier saying he had lost his left leg and all the toes on his right foot, 'but you know I do not get downhearted at all'.

Gwendoline Rice's National Egg Collection Certificate. (Devon Record Office)

Other major collections had the added attraction that the children would be paid. The shortage of medical dressings led the county council to encourage children as well as adults to collect sphagnum moss, which could be found in abundance in the water-laden moors and valleys of Devon. Soft and silky, its cellular structure contained the antiseptic qualities of iodine and also absorbed large amounts of moisture with minimal irritation to the skin. Working parties delivered hundreds of sackloads each week to local depots, such as those in Okehampton, Princetown and Totnes abutting Dartmoor, and in Budleigh Salterton and Hemyock in the south-east. There the moss was cleaned of impurities, dried and stretched, shaped into various sized dressings, sealed in muslin bags and then packaged, a hundred at a time, in waterproof containers for dispatch to local and national hospitals. In the summer of 1916 boys from schools in Moretonhampstead gathered 5½cwt of foxglove leaves, from which digoxin could be extracted to assist in the treatment of patients with certain heart conditions. Sadly the youthful collectors were urged to be more careful in 1917, as only leaves two or three years old were any use. In 1918 all Brixham schools made a concerted effort to collect date stones and nut shells, which were turned into charcoal for gas masks.

In August 1917 all schools received an urgent plea via the Board of Education from the minister of munitions and the food controller to collect horse chestnuts. They were, it was mysteriously yet enticingly announced, an effective substitute for grain 'in certain industrial processes essential to the prosecution of the war'. Each ton of chestnuts saved half a ton of grain. The chestnuts were delivered in bulk to local depots from where they were transported to a destination and for a purpose that were never made public – although the official sacks used by the schools had a definite clue in the address: 'The Director of Propellant Supplies'. The chestnuts had been found to be a suitable alternative to imported wood and maize for the distillation of acetone, a solvent used in the manufacture of cordite. They ended up in a secret processing factory near King's Lynn in Norfolk.

Schools responded enthusiastically. In 1917 three walks by children at St Philip & St James School in Ilfracombe produced 90lbs, 97lbs and ½cwt respectively. Heavitree Parochial School collected 3cwt, Topsham and Upottery Council Schools achieved half a ton each, and Haywards Boys' School in Crediton gathered an impressive 3 tons 7cwt. Perhaps not surprisingly Devon's chief constable reported that there had been lots of complaints about boys throwing horse chestnuts in the roads, and at houses and passing railway trains. In October 1916 a tragedy occurred in Exeter when Archibald Raymond, aged twelve, was killed when he fell from a wall after being chased out of a garden in which he had espied a chestnut tree.

At the same time a shortage of labour and the heightened demand for jam by the armed forces led to another official request for nature walks, this time in search of blackberries. The fruit, which had to be dry, not over-ripe and without stalks, was sold to local dealers for 3*d* a pound, and the money distributed among the youthful pickers. A few schools picked wild soft fruit in 1914, 1915 and 1916, largely to make pots of jam to give to local hospitals, but the bulk harvesting occurred in 1917 and 1918. Many schools took part, and some devoted six, seven or eight afternoons to the task. Among those recording the final totals were Lustleigh with 424lbs, Haywards Boys' School, Crediton, with 586lbs, Topsham Council School with 694lbs, Hatherleigh Council Boys' School with 1,360lbs, and the small school at Westwood, near Broadclyst, with a massive 3,247lbs – which was probably helped by access to the Acland family's nearby Killerton estate. Not everyone thought it was school time well spent. At Throwleigh the recurring bouts of sickness and several changes of teacher led parents to stage a successful protest in September 1918 against any further teaching time being lost to collecting soft fruit.

THE CHILD LABOUR CONTROVERSIES

The wartime loss of adult labour led to a resurgence of demand for older boys to be released from school before the age of fourteen. It provided the perfect opportunity for those who criticised elementary education as taking far too long to teach things of little practical worth to prospective labourers and artisans to receive a more sympathetic hearing than hitherto. In September 1914 Earl Fortescue suggested to the county education committee a formal relaxation of the by-laws which would allow children aged thirteen to enter full-time employment, either temporarily or permanently, if their school attendance and standard of work were sufficiently high. With varying degrees of enthusiasm a majority of members concurred. Some, though, disapproved of a general relaxation, arguing that local needs varied widely, while others thought the whole idea was merely a ploy by farmers to secure cheap and malleable labour. All these arguments were bandied about repeatedly throughout the war, but maintaining agricultural output easily prevailed over maintaining educational standards, and school logbooks duly recorded the erratic and generally low attendances of older boys. By February 1916 658 children had been formally exempted under the relaxed ruling. More came later, such as the twelve-year-old son of a Tiverton baker who wanted his lad 'to run about the outskirts of the town on errands'. Many other families did not bother with formalities.

The declining situation was complicated by four interwoven factors. Firstly, the education committee's continuing debates left people confused, or pretending to be confused, by what exactly had been decided, and secondly, the government decided that although labour was probably short in agriculture it would not incur the odium itself by being responsible for formally curtailing children's education. It left the decision about granting 'certificates of exemption' to the people it said knew the local situation best – the local authorities. Thirdly, many school attendance officers had enlisted and not been replaced, and fourthly, many magistrates had sympathy with the difficulties of farmers and were often farmers themselves, and therefore became increasingly less inclined to impose deterrent fines on parents. In the event, in 1916 the county education committee went so far as to allow children after the age of twelve to receive limited periods of exemption to work on the land if it could be proved that no adult labour at a reasonable wage was available. It acknowledged but otherwise ignored the protests from Newton Abbot's UDC, Trades and Labour Council, Independent Labour Party, Gas Workers & General Labourers Association and Shop Assistants' Union.

Not surprisingly there evolved a tacit understanding: provided no-one grossly abused the situation, older children could miss school and go to work without prosecution. But of course, as many headteachers wrote in their logbooks, the relaxed rules encouraged other children to stay away for a variety of reasons – shopping, helping at home, running errands, casual paid work and looking after younger siblings. 'Scores of girls are home from school for petty reasons,' bemoaned the headmistress of Plymouth's Ford Senior Girls' School in 1917. In addition touring circuses and menageries, and the annual agricultural fairs at Bampton, Barnstable, Hatherleigh, and Tavistock, with their sales, auctions and sideshows, continued throughout the war, and enticed children away from school as customers, onlookers or helpers. Dartmoor itself offered another lure. Many who lived on or near it customarily played truant to gather whortle-berries, or 'hurts', to sell to Tavistock dealers for jam making. The war led to whortleberry dye being used in the manufacture of blue uniforms, and the price rocketed from about 6*d* a quart to 2*s*, which meant families could add considerably to their income. In July 1917 Okehampton Council Boys' School lost forty to fifty boys – a quarter of its roll – to whortleberry picking.

Overall, logbooks suggest that normal attendance outside periods of exceptional illness and particularly foul weather dropped by 10 to 15 per cent during the war, from the mid-90s to the low 80s, but most of these additional absences were concentrated in the older classes. Typically, attendance at Beer did not get above 86 per cent during 1916–17 and was often much lower, and in September 1916 the headteacher at Woodbury specifically recorded that only 58 per cent of the top class was present.

Farmers welcomed the education committee's decision, and the president of Devon Farmers' Union publicly stated that 'he hoped that would be taken full advantage of by the farmers for beneficial employment in agriculture'. Some school managers agreed, one in Paignton seeing it as a significant educational opportunity, and asserting that 'if the boys were required, they would be learning a very useful occupation. It was unfortunate farm labourers had been looked down upon in the past. A farm labourer could usually turn his hand to anything.' The vicar of South Brent concurred, stating that many boys were best suited to manual rather than intellectual pursuits. Let them leave early if they want to, he wrote in the parish magazine, adding, with a low view of schools and schoolboys, 'If a boy cannot read and write well and express his thoughts clearly and intelligently at the age of 12 or 13 years, then it is either due to defective teaching or incapacity to derive much benefit from teaching.'

The Farmers' Union was outraged that the County Teachers' Association had the temerity to lodge a forceful protest against the decision, in which it said that the committee was 'making serfs of these little chaps', and what the farmers really wanted to do was to get children back on the land at the age of eleven. Once they left school, the association argued, the children would never return. In reply the supporters of child labour said that many poor parents depended upon the pennies their children were able to earn, stimulating the counter-argument that farmers should pay their labourers decent wages in the first place. Even grammar schools were not immune to the exigencies of the times. Their pupils helped on farms, and in 1917 the headmaster of Crediton Grammar School acknowledged the 'thinning in the ranks of the upper school' as older boys, especially farmers' sons, left early for full-time jobs.

Planting and harvesting were the primary times when attendances plummeted. Nevertheless, in March 1917 William Hiern, chairman of Devon Education Committee, said confidently, 'I dare say that the school attendance officers will not be very strict in cases of that sort' when asked if schoolboys could help till potatoes on school days. In addition, school managers were now granted flexibility to fix school holidays around peak agricultural demands for labour, and could also grant extra holidays for up to a fortnight a year in accordance with local farming needs. Full advantage was taken of both concessions – alongside a high incidence of illegal absenteeism. Among many examples, the schools at Inwardleigh, Heasley Mill, Ashburton and Ashcombe dutifully closed for a fortnight for the hay harvest. At Atherington boys over twelve were absent harvesting in September 1916 and then potato digging the following month, a pattern repeated in 1917 and 1918, but with an additional fortnight's working holiday and then late autumn fruit picking. At Beer and Thorveton the boys went haymaking in summer and in the autumn helped with the threshing, then with digging potatoes and mangolds. At Manaton the children went haymaking in the early summer, then potato planting, sphagnum moss gathering and finally potato digging in the autumn. Commercial fruitpicking absorbed a great deal of child labour around Topsham in the Exe valley.

Dr Adkins, the county medical officer, grew particularly concerned at the extent of child labour out of school hours on school days. In towns boys sold and delivered newspapers and milk and ran errands, and in the country boys helped on farms and girls worked in houses. At Westwood the headteacher complained when the farmers' cider made children who worked in the fields during the midday break 'very flushed, heavy headed and sleepy' in the afternoon. In a public lecture in Torquay an education committee member attacked the practice of children working from seven o'clock in the morning, and often ending up in school soaking wet, hungry and tired. School, he said, was merely a resting place before they went back to work at dinnertime and in the evening, and, he told his audience, 'it was a terrible reproach to their civilisation and humanity'. 'The children of the County', said a headmaster at a union conference, 'were already doing more than their own share of the additional work imposed by the war.' In the case of his school – a typical one, he said – a quarter of the children were employed out of school hours.

At Bolham, near Tiverton, boys worked on early morning milk rounds and often missed registration, even though it was delayed until 10 a.m. At a Tiverton Education Committee meeting a member asked the school attendance officer to explain why he had met eleven boys in the street after 9 a.m., some carrying vegetables, some fetching coal, only for them to say the headmaster had said it was all right to come to school at 9.30 a.m. However, most other members took a more relaxed view of children doing domestic or part-time jobs, and also agreed that newspaper boys should be treated leniently if the trains arrived late from London.

Adkins, though, believed that such regular work, with its attendant 'hurried meals, improper food, insufficient rest and insanitary conditions of the home', rendered the children more prone to disease as well as impairing their intellectual capabilities. In 1916 he found schoolboys in Seaton spending five hours in school and nine hours at work each school day. As always, he put the blame not so much on employers as 'on the home neglected by mothers who go out to work'. In 1917 the county education committee was forced to recognise that no statistics were available regarding the extent of children's employment on school days, and duly established an investigatory committee that confirmed the widespread nature of the problem. Unfortunately no statistics survive. Any stiffening of the by-laws, however, had to wait until the war ended.

In Plymouth the scandal of child labour centred on the likelihood of corruption and immorality, and amid considerable controversy in 1916 the city tightened up its by-laws just a little to bar any boy under twelve and any girl under sixteen from street trading, and limited their working hours to twenty a week on school-days. In the face of all the evidence, including a thirteen-year-old boy who earned 2s 6d selling newspapers for forty-eight hours a week outside school hours, one of the education committee's fiercest opponents of the reform was the Revd L. O'Loughlin, who said 'he considered it nothing more than a refined form of persecution against the defenceless poor'. 'If they went to the slums of Plymouth,' he asserted, 'they would find mother after mother between whom and starvation stood the money they now sought to deprive her.' Others agreed, some only too conscious of the extent of local poverty, and the abuses continued. In 1916 the headteacher of Keppel Place Higher Elementary Boys' School identified a dozen boys who undertook domestic chores before school, and thirty whose evening work meant they did not get to bed until after 10.30 p.m. In 1917 one boy 'aged between 12 and 14' was found to be working thirty-five hours a week in a Plymouth barber's shop over and above his twenty-seven-and-a-half hours in school, and another was employed as an errand boy for forty hours.

JUVENILE CRIME

There was a general feeling that a breakdown in family and school discipline was causing a rise in juvenile crime. No-one had any statistics; it was more an assumption that crime was caused by the combination of prolonged absences of fathers and older brothers, extra workloads descending upon hard-pressed mothers, the heady excitement of so many soldiers being in the county, and the poorer discipline that was assumed to be prevalent in schools.

Cinemas came in for special condemnation. Their 'sensational' films were held to keep children awake at night, arouse unhealthy emotions and incite them to imitate the attitudes and actions of heroes and villains, without necessarily discriminating between the two. Despite the views of others who thought films could be educational in content as well as having a value in taking ordinary people's minds off the dreary round of their daily lives, the general consensus was that their hold on impressionable minds was so great that some children were resorting to theft to pay for their entry tickets. In May 1916 Barnstaple Education Committee condemned cinema posters as 'very shocking – setting forth death, crime, killing, fighting, scenes of anguish, and unhealthy excitement'. Strident cries for tighter local censorship, and some form of national censorship, came from church groups and social reformers – and also doctors, who were concerned with damage to the children's eyes and ears. Although innocuous to modern audiences, some films undoubtedly possessed salacious titles. Among those shown in wartime Devon were *Be Sure Your Sins, Whoso is without Sin, and The World, the Flesh and the D—l*. One titillating advertisement sold *The Scarlet Sin* as 'the story of a woman throwing away the substance of a good man's love for the shadow of a gay life by a man without moral scruples'. The most that happened was a bar on children attending cinemas after 9 p.m., and of course the cinematograph industry fought a vigorous delaying campaign against effective censorship.

Certainly there were steady streams of detailed juvenile court cases reported in most local newspapers. The culprits were usually named and shamed, their offences described and their punishment noted. Small communities were not immune. In May 1917 two Shaldon boys under the age of fourteen were birched for stealing money, bicycles, chickens and eggs. Their mother had died and their father was away; they were looked after by a relative but they had 'been deluded' by a Shaldon gang that was blighting the neighbourhood. In September the well-publicised 'thieving mania' in the town continued, with two boys aged ten and twelve convicted of stealing money from bathing machines. The elder was birched, and the younger handed to his father for punishment. Probation had been available for more than a decade, but it was rarely used in Devon at this time; retribution was much preferred.

Most towns believed children were getting out of control. In 1916 the mayor of Tiverton visited schools to talk to teachers and children about the juvenile crime wave that the watch committee and education committee believed was blighting the town, largely as a result of cinemas and a lack of sound religious instruction. In 1917 two ten-year-old boys were birched in Barnstaple for robbing a newspaper boy of 3s. The borough's chief constable asserted that they, too, were just one part of a juvenile crime wave, and 'He could only suggest one way of putting that down, and that was by giving those boys a thorough good birching.' In Torquay that year the magistrates ordered the birching of two young thieves aged ten and twelve, and sent a third to an industrial school; they wondered whether these cases, and many that recently had gone before, reflected badly upon the quality of elementary education in the town. 'Hardly a day passed', added one magistrate, 'without there being some depredation of gardens in the vicinity of his house.' The *Paignton Observer & Echo* thoroughly approved of the naming and birching of the resort's high number of 'bad boys'. In Plymouth it was common for initial offenders to be birched and repeat offenders to be dispatched to industrial schools.

In 1916 members of an Exeter gang were birched for stealing and selling chickens in order to play on penny slot machines – an occupation incurring condemnation second-only to the cinema. Exeter errand boys, like those elsewhere, sometimes found the goods and money they were carrying tempting enough to try to defraud customers and their employers; the boys were invariably birched. In January 1917 a string of juvenile cases in the city led to headlines of 'Thieving Epidemic', and the chief constable's annual report for 1916 said that children contributed 30 per cent of all the city's crimes. Exeter's juvenile court was busy throughout 1918, and gangs seemed to be the biggest worry. Five Exeter boys aged nine, ten and eleven in one gang were fined, and the ringleader sent to a strictly disciplined industrial school, for vandalising St Mary Arches Church, and another three aged ten birched for stealing sweets. An older group of fourteen and fifteen year olds, known as the Silken Cord Gang, who wore black masks and carried weapons including an old army pistol, was dealt with severely for consistently terrorising passers-by and robbing shops and lock-ups at night. Perhaps the cinema had had a deleterious effect after all. No wonder Alderman John Stocker, chairman of the city's education committee, was lavish in his praise of the Boy Scouts, Girl Guides and Army and Sea Cadets, and especially 'how these organisations tended to make the rising generation subservient to lawful authority and to be instantly obedient to the word of command'.

CHILDREN'S HEALTH

The fear of juvenile crime was great, but the fear of infectious diseases must have been terrifying. There is just one surviving wartime annual report by Dr Adkins, although it excludes Exeter and Plymouth. It is for 1915, and shows there were 1,089 reported cases of adults and children with scarlet fever, which resulted in 141 deaths, 716 cases of diphtheria and 58 deaths, and 59 cases of typhoid fever and 8 deaths. There were also 81 deaths from measles, 71 from whooping cough and 390 from tuberculosis. Numerous schools had to close during epidemics – 4 from chicken pox, 11 from diphtheria, 71 from measles, 18 from scarlet fever, 30 from whooping cough, 5 from mumps and 4 from influenza. Adkins had a particularly low view of parents, placing much of the blame for epidemics on their not taking the early signs of illness seriously and delaying reporting infectious diseases to schools, doctors and the local authorities. In addition, he condemned the failure of breast-feeding, mothers going out to work, inadequate diets, the piles of rubbish that lay near houses and bred fly-borne diseases, and poor sanitation, including the badly polluted water supplies from the rivers Axe, Culm, Harborne, Lew, Otter and Taw. In what he took to be the final proof of inadequate child-rearing, he drew attention to 'the degenerate type of youth which is so frequently seen in the county'.

Other years were probably just as bad. Measles closed at least twenty-two schools for two weeks or more across the county (excluding Exeter and Plymouth) in 1916, thirteen in 1917 and forty-one in 1918, and scarlet fever remained ever present, shutting at least five schools in 1916. Logbooks hint at the alarm and disruption epidemics caused. In June 1915 a headteacher at Honiton wrote, 'Whooping cough is worse than ever. The numbers are so bad and the coughing in school so distressing that the working of the school is being seriously upset.' In November 1915 the headteacher of Mary Dean School in Tamerton Foliot just outside Plymouth noted with exasperation that diphtheria had returned to haunt the neighbourhood for the fourth year in succession, and it returned again in 1916 to wreck lives, attendances and syllabuses. A plaintive logbook entry for September that year reads, 'Shall we ever be free here from diphtheria; there is very little interval between the cases.' The Germansweek headteacher recorded how frightened village families became when diphtheria appeared among them; it was little different to a plague and each family tended to avoid contact with other people as much as possible.

Sometimes localities suffered multiple outbreaks. Whooping cough and diphtheria closed Ilsham School in Torquay in autumn 1914, measles, ringworm and diphtheria hit Atherington in the winter of 1915–16 at the same time as Great Torrington endured scarlet fever and whooping cough. Mumps and whooping cough swept through Lustleigh in the summer of 1916, and impetigo and whooping cough struck Loddiswell the following year. And, of course, the vast majority of schools closed for several weeks on end during the devastating Spanish influenza epidemic in the autumn and winter of 1918–19. There was little the medical profession could do to counter it, except publicise the precautions families should try to take, such as avoiding crowds, keeping windows open, eating well, drinking plenty of water, washing frequently and wearing clean clothes. Small wonder, therefore, that Plymouth's *Western Evening Herald* gloomily commented on the gross overcrowding in the city's tenement blocks, which 'lends itself to the spread of the disease'. A doctor lamented, 'The people are going down all around us and we cannot help them.'

The patchy evidence suggests that the recently established school medical services provided effective inspection regimes and a steadily growing range of treatment facilities, despite several medical officers enlisting and a number of nurses transferring to war hospitals at home and abroad. In 1915 in the area under Devon County Council's authority, 577 visits were made to schools by the three doctors, and 18,152 children inspected, an increase of 1,400 over 1914; 140 older children were treated for flat feet or hammer toes, and many others for eye, teeth and breathing disorders. There were many home visits by the nurses to give advice and ensure effective treatment had taken place. Across the Borough of Plymouth 12,113 children were examined or re-examined that year, with particular attention being paid to treating the high incidence of rickets, physical defects such as spinal curvature, wry necks and flat feet, and vermin-ridden heads and bodies.

By the end of 1916 public attitudes to the ill-health of so many schoolchildren were changing fast. The statutory inspection and subsidised treatment of thousands of Devon schoolchildren had provided medical officers and local authorities with an array of statistics that revealed the vast extent of the problems but also the positive impact of treatments. Many more children could hear and see better, their mouths were healthier and their bodies cleaner, and a combination of the new clinics and nurses' domestic visits to advise, persuade and in the last resort threaten parents were helping families to help themselves. The war had helped in three key ways. First, it had focused further attention on the thousands of young men unable to pass the army's basic physical test. Second, the appalling casualties had become a stimulus for welfare reform. As Lloyd George, the prime minister, acknowledged in the darkest days of war, the people's sacrifice deserved a people's reward in terms of better educational opportunities, health facilities and housing. Third, the war was soon perceived as the direst threat yet to Britain's imperial trading networks. All these factors stimulated the moves to ensure the rising generation was sufficiently fit to defend the empire, and fight the next global challenge.

By the end of the war Devon's local authorities had made a range of treatments for eyes, ears, teeth and skin conditions far more easily accessible to parents in clinics and hospitals, although those who could afford it still had to pay, and far more children with chronic physical and mental conditions were being catered for in special day schools or residential institutions. Exeter had had St James Street School for Crippled and Delicate Children for a number of years, but in 1916 the children were dispersed to several specialist institutions. Plymouth Education Committee estimated that 3,000 delicate and anaemic children lived within precincts. In April 1918 it agreed to open two open-air schools for at least some of them. The first, Little Efford, opened at the end of the year. Each specially designed classroom had sides that could be lowered to the ground, the children were given good meals and they were encouraged to rest in the afternoons. The education committee also agreed to improve physical education provision for all children by employing more specialist staff, make far better educational use of the playing fields donated to the borough by the Astors, and open a remedial exercise gymnasium. By the end of 1918 the borough possessed several school clinics, and much more preventive as well as curative treatment was being carried out. Nevertheless there was still a long way to go, and the borough's medical officer rarely stopped complaining about parental failure to notice the signs of impending ill-health in their children.

CHILDREN IN INSTITUTIONS AND ASYLUMS

Poor surroundings and ill health were held to be major contributors to mental deficiency. It was a short step from this assertion to say, as many did, that inadequate parents were to blame and children would be better off, and less of a menace to their localities in residential schools, where long-term health could be restored, strict routines established and ingrained, and a modicum of possibly wage-earning training carried out. Miss Cecile Matheson, an 'expert' lecturing in Exeter in 1918, publicly reinforced all these points by arguing that mental defectives 'constitute a serious national danger'. They should be identified early, removed from the home environment, cared for in residential communities and 'should not be allowed to propagate their kind.'

Voluntary efforts complementing and supplementing the statutory ones had expanded during the war. In 1917 Plymouth's Civic Guild of Help was pleased that 61 of the 114 boys and 26 of the 98 boys from the borough's Defective School were wage earning, but far less so that six had married and might have children. The city's Voluntary Association for the Care of Mental Defectives came into being that year to monitor and guide, and 'keep in friendly touch', with children who left the special school. It followed in the wake of the wider Devon Voluntary Association, which primarily advised and supported families whose children might be suitable for admission to Starcross, the Homes for Girls, the workhouses or other specialist institutions, or merited careful control at home.

By the end of 1918 a county council-certified institution for boys aged five to twelve was planned in Exmouth; far too many cases were being identified across the county for acceptance in the asylum at Starcross. By then Starcross itself was viewed with unconcealed suspicion by local families, and many fought against their children's incarceration there. Probably its Victorian origins and institutional appearance made it appear as a singularly unwholesome combination of madhouse, prison and workhouse to many working-class parents. Probably, too, its regime appeared harsh as it attempted to reverse what it saw as the adverse influences of the home environment. A 1915 Starcross report spoke of its intake growing up 'in habits of idleness, accustomed to have their own way, and often petted and spoilt by the injudicious treatment of friends.' Therefore, it went on, 'before any progress can be made, much has to be unlearned, bad habits have to be eradicated, and good ones substituted; this, of course, took time'. Vocational training in useful skills was its ultimate objective, and despite its popular image in 1916 its cheerful rooms, well-cared-for inmates and varied training programmes were praised by Sir Frederick Needham from the Board of Control. Some significant success was achieved, perhaps against the odds, in 1914 when thirteen members of staff enlisted and a few carefully selected older boys became temporary assistant staff and 'proved themselves worthy of the trust'. In addition the girls produced several thousand socks, mittens and jerseys, as well as making hundreds of sphagnum moss pads – a delicate and time-consuming task. This was on top of knitting all the blue jerseys worn by the boys and the socks and stockings worn by the staff.

CHILDREN IN WORKHOUSES

Even more unpalatable to the vast majority of families was the thought of being forced by poverty to seek admission to local workhouses. Nevertheless the Boards of Guardians controlled several thousand lives across Devon, and the bleak external features of the numerous workhouses reflected the bleak existence of those inside them. Their reputation as publicly funded refuges of the last resort, and institutions in which all personal independence was taken away, was well-deserved. It was long-lasting too. For example, in 1914 all the inmates, whether young or old, still wore a distinctive uniform publicly proclaiming their status. In a particularly revealing incident, on 1 January 1916 Exeter's Board of Guardians debated the rising prices of food and fuel, fearing that the number of people needing relief might soar. When a small rise in allowances was suggested, a member angrily retorted they must not be 'led astray by the Christmas spirit', and he reminded the Board that it was not a charity but a guardian of the public purse. The rise was denied. This Dickensian perception of the Guardians' role was widespread across Devon, and it persisted throughout the war.

In 1914–15, 363 children lived in Devon workhouses, another 187 were boarded out and 3,015 were financially supported while still living with their parents. Reforms were reluctantly undertaken. The Guardians in Okehampton and Holsworthy dragged their heels for years when the Local Government Board urged them to create Scattered Homes, and Plymouth's initial interest, which resulted in the provision of a few house groups, greatly diminished when members fully appreciated the extra costs involved.

The Exeter Guardians were highly selective in their concern for the public purse. In June 1915 they reduced the inmates' meat allowance to 2oz a meal, abolished the bacon allowance on Saturdays and agreed that most days the dinners should be bread, cheese and broth with lentils. Later that summer the headmistress of Newtown Girls' School lamented the mental and physical lethargy of the children from the workhouse, and soon afterwards two official workhouse Visitors criticised its stultifying atmosphere during the long summer holidays. The children 'had to remain in a big room or in a yard with a very high wall', with little to do. The Guardians were unmoved. Much to the anger of ratepayers, that summer they had opened their new 'palatial offices' complete with a fully upholstered boardroom in prestigious Southernhay. Playing up to its readership, the *Western Times* said the Guardians had found their old buildings in Castle Street 'inconvenient and objectionable, and not consistent with their dignity'.

Inspections during the war revealed numerous glaring faults. In 1916 the Devonport Guardians were informed that their after-care of the 100 boarded-out children was inadequate, notably regarding the quality of foster-mothers and the employers they allowed to train girls as domestic servants. Under pressure, they introduced a new register with a record sheet for each child, agreed greater attention should be paid to ensuring sympathetic as well as systematic training, and promised that every case would be reviewed once a quarter by the children's committee.

In 1916 the inspection of the Stonehouse infirmary, maternity ward, nursery and children's quarters revealed an institution wedded to absolute economy. The infirmary food was largely 'thin and watery' soup, the bedsteads were thick with dust, the remains of food littered the ledges and lockers, and mice and plagues of flies were endemic. It was much the same in the maternity ward, with the additional problem of ill-kept records. The nursery was dirty, cot mattresses were in holes, the women's bedding in need of repair, and no records existed of the doctor's visits. Twenty-six children lived in the workhouse, with just one attendant, and there was no evidence of after-care. Many of the girls had head lice, and the diet was grossly inadequate, comprising oatmeal porridge and tea for breakfast, meat, vegetables and boiled rice for dinner, and bread, margarine and tea for tea. Little was done, complaints mounted, and one Guardian admitted that 'if some of us had to live on the dietary of this house we should soon be carried away somewhere else'. Others agreed. 'The inmates were getting thin and looking wretched' said one. 'The little girls are looking pale and hollow-eyed' asserted another. Nevertheless, the Board declared itself satisfied that inmates received meals in accordance with the Local Government Board's recommended wartime levels, but agreed with their doctor's suggestion that potatoes fried in beef dripping should be alternated with oatmeal at breakfast. Another 140 children lived in the Scattered Homes in Newton Abbot and here, too, their very basic diet disturbed some Guardians in 1917. However, far from offering anything better, the Board reduced the bread ration and sought cheaper cuts of meat, using the argument that even the paupers must share the 'national self-denial' regarding food. There was little sign that these workhouses were sensitive to the mounting pressures for welfare reforms.

CONCLUSION

The cessation of hostilities was a time for celebration for children as much as adults. On 11 November 1918 the headteacher of Great Torrington Council Boys' School wrote, 'The boys broke into loud cheers which needless to say we did not check.' Lessons stopped, flags were hoisted, 'and general shouting, cheering and merriment took place'. In Tiverton the boys of Heathcoat School were, at least initially, more restrained. They listened to Sir Ian Amory, who told them 'it was the greatest victory ever known in History', then ran up the Union Jack and sang the National Anthem. Sir Ian, whose son had been injured and brother killed, recalled the 'sad hearts ... overwhelmed with grief' trying to come to terms with the sacrifices their families had made. Only then were the boys allowed to rush out to join the cheering crowds in the street. Some days later the villagers of Uffculme expended their pent-up feelings at a celebration where 'the Kaiser was tied to a stake, well soaked in tar, and ignited amid loud cheers'. Early in December hundreds of Plymouth schoolchildren were taken to see the clearest sign of British triumph as the Royal Navy escorted surrendered German submarines into the Hamoaze.

For a brief period it looked as though a golden dawn would follow the nightmare of war for the nation's children. The war had heightened the value that the nation at large placed upon young children as future workers and defenders of its empire, and politicians acknowledged that greater investment in education and health care was an appropriate means of meeting the nation's expectations once peace was declared. As a result the 1918 Education Act promised much. It sought to address many long-standing issues highlighted by the war, such as the brevity of elementary schooling, the high incidence of early leaving and the blighted health of many children. All exemptions from attending school between the ages of five and fourteen were abolished, no child was to be employed on a school day before the end of the afternoon session, and the provision of medical treatment as well as medical inspection for elementary schoolchildren became mandatory. It allowed local authorities to extend secondary education and make more scholarship places available by increasing the rates, although it did not abolish admissions through the payment of fees. It did, though, provide the opportunity for elementary school leavers to study beyond the age of fourteen while also earning a living. It planned the gradual introduction of a system of free and compulsory day continuation classes for eight hours a week for young people aged between fourteen and eighteen.

As many critics noted at the time, though, the 1918 Act did not remove the social class basis of British schooling. Elementary and secondary education remained on parallel rather than converging paths, even though the scholarship admission gates of the secondary schools were to be pushed slightly more ajar. The Devon County Teachers' Association lamented the missed opportunities to abolish fees and to provide maintenance grants to support poor children in secondary schools. As a speaker said, a significant number of scholarship winners could not take up their places as their parents could not afford the travel, books and uniforms, or do without their children's wages.

The encouragement the Act gave to practical subjects such as handwork, gardening and domestic science in the elementary school ensured those schools continued to pursue very different programmes of study from the secondary schools, and thereby tended to channel the children into very different career paths. Despite the greater investment in elementary schools they remained essentially utilitarian and vocational. In the 1920s the vast majority of children in Devon still left school at fourteen and looked to estates, farms, factories, shops, ports and offices for jobs. The most glaring failure was the abandonment of the continuation school proposal under the pressures of the economic downturn in the early 1920s. A great deal of planning came to nothing. It would need another world war, and another war-stimulated Education Act in 1944, to bring about the abolition of 'elementary education' and to create the modern universal and free primary-secondary school system.

CHAPTER SIX

COMMUNITIES UNDER PRESSURE

National priorities, local turmoil, making a living

The outbreak of war saw dislocations not only to family life but also to a host of occupations in towns and villages right across Devon. The reluctance to impose any barriers upon voluntary recruitment, and especially the failure to bar key employees from enlisting, meant that factories, farms and offices were suddenly deprived of many of their young and skilled workers. As the war dragged on and the casualty rate soared, the demand for more men was never-ending. Employers everywhere were subjected to consistent pressure from government departments and military tribunals to maintain their output – be it farm produce, government contracts or public services – with fewer and fewer staff, or by resorting to the greater employment of women or men too old, too young or too infirm to fight. On top of all this, firms were called upon to change production lines to fulfil strict government contracts, and in agriculture farmers were obliged to implement drastic changes in land usage to meet the government's wartime food production targets. As these wartime expedients occurred while the prices of virtually all domestic commodities and raw materials soared alarmingly, it is hardly surprising that general support for the war did not preclude bitter criticism of government policies, especially when manufacturers and agricultural producers were strongly suspected of making large profits, and neither did it stop strikes. Indeed, a small but vociferous minority of workers possessed little sympathy with what they condemned as a capitalist war, and were far more concerned with using every opportunity to bring about a far fairer distribution of national wealth. Anxiety, uncertainty and frustration were just a few of the emotions associated with making a living on farms or in factories in wartime Britain.

WAR CONTRACTS

Work patterns and relationships were dislocated everywhere. Firms had to adapt to wartime conditions and pressures, and many flourished with new wartime contracts. From a host of examples, Trusham quarry in the Teign valley supplied granite, Shapland and Petter's cabinet works in Barnstaple made ammunition boxes for the army and wooden propellers and struts for aircraft, the textile mills of Buckfastleigh, Tiverton and Uffculme provided khaki cloth, puttees and other items of military clothing, the paper mills at Hele, Silverton, Stoke Canon and Ivybridge supplied huge quantities of government forms, the family firm of Ellis in Ilfracombe made motor lorries for the army, Messrs Wildish and Son in Paignton harbour made shell cases, and the Deco Company, also in Paignton, constructed Admiralty whalers.

Around the coast, Devonport Dockyard repaired and maintained warships, and also completed the light cruiser HMS *Cleopatra* and the submarines *J5* and *J6* in 1915, *K6* and *K7* in 1916 and *J7* in 1917. As mentioned earlier, Appledore shipyard secretly fitted out Q ships. A boatyard at Barnstaple built and launched two ships with experimental reinforced concrete hulls under contract to the shipping controller. The first, named *Cretepath*, grounded on a sandbank after its launch in September 1918 and broke its back. By the time the wreck was cleared, and the second one, *Cretepond*, was ready to launch, the war had ended. *Cretepond* was completed successfully in 1919, sold to Joseph Bowles of Cardiff, and eventually sunk as part of a pier construction in 1927.

In 1919 the directors of Willey's ironworks on Haven Banks by the river in Exeter celebrated the company's wartime achievements. It had repaired 1,800,000 cartridge cases, made 1,168,000 new primers, repaired 2,245,000 primers, made 500 mine sinkers, 7,000 cast iron plummets for anchoring mines in the sea, 30 cast-iron engine beds for tugs, 3,360 cast-iron pipes for use with poison gas, 300 backsights and 300 foresights for machine guns, 100 tons of castings for dockyard cranes, 10 tilting furnaces for melting brass, 30 huge riveted petrol storage tanks holding 250,000 gallons each, 300 sets of balance weights, 60 concrete mixing machines and 8,000 ploughshares. In 1915 the company lent a manager to assist a new munitions firm, created by a consortium of Exeter businessmen, which was establishing itself in the Vulcan Stove Company's premises and had a contract with the Bristol National Munitions Company to turn out high explosive 18lb shells.

In Plymouth the Astor family was influential in securing a contract with the Royal Army Clothing Department for the production of 5,000 shirts a week, later raised to 10,000, by seamstresses who might otherwise be out of work and servicemen's wives who were hard-pressed financially and willing to be trained.

By April 1915, 1,175 women were employed on the scheme and 221,194 shirts had been made. A different scheme was introduced in Exeter when fifty young women, many aged between fourteen and seventeen, were thrown out of work because a collar factory found itself without orders soon after the outbreak of war. The Mayoress of Exeter, the city's education committee and a local charity organised training classes so that the women could be employed making and mending shirts, mufflers, ward suits and other garments for war hospitals.

LABOUR DIFFICULTIES AND STRIKES

It was a volatile period in industrial relations, and it is significant that the promoters of the Plymouth shirt-making scheme ensured that no commercial manufacturers in the borough would be adversely affected by it. Trade unions had been flexing their muscles before the war, and large-scale strikes had severely disrupted many industries, especially the docks, mines and railways. Unsatisfactory working conditions, the right to union membership within a company and relative wage levels were the main triggers for action, and underlying early twentieth-century employer-employee relationships across all industries lay a deep mutual distrust, as older notions of patrician control and deferential subservience were slowly but surely eroded. Employees were gradually learning that solidarity could prove a powerful lever in negotiations, and employers were learning the unpalatable lesson that the nation's social hierarchies did not necessarily ensure a malleable workforce.

Despite all the wartime talk of national unity, a vocal minority of workers believed that these patriotic words largely masked an opportunity for the government and its major allies – the great landowners and commercial entrepreneurs – to ensure that the war was fought in their economic interests largely with the blood of the lower classes. Such extreme political views attracted much criticism. Indeed, a number of prominent trade union leaders passionately supported the war effort, not least because they believed that closer contact between the social classes would bring about greater understanding. When Will Thorne, the veteran general secretary of the Gasworkers' Union, visited Chudleigh in January 1915 he urged the workers in his audience to see the war through to victory, after which their patriotic efforts and solidarity would ensure their calls for a fairer society would be heard sympathetically. Some in his audience approved, but others saw him as far too moderate.

Thorne visited Chudleigh in connection with the ill-tempered strike that had just petered out at the nearby Trusham granite quarry in the Teign valley. Since May 1914 over 120 strikers had challenged the company's reduction of each man's wages by a 1*d* per ton produced, on the grounds of falling prices.

The company closed the quarry when talks broke down, but when war was declared the decision was revoked – although no concessions were made to the workers. Pickets were placed, and the few men who returned to work were the targets of both verbal abuse and stones thrown by angry strikers invading the quarry. One man was seriously injured. Twenty strikers ended up in Newton Abbot magistrates' court, and six were found guilty of assault – a decision that prompted further violent scuffles outside the courthouse and around the quarry. The hard core of strikers never returned to work, and were forced to leave their cottages and the area. Their leaders were deeply imbued with Socialist ideologies. They attacked the company's managers, directors and shareholders, who included the local MP, Captain Morrison-Bell, as grasping and unfeeling capitalists, and the police and magistrates as their willing lackeys, and condemned all working-class sacrifices taking place in a fundamentally capitalist war. In a typical speech in the first week of August 1914, W. Bond, the strike leader, warned colleagues that:

> if they allowed themselves because of the quarrels of kings and princes, priests and nobles, to be dragged into a war which the latter would not fight, but in which the peoples of Europe would, it would be another means of keeping them down, and retarding the work for the better conditions of the people. It would be their brothers whose corpses would be on the battlefield and their bodies that would be torn to pieces by the will of the ruling classes.

His resolution against the war was passed with acclamation.

The quarry strikers were defeated but not humiliated, and they were not alone in the radical views they held especially in and around the industrial and railway centre of nearby Newton Abbot. Many conscientious objectors came from the town. Interestingly, in 1915 Thorne's Union was successful in negotiating wage rises in several Newton Abbot firms. The tanners J. Vicary & Sons raised the wages of men by 2s 6d a week, of boys under eighteen by 1s and girls by 6d. Watts, Blake & Bearne agreed a rise of 1s per week, bringing a man's wage to 4s a day, with extra payments for their lightermen when they worked the barges by hand. Perhaps both sides in this politically aware town saw equitable working relationships as mutually beneficial.

Other groups of workers decided strikes were the only option as prices rose and wages failed to keep up. An unsuccessful strike by workers at Frederick Tremlett's paper mills at Stoke Canon in 1915 resulted in a bitter court case and a dozen families being evicted from their tied cottages in the village. For a time they lived in tents by the roadside alongside a large board saying 'Evicted Paper Mills Workers' Camp, Stoke Canon', but gradually they left to seek jobs in Exeter and Bristol. A few weeks earlier a similarly unsuccessful strike at Ivybridge paper mill led to a few men returning under their old terms, but most refused and left the area. The government contracts were being done 'under sweating conditions', complained the Plymouth Trades and Labour Council, and condemned the wages of 15*s* to 16*s* as a disgrace. Certainly they were no higher than those of farm labourers.

A strike in 1915 brought production to a halt at Shapland & Petters cabinet works, the largest employer in Barnstaple. The men wanted increases of 4*s* 6*d* a week to bring their wages in line with similar industries in the industrial north of England. The company protested that output was declining as a hundred workers had enlisted, and offered a 2*s* increase for all men earning 25*s* a week or less and a 1*s* increase for everyone earning more. The men refused, and against a background of considerable hostility within the town the strikers installed pickets and organised public meetings in an attempt to explain their position. They held out for a month before sourly settling for the company's slightly better offer, but lingering dissatisfaction lasted throughout the war and from time to time erupted into sudden walkouts over relatively petty issues.

In September 1916 a rumbling dispute over wages erupted into a lengthy strike by male and female employees in the numerous depots and departments of the vast Plymouth Co-operative Society. Both employers and employees felt determined enough to hold public meetings and issue press notices defending their positions, and supplies of coal, oil, timber, vegetables, fruit, bread, milk and dairy produce throughout the borough were seriously threatened. Pickets were posted outside Society shops trying to stay open, delivery lorries had to be escorted by policemen, and shoppers braving the strikers were 'greeted with obvious disfavour'. Convalescing soldiers and sailors proved unsympathetic, and strikers' meetings were wrecked by barrages of taunts and accusations of cowardice and treachery.

One striker, a sixteen-year-old boy, was cautioned for throwing stones at the windows of a Society building, a second ended up in court accused of intimidating a saleswoman driving a horse-drawn delivery cart and a third was fined £3 for covering a working warehouseman with a sackful of soot and flour. Ben Tillett from the Transport Federation arrived to reassure the strikers that they were fighting for democracy and against the 'slavery and despotism' of the Co-op 'Junkers'. The local dockers and carters proved sympathetic and coal ships remained unloaded. Over 1,000 men and women were being paid strike money by early October 1916. Eventually arbitration took place between senior unionists and Sir George Askwith, the chief industrial commissioner at the Board of Trade, and the strikers achieved small increases in wages.

Labour relations remained sensitive throughout the county. In 1917 building workers in Torquay went on strike for nine weeks. They wanted 2*d* an hour but settled eventually for a penny. In August 1918 Teignmouth's council workers stopped work until they received more than the 1*d* an hour offered by the council, and in the same month 650 dockers there struck for a week until they agreed to arbitration over a rise from 3¼*d* to 4¼*d* per ton handled. The following month 200 train drivers and firemen at Plymouth stopped work in support of the general grievances of footplate-men, especially in South Wales, over wages, and the shutdown spread to Newton Abbot and Exeter despite official threats that interference with troop movements was illegal in wartime. It was the ill-tempered prelude to the more extensive railway strike of 1919.

WOMEN TAKING ON MEN'S WORK IN THE TOWNS

Once the nation appreciated that the war was not going to be won quickly and Lord Kitchener sought hundreds of thousands of servicemen, the calls for women to take over the jobs of young men grew loud and incessant. In Torquay Admiral Sir William and Lady Acland publicly targeted taxi drivers, barbers and drapers' assistants as potential recruits, claiming that women could easily take over their roles. A female correspondent in the *Western Evening Herald* suggested that women should take over men's jobs as deliverers of milk or serving in 'stores, where so many of our useful countrymen are employed in such soft work as selling tea and sugar, caps and canes'. In April 1915 the first two female ticket collectors started work on Devon railway stations: Miss Harris was appointed at Teignmouth, and Miss Hopping, the daughter of a local railway official, at Exeter St David's station – both direct replacements for male colleagues who had enlisted. As no uniform was available they wore white bands on their left arms bearing the letters 'GWR' in red. In Topsham the novelty of a group of young women painting the station railings was the subject of a photograph, sadly rather fuzzy, in the *Western Times*. In late 1915 the first twelve female

Dorothy Prouse in her Exeter tram conductress uniform. (*Western Times*, 18 October 1918)

tram conductors were employed in Plymouth, and in due course special headwear had to be ordered by the Tramways Committee as, according to the *Western Evening Herald*, 'the ladies by the arrangement of their hair, had some difficulty in making the hats fit'. Exeter's tram company also employed women conductors: there were 104 applicants for six places. In Cullompton Mrs Lee took over her husband's job as a chimney-sweep when he enlisted, and in Pinhoe, near Exeter, Daisy Rogers took charge of her husband's bakery business. Each day she drove the horse and cart on its rounds with the bread she had baked that morning.

The unions and the Trades and Labour Council constantly bemoaned the lowly wages of women and girls, citing examples of those getting 4s or 6s a week and lamenting that few received more than 15s, but they failed to arouse any concerted action against employers.

In 1918, however, attitudes towards women workers changed very suddenly. As early as 2 November 1918, before the war ended, the *Mid Devon Times* printed a blunt letter from the leader of the Gasworkers' Union in Plymouth, complaining that women were occupying jobs that rightfully belonged to discharged servicemen who often possessed inadequate pensions and needed to redeploy to full-time civilian work to restore their war-shattered confidence and pride. In addition, he argued, female clerks, typists and ticket collectors should make way for the thousands of wounded and disabled servicemen who could undertake these less physically demanding tasks.

Men and machines in agriculture

Rural employment changed differently but equally dramatically. By 1914 farmers' local markets had been supplemented and then overtaken by the distant ones opened up by the railways. Mixed farming existed nearly everywhere, although cattle and sheep predominated in north Devon, pigs and poultry in the east, potatoes in the Teign valley and early vegetables, flowers and fruit in the Tamar valley and Exe estuary. The late Victorian changes in agricultural practice as cheap imported American grain poured in the country had exacted their toll, and that was the harsher attitude towards labour costs as farmers strove to adjust to the challenging economic times. Efficiency savings contributed to a marked reduction in the rural population and a tight rein on wages, and in turn these decisions contributed to a sharp rise in migration as young men sought better prospects overseas, especially in Canada, South Africa and Australia.

Nevertheless farming was still a labour-intensive occupation, despite the introduction of machines for specific tasks. Most noticeable were probably the steam-driven threshing engines that visited many farms each year under a contractor and his team. Horses were still the main sources of power, however. They drew the vast majority of ploughs, harrows and seed drills back and forth across the fields, and pulled the carts full of manure and lime – needed to enrich and stabilise the soil. Many farmers, though, still sowed seed by hand, and on all farms bird-scaring, and essential hoeing and weeding, especially of root crops, were also time-consuming chores. The early autumn corn harvest was gradually being mechanised, with horse-drawn reapers and binders speeding up the processes. Nevertheless, just as valuable horses required skilled care and control so farm wagons and machinery required not only a competent operator but also maintenance and repair. Local blacksmiths, wheelwrights and agricultural engineers provided an essential range of services. Another skilled task was thatching, and not only of cottages. Once dry, corn had to be loaded in wagons and carried to the barn or made into ricks, in which case their sloped tops needed to be made waterproof.

Haymaking in summer was a team effort, with lines of mowers with scythes laying the cut hay in swathes on the ground. It was regularly turned over, perhaps more than once a day, until dry, and then loaded onto wagons to be stored in a barn, or ricked and carefully thatched to avoid rot and infestation. It was an anxious time, and the days of haymaking could vary each year as farmers tried to balance the maturity of growth against the likelihood of dry weather. By 1914 the processes could be speeded up with the use of horse-drawn machines, which turned the hay or raked it into windrows ready for carting away. Well-watered meadowland was particularly valuable as it made the best hay, ideally full of herbs and natural grasses. In recent decades, though, more and more Devon cornfields had been sown with grass and clover; these were known as ley land.

Under wartime pressures farmers repeatedly argued that the efficient planting, care and harvesting of crops required skilled hands and a healthy constitution. The same argument was applied to the efficient production of livestock. The births of calves and lambs could be as labour intensive for the farmer as for the cow or ewe, and the multitude of diseases blighting herds and flocks was another source of anxiety in the days when local folklore and home remedies were far more prevalent than professional veterinary care. On the larger farms a skilled cowman or shepherd was deemed essential, and a good one was highly valued, if not very well paid.

A diary written by Miss Edrica de la Pole, who personally worked her farm near Kingsbridge, records her perennial and probably typical anxieties. The weather was a constant concern, affecting not only farming operations

Haymaking outside Cullompton. (Devon Record Office)

Haymakers and thatched rick. (Tiverton Museum)

such as preparing the ground, harvesting, and feeding stock in the fields, but also her ability to travel by dogcart to local towns and markets along the narrow unmade lanes of south Devon. She was always worrying about the next task, be it hedging, ditching, spreading manure, planting vegetables, selling or buying animals, harvesting the hay, negotiating deals with neighbours and tradesmen, and ensuring she had enough home-produced meat and vegetables in stock to prepare the next week's meals. Although she welcomed the occasional opportunity to combine pleasure with business when she visited Newton Abbot, Exeter, and even London by train, her overriding concern was making the farm pay its way. She supported the war, knitting socks and scarves, donating blankets, encouraging local men to enlist and attending charity committee meetings with 'the usual confusion of tongues', but she retained grave suspicions about the attitude of military authorities and government departments towards agricultural production. She shared the general conviction of farmers that they were grievously misunderstood by all those unfamiliar with the hardship and vicissitudes of their lives.

LAND OWNERSHIP IN TRANSITION

The agricultural community was a self-contained one. Immersed in the countryside and largely self-sufficient, it relied upon succeeding generations taking over ownership or tenancies rather than embracing newcomers. The enforced changes in practice over the last thirty or forty years had been particularly unsettling, but by 1914 profitability and stability seem to have been restored and a new conservatism was prevalent among farmers.

The ownership of their land was in significant transition, however, and the war saw the continuing sale of great estates across the county as landowners rationalised their holdings in uncertain times. In June 1915 the Devon land owned by William Wyndham, whose main property was in Wiltshire, was sold by public auction. This included the extensive Silverton, Kentisbeare and Blackborough estates and numerous farms, woods, mills, shops and cottages in and around Bradninch, Cullompton and Halberton. There were ninety-eight lots in all and the three-day sale made £146,214. The *Crediton Chronicle* noted that many localities, farms and families would be deeply disturbed by the sale. The estates had been prosperous, rents had been reasonable and many tenancies had stayed in families for several generations, but not all tenants had been able to buy their farms in the auction. In November 1917 the northern part of Lord Clinton's vast Devon estates was auctioned in Barnstaple, and £91,000 was realised from 5,790 acres comprising fifteen farms and numerous other smallholdings, fields, cottages and woods around Great and

Little Torrington, and St Giles-in-the-Wood. In July 1918 the 683-acre Shute estate owned by Sir Frederick de la Pole was sold, mainly to tenants as he had wished, and that month, too, much of the Haldon estate, comprising twenty-three dairy, stock and corn farms, was broken up and sold by the Commercial Union Insurance Company, which had secured the properties after the bankruptcy of the second Lord Haldon in 1891. A few months later the estates at Down St Mary and around Tavistock and Barnstaple owned by Lord Alington, whose primary residence was Crichel Down in Dorset, were auctioned. The sixty-three lots covering 2,630 acres with nineteen farms and numerous cottages raised £61,165.

THE INITIAL IMPACT OF WAR ON COUNTRY LIFE

Farmers suffered three blows as soon as war was declared. First, many men from farming communities were officers and troopers in the Territorial units scattered across the county, and therefore were deemed sufficiently well trained for immediate posting to coastal areas around southern and eastern England to face a possible German invasion. Second, the army commandeered many horses, some of them no doubt much-loved family mounts although most were more used to the rhythm of seasonal work in the fields. Their owners were required to take them to local market towns where the army selected and paid for the ones it wanted. The army paid good prices, as a farmer at a Devon Farmers' Union meeting rather surprisingly acknowledged – but the fate of most of the horses was not enviable. Many endured considerable hardship when they were shipped to the Western Front, being used to haul military stores and equipment in all weathers and across all types of ground, often close to the battle zone. A large number were lost on the embattled Allied retreat from Mons. Soldiers' letters home spoke of horses as well as men being injured and killed as enemy artillery and aeroplanes struck areas behind the front line. The army also had the first call on local hay to ensure its horses were adequately fed, and no farmer could sell hay privately without permission from the army. The third blow was the cessation of imported fertilisers from Germany and parts of Europe behind enemy lines, and the compelling need for farmers to use home-produced alternatives. The suitability, availability and price of various domestic products were the source of perennial complaints.

Soon after war was declared the government decided that farmers should grow more wheat. This idea split local opinion. A few farmers thought patriotism demanded cooperation but others distrusted the government's integrity – and this rural divide greeted every national initiative throughout the war. Suspicions abounded. One farmer thought the government would commandeer all the extra wheat at a lowly price of its own devising, while a second feared the country would soon be flooded with cheap Canadian wheat and a third refused any cooperation until a favourable grant or price was announced. Many farmers hated the idea of ploughing up meadows or ley land.

As 1914 turned into 1915 farmers bitterly resented the widespread accusations that they were holding back their sons from enlistment. At local meetings they protested that there was a need for adequate labour while asserting their support for the war, but there was always the reluctant admission that a few farmers might be holding more men back than others and thereby giving everyone a bad name. Nevertheless they felt victimised. In a typical exchange one Okehampton farmer asserted, 'They all desired to be patriotic … but he did not think that for each and every man on the farm to drop tools and go to the front was the only way of showing patriotism – (applause).' Another agreed, and added, 'Let them go into the towns and they would find many men in the shops who could well go. It was common to see four or five able-bodied young men behind the counter waiting to hand a customer a pound of sugar or a yard of cloth.' As anger grew, a third claimed (to yet more applause) that 'the way farmers had been "knocked about" was insensible'. Police forces and Inland Revenue officials were other groups that angry farmers charged with evading active service.

Details of the Farmers' Union meetings were published in local newspapers, and this meant that counter-accusations were often printed in the following week's edition. In December 1914, for example, a letter in the *Crediton Chronicle* poured scorn on a recent Tiverton meeting that had adopted a provocative resolution: 'that greater sacrifice in men and horses had been made by the farming community than any other industry in England'. The writer asserted that the army had paid good prices for the horses, many of which the farmers had been keen to sell as unsatisfactory for agricultural work, and in a grimly mocking tone repeated the recruiting officers' assertions that few farmers' sons had enlisted. Reports of the troubled recruitment marches criss-crossing the county hardened public opinion against the farmers, who increasingly saw themselves as the targets of a sinister urban and army campaign.

Schoolboy labour

At a meeting in Crediton in October 1914 farmers were particularly enamoured by the report of a member who had just returned from a County School Attendance Committee meeting. He said that 'he had seen at their meeting that day more exemptions for boys to go on the land than ever before, and this, at any rate, was a good sign'. G.C. Smythe-Richards, a well-respected Devon farmer and land agent, told the *Western Times* that schoolboys were the best hope for farmers short of labour. The three alternatives, he argued, were unsatisfactory. Adult farm labourers could be offered overtime, but they had very limited spare time and needed to cultivate their own plots. Some Belgian refugees were available, but besides the language and cultural issues not many of them were rural workers. The county council had offered some of its road maintenance men to work on the land, but they were too few to make a real difference.

In February and March 1915 MPs debated the alleged severity of the shortage of labour in agriculture. Sir Harry Verney, parliamentary secretary to the Board of Agriculture, estimated the overall deficiency at 10 per cent, and although he felt that farmers should employ more women he recognised that they preferred boys as they were, he suggested, cheaper, easier to order about and wore more convenient clothes. Keir Hardy, the veteran Labour MP, and Sir James Yoxall, a Liberal MP and general secretary of the National Union of Teachers, spoke against any relaxation of the school leaving regulations as the years of elementary education were so brief, and Yoxall argued that farmers could easily find alternative labour if they paid better wages. Other MPs showed more sympathy for the farmers. Rowland Prothero, soon to be president of the Board of Agriculture, and Henry Chaplin, a keen huntsman and agriculturist, spoke firmly in favour of children being allowed to forgo the last year of their elementary education to undertake farmwork where a proven local need existed. Chaplin was particularly blunt, condemning rural elementary schools out of hand for educating the children to scorn agricultural occupations. Herbert Asquith, the prime minister, was sympathetic too: 'we ought not to be bound by any pedantic regard for rules, conventions and usages which have prevailed when the circumstances were normal'. In the end, as we have seen, the government fell short of decreeing that children could be exempted from school attendance in order to work full time. However, its carefully phrased public statement that it would not interfere with local education authorities who granted exemptions where the work was suitably light, wages were fair and other sources of labour were exhausted, was enough to convince many farmers, and indeed many parents, local councillors and magistrates, that child labour was available merely for the asking.

As we have seen, Devon farmers were delighted with national and local news regarding the relaxation of school attendance regulations. Now was the time, one farmer asserted, to reverse the elementary schools' practice of educating the children of agricultural labourers 'above their position' and encouraging them to find jobs in the towns. Once again, many children could begin the practical training for their life's work at the age of thirteen. And, not surprisingly, some of the local attendance committees, which determined who should receive exemption from school, agreed with this sentiment. In December 1915 a discussion took place at the Totnes School Attendance Committee about a farmer who wanted a twelve-and-a-half-year-old boy to work on his farm. To general agreement a member stated that 'these children were useful, and were learning more by going to work than by continuing at school to learn things never likely to be useful to them as long as they lived. These boys were receiving training for smallholders by learning something about cattle and work in the country, as boys who were helping their fathers in the town were likely to become more useful than if they were at school.'

Boys from secondary schools and major public schools as well as elementary ones worked on Devon farms. In the summer of 1916 most secondary schools across Devon offered older boys and girls to help with the harvest, as did the Boy Scouts Association and the *Mount Edgcumbe* training ship. 'This is an exceptionally good class of labour and has been doing really good work in the country and is being eagerly sought after,' declared a member of the County Executive Food Production Committee. Over the Easter holiday in 1917 forty boys and five masters from Rugby School worked for farmers around Chudleigh, planting potatoes, fencing and clearing rough ground, and were highly praised by their employers. Between 7 August and 22 September 1917 schoolboys from Islington camped at Lapford, and were commended for their good behaviour and soundness of work hedging, weeding and harvesting; the exercise was repeated here and at Copplestone in 1918. A Crediton farmer said much the same things about the thirty Exeter Boy Scouts who camped and worked as harvesters on his farm, and the Devon Farmers' Union was equally pleased with the twenty-five secondary schoolboys from Newton Abbot and Tavistock who spent twenty-six days with several teachers harvesting around South Molton.

THE HOSTILITY TOWARDS WOMEN WORKERS

In 1915 the National Farmers' Union sent the Board of Agriculture a resolution 'that recruiting should be closed down as far as skilled hands were concerned', but when the Board's representative addressed the Devon Farmers' Union his message was bleak. He said the Board supported the resolution but military needs were paramount. With unfounded optimism he said, 'He was sure that if, after most careful consideration, it was decided that the skilled farm labourer could not be given preferential treatment, the farmers would cheerfully accept the situation, and do their best to carry on their farms under the very difficult circumstances with which they would then be faced.' He darkened the mood even further by saying he could not understand why 'there was considerable hesitation about women coming forward to do the lighter forms of farmwork', to which his audience repeatedly cried out 'No'.

This did not mean, of course, that Devon farms had no women workers – far from it. Farmers' sons usually married other farmers' daughters, and the wives put the skills they had acquired while growing up to good use in their new homes. Wives and daughters looked after the house and undertook all domestic chores, and they took charge of the dairy and the making of butter, cheese and cream. Poultry were usually their responsibility too. Women often worked in the fields at hay harvest times, and certainly many were skilled animal handlers. A few such as Edrica de la Pole turned their hands to everything alongside any labourers they employed. The wartime controversy throughout Devon centred upon the employment of women who were not part of the farmers' households.

It has been estimated that by the summer of 1915 about 15 per cent of men employed in agriculture had enlisted, thereby creating a sizeable gap in the rural working population. In a House of Commons debate in May 1916 two local MPs, George Lambert of South Molton and Sir John Spear of Tavistock, made it clear that not only were farmers lacking in any official protection regarding vital labour but also, they asserted, local tribunals were blatantly unsympathetic towards applications for exemption. Lambert insisted that the employment of female workers was not a solution welcomed by most Devon farmers. Unfortunately for Devon farmers, not only did military needs continue to transcend agricultural ones but it was common knowledge that women workers were welcomed by farmers in many other parts of the country, including neighbouring Cornwall. Indeed, in the early summer of 1916 the Board of Agriculture published a pamphlet extolling the successes of trained female farmworkers in various counties. They were rearing calves, caring for dairy herds, carting manure, lifting potatoes, cutting thistles, white-washing sheds, hoeing roots and harvesting. Interestingly, and in contrast to Lambert and Spear, Lord Fortescue believed that Devon's rural tribunals 'have given more weight to the needs of agriculture which they thoroughly understood than to the necessities of the Army which they only imperfectly appreciated'. His memoirs reveal that he suspected many 'plausible shirkers' beguiled the panels.

The Women's War Work Committee

A vigorous Women's War Work Committee was established in Devon, with Miss Calmady-Hamlyn, from a wealthy county family in Bridestowe, and Mrs Mildmay as its leading lights. In January 1916 Mrs Mildmay told a public meeting in Totnes that farmers would soon be seeking replacements for the men they would lose when military recruitment intensified later that year. She urged women to come forward, while at the same time lamenting the unusual prejudice of many Devon farmers. Cries of shame greeted the story of a woman who was 'blackguarded by the farmers' when she went into the fields pulling mangolds wearing breeches and leggings.

At another meeting in Totnes in October Miss Calmady-Hamlyn had no hesitation in condemning the inadequate wages farmers were offering women. In one district 'a prominent farmer expected a woman to walk four miles a day, milk 10 cows, and at the end of the week, of six days, gave her 2s 6d. She did not blame the woman that she did not work; it was not worth wearing out the shoe leather for.' Several men, including the mayor and county councillors, supported her, one stating that Seale-Hayne Agricultural College near Newton Abbot trained women to drive and milk cows, and 'make a good bargain if they wanted to sell a beast'. The meeting ended with several expressions of faith that farmers would come round to seeing the benefits of employing trained women on the land.

They were wrong. Later in October it was calculated that 2,254 women were available for war service in Devon – 329 whole time, 1,785 part-time and 190 for milking only. Currently just 835 were working on farms, and once again Miss Calmady-Hamlyn denigrated the paltry wages many women were receiving. In south Devon, she said, 6d an acre was offered for weed cutting and 7s 6d an acre for pulling mangolds, whereas in Bridestowe, her home parish, the payments were at least 1s and 12s respectively. She did not baulk at implying farmers were prolonging the war, even jeopardising victory, by pleading a labour shortage and then refusing to offer women reasonable wages despite the high prices that agricultural produce was achieving. She labelled them 'insular' and 'conservative', adding that 'it was a type of mind very difficult to deal with'.

In the same month Totnes Rural Tribunal discussed a letter about three women trainees at Seale-Hayne College who gained good reports but could not find jobs. The chairman said: 'it is a disgrace to the agricultural community that these young women, who had paid for instruction, given their time to it, and in many cases put themselves to considerable inconvenience for the national good, were not employed'. The four-week course in manuring and harvesting and animal husbandry was demanding – and tiring, as one student recorded. On a typical day she was up at 5.15 a.m., groomed and fed the horses, cleaned the harnesses and stables, milked several cows and took the milk to Newton Abbot, fed and cleaned the pony, drew loads of mangolds from the fields to the store, helped with threshing, milked the cows again and took the milk to town, then stabled the pony before going to bed.

The agricultural historian Edith Whetham argues that the reluctance of farmers to raise wages shows they were not dangerously short of labour however much they complained. She is probably right, and substantiating this suggestion is the fact that in autumn 1916 the army allocated 1,800 soldiers from labour battalions to Devon to help with the harvest. The campsites were made ready but the order countermanded as so few farmers applied for the

Dorothy Hatherleigh and her horses. (*Western Times*, 22 March 1918)

men. They said the men would be ill-trained, lack stamina and commitment, and not be worth their wages – unlike the schoolboys, it seems. Certainly as late as 1917 farmers were getting away with paying male labourers around 23s a week, which was an increase of only 40 per cent since 1914. Retail food prices had risen 87 per cent in that time.

CONFRONTATION

By Christmas 1916 farmers were feeling hard pressed, and not least by the well-publicised criticisms levelled at them by leading female figures. At a Totnes Farmers' Union meeting emotions ran high. Alongside the annoyances that home-produced superphosphates were 'in the opinion of their chemists in Exeter almost worthless' and nitrate of soda and sulphate of ammonia were virtually unobtainable, the 'bullying' of farmers was top of the agenda. There were many complaints. First, the government's recent labour survey asked for the number of men who had enlisted but ignored the fact that many others had left for jobs in the towns. Second, farmers were the victims of newspaper vendettas regarding 'shirkers', but clergy who stayed at home remained immune from criticism. Third, the gentry and their wives attacked the farmers but still employed 'chauffeurs, male servants and game-keepers and numerous other people who did nothing in the national interest'. And finally, just because a few women were working on Devon farms for decent wages those farmers not employing them should not be accused of being miserly and unpatriotic. Particular criticisms were reserved for Mrs Mildmay and Miss Calmady-Hamlyn. Recently Mrs Mildmay had advertised for a male worker, and her children had been seen at Modbury market with a pony and trap and a man looking after them. The meeting unanimously agreed that 'a girl' could have done both jobs. The two women were ridiculed for asserting that women could work with teams of horses, and contemptuously advised that 'they might have done very much better with women's labour by taking vacant farms and showing how they could produce poultry, pork and dairy produce. They had not done it but they were telling farmers to do it.'

The barbs drew blood, and Colonel Mildmay MP issued an open letter from France explaining that the man with his children was a stud-groom well over military age, and his family currently employed no men in the house or on the estate who could serve in the armed forces. Farmers had also criticised pheasant hunting on his estate, and he replied that the farmers' great pests – rabbits – were the primary targets of the shots his critics must have heard. He expressed his full support for his wife's encouragement of women farmworkers.

Miss Calmady-Hamlyn bravely accepted the challenge. By the autumn of 1917 Great Bidlake Farm near Bridestowe became an all-female undertaking under the auspices of the government's Food Production Department. It extended to 140 acres, of which 75 were tilled by horse-drawn ploughs, with a further area gradually being cleared of undergrowth by the women. Fourteen cows were kept and the milk sent by railway to Plymouth. In March 1918 a well-publicised demonstration of the women's prowess was held at the farm, and similar events, including competitions in horse management, milking, and manure loading and spreading, were held in Lapford and Exeter.

A VICTORY OF SORTS

At tribunals Sir Ian Amory did not hesitate to imply that Devon farmers refusing to employ women were less than patriotic, but members who were farmers vigorously defended themselves. One said that a woman he employed refused to dig out thistles, and another complained that women soon left to find better-paid work in munitions factories. Other farmers were equally obdurate. The Exeter branch of the Farmers' Union agreed that a woman could not be trusted with a valuable pair of horses, and that no women from the city's slums or any female factory worker would possess the mental and physical strength to stand a day's work on a farm. In Dartmouth one farmer asserted that a woman was worth a quarter of a man and therefore a quarter of his wages, and another stated that a willing boy of twelve was worth two women. In a particularly unsavoury incident two women felt obliged to defend their skills in public when an Ottery St Mary farmer tried to secure exemption for three male labourers by arguing that the women whom he paid 2s 8d a day for seven and a half hours' work were not worth 1s a day.

The tribunal reports revealed the farmers' other concerns about women workers. Some blamed the antipathy of their wives and daughters towards strange women coming into their midst. Others claimed that it was impossible to find appropriate accommodation for them. Few empty cottages were available as the families of enlisted labourers were still occupying them, and most farmhouses were full of the farmers' extended families. A farmer from Ermington explained that the surrounding roads were so poor in winter that no women could use them – if she tried 'she would have to be pulled out'. However, Edith Whetham argues that many farmers did not want strange women on the farm intruding on male company and inhibiting their conversations during breaks, or working far fewer hours than their wives, daughters and sons were used to each day.

A few disagreed with the general condemnation. Lord Fortescue said that women successfully pulled fields of mangolds around South Molton when paid a decent wage, and Sir Ian Amory said that he proved his tenant farmers' assumptions of female inadequacy wrong by enticing them to employ women at 2d for each cow they managed to milk twice a day. The Archdeacon of Exeter took an elevated view, proclaiming that 'educated women' would find little difficulty in adjusting to farming life. 'The best blood in England was not in the least afraid of labour,' he stated, 'and educated women were willing to dignify labour by taking part in it as labour dignified them.' The headmistress of Exeter's Maynard School was equally confident that her older girls could cope, although a farmer who employed them cautioned that they should come more appropriately dressed. He 'would not think of going digging mangolds in his best clothes'.

The campaign to encourage women to train as farmworkers, and to persuade farmers to employ them, continued to the end of the war. At a time when the German submarine menace was at its height, in May 1918, a large rally took place in Exeter under the banner 'Women of Devon – the Nation's Food Supply depends on you'. A procession through the city was headed by a Devon Regiment band, which was followed by a corps of female farmworkers marching under other banners inscribed 'Great Bidlake Women's Farm' and 'Recruits wanted for Land Army – Apply Employment Exchange'. Then there were representatives from the Forestry and Forage Departments, a team of women gardeners including two daughters of Lord William Cecil (Bishop of Exeter) and wagons and implements from the Devon Ploughing School, based just outside Exeter. Countess Fortescue presented proficiency certificates to women who had recently completed their training, and her husband, the bishop and the mayor spoke about the bitter war against the U-boats, the need for increased food production, the desperate shortage of labour and the proven success of women workers. The day was a modest success, with forty-seven recruits.

A similar event in Plymouth was reported in terms reminiscent of a carnival. Except for the military band the procession was composed entirely of women, and 'admiration was loudly expressed at the healthy, hefty farm-workers in smock and sun-bonnet, or gaiters and overalls, each armed with rake or hoe or spade, the mounted division of women-workers on upstanding farm-horses and the two damsels reposing on a load of hay, one chewing a straw in the approved manner. Other women drove farm-carts and wagons with all the skill of experienced drivers, and all seemed to thoroughly enjoy their outing.' The Plymouth event recruited seventy women, and another in Torquay

The Devon Land Workers Rally in Exeter, May 1918. (*Western Times*, 31 May 1918)

recruited forty. Miss Calmady-Hamlyn was heartened that at least some
farmers recognised the worth of women workers. Twenty-seven Devon farms
in addition to Great Bidlake were now training women. Possibly the scenes
at Ottery St Mary in the summer of 1918, where several hundred acres were
harvested and safely ricked by teams of elderly men, schoolboys and women,
were replicated in at least a few other parishes across the county.

Nevertheless progress was patchy. In August 1918 a survey shows that just
176 trained women were employed on Devon farms, together with 525 other
female war volunteers, a total of 701 and a fall of 134 since December 1916.
In contrast, a number of conscientious objectors worked on Devon farms and
there is no record of hostility towards them, unlike the 'absolutists' who refused
all war-related work. Indeed even Sir Ian Amory, who usually took a hard line
towards their exemption, felt that Lieutenant Stirling, the military representative on the local tribunals, was too vindictive in appealing against the wife of
Albert Pethick, a conscientious objector from Holsworthy, joining him on a
farm at Sidbury, and brusquely overruled his objection.

The timber cutters

With justification, Miss Calmady-Hamlyn was proud to publicise the
successful work of forty women 'drawn from all classes, educated ladies,
factory girls, servants etc.' who were engaged in timber felling and barking
on a government contract in Lydford Wood. However, most of the extensive
forestry work in Devon was undertaken by two large contingents of male
workers drawn from overseas. Supplies of timber from countries around
the Baltic Sea had been cut off by the war, and thousands of trees had to
be cut down across south Devon for military and industrial use, notably as
huts, trench supports, pit props and railway sleepers. Two hundred and fifty

men of the 224th Canadian Foresters were engaged in felling 700 acres of forest around Stover near Newton Abbot, and preparing the timber in a steam-powered sawmill for transportation by railway from Heathfield station yard. They lived in a tented encampment deep within the forest, although from time to time they made their presence felt locally, occasionally by organising local sports days to celebrate Empire Day and the founding of the Dominion of Canada but more often by appearing in the magistrates' court for disorderly behaviour and theft, usually when drunk. The Canadians were usually treated leniently by magistrates, and two even escaped with a caution when obviously guilty of house-breaking. Women came into their own, though, early in 1918 when Colonel and Mrs St Maur, owners of the Stover estate, arranged for a group of female landworkers to plant 15,000 mixed conifer and deciduous saplings to replace the lost trees.

The other felling contingent came from Portugal. The men lived in a self-contained settlement of wooden huts at Mamhead in the Haldon hills to the west of Exeter and worked under an English manager. Relations were volatile; the Portuguese were easily crossed and the English courts reacted severely towards their inclination to use strikes and violence as first rather than last resorts. In autumn 1917 a small group stopped work as a protest against their rations and tried to incite a total strike, but were dealt with summarily under the Defence of the Realm Act and imprisoned. A few months later another Portuguese logcutter was equally severely punished for threatening officials when he was fined for attempting to decrease his gang's workrate. Imprisonment was also meted out to several Portuguese who attacked a

Women workers undertaking efficiency tests at Woodwater Farm near Exeter. (*Western Times*, 22 March 1918)

group of Canadians with knives at a dance in Kenton, after taunts over the village girls got out of hand. When a new forest camp was established near South Molton forty-six Portuguese decided they did not like the conditions there, but were arrested on a train heading in the opposite direction for failing to pay their fares, contravening the travel restrictions on aliens and disobeying instructions linked to a military contract. The *Western Times* said that Portugal was 'our Oldest Ally', but a proportion of the timberworkers were 'frankly, undesirable'.

PROTECTING SKILLED WORKERS

The exemption tribunals recognised that some country occupations merited skilled personnel who were irreplaceable. Small businesses would collapse if their workforce was reduced beyond an acceptable minimum, and their failure could threaten the livelihood of clients throughout the neighbourhood. In May 1916 the Crediton panel gave 'absolute exemption' to the twenty-one-year-old son of Mrs Davey, who ran Copplestone Mill. Her husband had died two years earlier, she had a small daughter to care for, the mill ground between 120 and 150 sacks of cornmeal a week and her staff was reduced to a delivery man and 'a small boy'. Other successful applications in that district that year were a rabbit-catcher from Morchard Bishop, a wheelwright and carpenter from Wemworthy and two agricultural mechanics from Poughill and Newton St Cyres. In 1917 the County Appeal Tribunal summarily dismissed the army's appeal against the exemption of Walter Abrahams, the sole rabbit-trapper around Silverton. Sir Robert Newman was one of the many landowners who confirmed the damage rabbits could do: a hundred, he said, had been caught in just one field of corn when it was cut a few days earlier. In Exeter the remaining two thatchers in an extensive district covering Lympstone, Topsham, Budleigh Salterton and East Budleigh were exempted. A thatcher from Dunkeswell was exempted too, but strictly charged that 'the thatching of ricks must come before the thatching of cottages', and early in 1918 the Crediton tribunal rejected Captain Stirling's argument that one more thatcher could be taken from the district.

In autumn 1917 a county survey revealed how hard enlistment and conscription had hit rural craftsmen notwithstanding the trickle of exemptions. In Tavistock farmers publicly railed against the chronic shortage of blacksmiths and agricultural machinists. A Mr Steer, an agricultural engineer from Kingsbridge, complained that he had sixty new ploughs and corn drills on his order books, and 'his place is full of implements to be repaired'. He had plenty of plant and materials but too few men, and he argued that agricultural production throughout the district would suffer unless his two sons were released from the army. Returns from 299 out of 452 parishes indicated that 94 blacksmith shops had closed, 134 were understaffed and 232 skilled men were needed to restore the pre-war position. Fifty-five wheelwrights had closed, 124 were understaffed and 225 men were required. Sixty-three parishes reported delays in getting horses shod, and in fifty parishes farmers had to go up to 7 miles to find a blacksmith. Thatchers and rabbit-catchers were also scarce, with ricks in danger of rotting and crops facing severe damage.

Farmers' sons excited far less sympathy, and their cause was not helped by a revelation in the *Mid Devon Advertiser* in May 1916 that some farmers were seeking insider knowledge on how to secure their sons' exemption. That month William Selly, aged twenty-four, was fortunate to be granted absolute exemption because he was the joint tenant of a 135-acre farm with his infirm father, and their additional help had been reduced by enlistment to just a thirteen-year-old boy. However, the Culmstock tribunal thought little of the argument put forward by a Burlescombe farmer that all three of his sons, aged nineteen, twenty and twenty-one, were unfit for military service but vital to his mixed arable and dairy farm. If they passed a medical examination, the chairman said, some or all of them would be taken. In Barnstaple the tribunal quickly rejected the exemption application by a Parracombe farmer's son when the military representative said he had disgusted villagers by laughing at the soldiers on the previous year's recruitment march. In 1917 exemption proved even more difficult to obtain. It took a particularly heated interview to secure the release of the son of a Drewsteignton farmer with 197 acres, 48 bullocks, 170 sheep, 5 working horses and 3 colts, and no other labour than a daughter. Barnstaple tribunal swiftly rejected a West Down farmer's plea that paying 24*s* a week for a substitute soldier for his son was poor economics, as he would not work nearly as long and hard as a family member. It might have been a common argument put forward at farmers' meetings, but it met with little sympathy elsewhere.

THE PATH TO CENTRALISED GOVERNMENT CONTROL

By 1917 the government had taken firm control of agricultural policy, and this had a dramatic impact upon Devon's countryside. The decision had taken several years to reach fruition, and of course owed much to Germany's intensification of its U-boat campaign.

In the summer of 1915 a report of a committee on agricultural output chaired by Lord Milner recommended that the government guaranteed farmers a minimum price for wheat for the next four years. This would encourage greater production, not least because thousands of acres of 'inferior pasture' could be put under the plough, and farmers would benefit from the high wartime prices, thereby being able to offer higher wages. The report said that county councils should set up agricultural sub-committees to encourage greater output from farms, allotments and gardens through specialised education, advice and support. Asquith's government rejected the report, not only wishing to avoid additional expense but also erroneously believing that the navy had contained the U-boat threat.

Two years later the situation was dramatically different. Casualty lists were growing longer, imports were declining and retail prices were soaring. Another committee under Lord Selborne sought to identify a solution, and its report, published in March 1917, advocated a dramatic extension of arable farming, a guaranteed minimum price for wheat and oats, the formation of district boards to fix minimum wages for farmworkers and the creation of local assessors, who could terminate tenancies and take over farms that were badly cultivated or neglected. The committee deliberated against the background of appalling weather, a lamentably poor harvest and resounding U-boat successes, and several weeks before its report was issued a Ministry of Food was established to oversee distribution and prices, and consider rationing; and a Food Production Department was created to stimulate and control output. Many of the Selborne and Milner recommendations were speedily implemented. Increasing the area of arable land devoted to wheat, barley, oats and potatoes became the top priority. Minimum prices were guaranteed to cover the farmers' investment in these changes, which were mandatory and backed up with stringent surveys by local assessors. The powers to control agricultural developments were delegated to County War Agricultural Executive Committees, whose members comprised key figures from the temporarily suspended county agricultural committees and influential nominees of the Board of Agriculture.

LORD FORTESCUE AND NEW DIRECTIVES

Not surprisingly the indefatigable Earl Fortescue became the chairman of Devon's War Agricultural Executive Committee. The county was divided into four administrative and operational divisions, the north under Lord Fortescue, the east under Sir Ian Amory, the south under William Coulton and the west under Sir Henry Lopes. Farmers were told bluntly that high levels of recruitment must not jeopardise high levels of food production. Fortescue dismissed the labour difficulties, saying that with help from trained women workers and German prisoners of war with rural backgrounds most farmers could till an extra field of 10–15 acres the next year without great difficulty. He asserted that much farmland across Devon was underused, even culpably neglected, and he expected between a quarter and a half of the temporary pasture in every parish to be tilled. The target was 130,000 extra acres of corn, and it had to be met. In addition, he announced that the divisional committees would be encouraging all parishes and schools to extend their allotment provision, and all cottage gardens had to concentrate on vegetables.

Action was swift. A series of well-coordinated and well-reported local meetings publicised the Executive Committee's terms of reference and powers. The new demands were shrewdly interspersed with appeals for greater personal endeavours in the nation's hour of need. Faintheartedness at home was a dishonour to the gallant sacrifices of men at the Front, said Sir Henry Lopes. William Coulton was equally clear, asserting that farmers were not any worse off than other sections of society, and that if they refused to cooperate and reduced the country to starvation the townsfolk would no doubt hang them from their trees, and deservedly so. At the Devon Farmers' Union AGM early in 1917 members were reminded that agricultural prices were high and that a recent survey had revealed that three-quarters of Devon farms were adequately staffed. Devon had 13,204 farms of which 9,571 had sufficient labour, 1,705 had excessive labour and only 1,928 not enough. Not surprisingly farmers contested the survey, saying it included all men and women whatever their quality, and its criteria of 'sufficiency' rested upon unreasonable assumptions of minimum wartime requirements. Nevertheless it was proving difficult for farmers to argue against the Executive's demands.

The Executive Committee announced that the acreage under tillage in Devon must be increased to at least the total recorded in 1872, just before the depression forced changes in practice. This must happen, it declared, without significantly decreasing the number of cows, sheep and pigs. It would mean, the committee acknowledged, 'a ruthless upheaval of many systems which we now think unalterable'. The comparative past and present figures were:

Crop acreage	1872	1915	Livestock numbers	1872	1915
Corn	308,000	208,000	Cattle	210,000	310,000
Green crops	156,000	93,000	Sheep	930,000	830,000
Clover/grass under rotation	172,000	164,000	Cows in milk	70,000	80,000
Bare fallow	32,000	5,000			
Permanent grass	400,000	729,000			

Captain Hunter from the Board of Agriculture told Devon farmers that 330,000 acres of corn was the county's target; tens of thousands of acres of permanent grass would have to be ploughed up. The divisional committees would determine what was the appropriate extra acreage for each farm bearing in mind its current efficiency and specialisms, but 'what nobody would have was the man who would do nothing … If common decency would not induce them to break the land the State would make them.' The County Executive Committee started as it meant to go on, and straightaway ordered an intensive survey of a dozen farms known to be poorly run.

The pressure was relentless. In May Sir Ian Amory told Eastern Division farmers that they were falling short of the extra tillage targets, and warned that compulsion was a ready-to-use option; in the following months Lord Fortescue said much the same thing at South Molton, Great Torrington and Honiton. To make matters worse, several farmers around Crediton were found to be falsifying their returns regarding the amount of extra land they were tilling. Not surprisingly, the complaints came thick and fast. In Totnes farmers complained that a 30 per cent increase was beyond them, in South Molton the primitive tractors introduced by the government were condemned as useless, and in Barnstaple angry farmers left corn rotting in the fields, saying that the tractors were too expensive to hire and no additional labour could be obtained.

Tractors and horses

As early as March 1917 the farmers of Okehampton decided they did not like mechanical tractors – their land was too hilly, their lower ground too wet, the machines too unreliable, the cost too high, the paperwork too onerous and, unlike horses, the machines missed the corners of their fields. Nevertheless the Board of Agriculture persevered with their promotion, and by November 1917 fifty-four tractors were working, with varying degrees of efficiency, on farms across Devon. Their highly disputed success rate reached the House of Commons that autumn, when George Lambert ridiculed the huge cost of the initiative's numerous supervisors, clerks and mechanics. Sir Richard Winfrey, parliamentary secretary to the Board of Agriculture, had to acknowledge that the 2,600 Devon acres ploughed by them worked out at a massive £2 8s 9d an acre. Current experience, he added optimistically, would guide future improvements.

Although privately Fortescue was sceptical about tractors, and even more so about their drivers and mechanics, early in 1918 he used his authority to promote government policy by establishing a prize scheme largely out of his own pocket for the work they achieved. Using an upbeat patriotic analogy, he asserted: 'The tractor plough is almost as new a thing as the aeroplane. Just as our airmen have done service of untold value by their skilful handling of their new weapon, so can you render immense service if you imitate them and get the utmost possible out of your new implements.' Detailed monthly totals of the tractors' performances were kept. For example, during one week in February 1918 twelve tractors ploughed 156 acres in north Devon, and in July six tractors ploughed 75 acres in a week around Crediton.

These were well-regarded, if belated, achievements, and seemed to confirm suspicions that it was the inexperience and recklessness of the drivers rather than the inadequacies of the machines that led to so many accidents and breakdowns. In summer 1917 the Devon Ploughing School at Woodwater Farm just outside Exeter demonstrated the versatility of the American tractor-plough, the Moline Universal. It tackled sloping ground covered with tough lucerne roots, dug up to 10in deep, turned within 16ft, had a two and three furrow attachment, and the driver controlled both the tractor and the plough. One man and a machine ploughed 6 acres in a day and a half, whereas a man and horses could manage only an acre a day. The future of the tractor was assured, and Fortescue records, with cynical amusement, that the much-criticised machines were snapped up by the farmers when they were sold off in 1919.

Horses, though, were in far greater demand. In September 1917 the army at last agreed to lend them out in teams of two, three or four, each team accompanied by a ploughman, or at least a horseman. The rate of pay would be 5s for a ten-hour day for the hay harvest and 6s a day for the corn harvest, with the men finding their own lodging and food. In March 1918 Sir Ian Amory reported that 483 horses had been returned to Devon by the army, but in widely varying condition. At least thirty-one were too sick to work, and most of them had to be destroyed.

BRITISH AND GERMAN SOLDIERS ON THE LAND

In marked contrast with previous years, 1,639 soldiers had been requested for farm work in 1917, and 1,450 were actually working on the land. By March 1918, 2,007 soldiers were recorded on Devon farms, and by mid-September the number had peaked at 2,611. They were paid 2s 6d a day with board and lodging or 4s a day without. Farmers, of course, complained, especially when some who had settled in well were recalled for active service. A few, though, were 'awful rotters', claimed a farmer at Totnes. It is likely that commanding officers were tempted to identify for farm duties a proportion of men they were glad to see as far away as possible, even though officially efforts were made to recall skilled horsemen and rural craftsmen. The army had complaints too. In the autumn of 1917, for example, two farmers from

Huxbeare and Chillington were found guilty of ill-treating soldiers they employed. Investigation revealed their farms to be poorly managed, and they were placed under Executive Committee control orders.

Suggestions that German and Austrian prisoners of war could offset the shortage of labour had been made earlier in the war but met with numerous local grumbles about language, aptitudes, numbers, organisation and security. As late as December 1916 South Molton Rural District Council was opposed to employing them on the roads or farms, as one 'can't put a tailor in a quarry'. By then, however, food shortages were causing mounting anxiety, and Sir Henry Lopes accepted prisoners of war to break up 4,000 acres of land at Willsworthy for potatoes. At the same time Sir Ian Amory accepted a dozen German prisoners to cut pit props at his family's Hensleigh and Knightshayes estates. They were good workers, he said, and had no interest in escaping back to the trenches.

Many more arrived in 1918. Groups of thirty-five to fifty prisoners of war with several guards were housed in eleven district depots across Devon. They worked on local farms either in groups of four or five with a sole guard or singly under the care of the farmer himself, although the farmer was not responsible if the prisoner absconded. Forty-two were reported working around Ashburton, another forty-two around Newton Abbot and fifty around Cheriton Bishop; all of them, said Sir Ian Amory, being good with horses. German prisoners with agricultural backgrounds were also recorded on farms around South Molton. All were considered peaceful, and happy not to be back in Germany. Indeed, Lord Fortescue remembered one group being escorted back to camp in the evening by a farmer's young daughter.

The prisoners received 25s a week, with 15s deducted by the army for board and lodging. At the height of the 1918 harvest 600 of them were on Devon farms, but the isolated farms, poor roads and steep hills rendered the organisation of work schedules, transport and security difficult, especially as no prisoner was to be placed within 5 miles of the coast, a tricky regulation to adhere to in Devon with its sinuous coastline and deeply penetrating tidal estuaries. Not surprisingly the farmers had complaints: they said prisoners left their rations at their base and tried to cadge refreshments from the farmers, and they suspected that many prisoners wilfully misunderstood instructions. Conversely, an official inspection of prisoner-of-war camps in Devon revealed several worrying abuses. The quality of the food was 'not above suspicion', the guards were unfit and slack, and one was found in the local town when he should have been on the farm. Lord Fortescue himself recalled that a guard, a prisoner and a barmaid had been found blind drunk after a joyride in an army car.

POTATOES, POULTRY AND PESTS

Every village and town was encouraged to grow vegetables, especially potatoes. Early in 1917 Devon Education Committee agreed the extension of five school gardens and the creation of eight new ones, with potatoes as the sole crop. Exeter City Council decided to create new allotments on a 2½-acre 'pleasure ground' in Heavitree, on an unused part of Exwick cemetery and on wasteland in Blackboy Road, where several houses had been demolished. Enthusiasm in the city was high but skills were lamentably low, and the crops were desperately poor according to the *Western Times* that summer. The Bishop of Exeter permitted potatoes to be grown on spare consecrated land in Tiverton, and hoped the poor would have first call on the produce. In Plymouth four council plots totalling 8 acres, including a large recreation ground, were earmarked for conversion into 140 new allotments, and others were added on vacant land adjoining Burrator and Crownhill reservoirs and abutting Mount Gold and Swilly hospitals. By May 1918 Plymouth had 1,903 new plots. In addition, the Earl of Mount Edgcumbe, Lord St Levan and Sir Henry Lopes handed over part of their extensive parkland for vegetable production in partnership with the borough. In North Molton Lord Poltimore doubled production on his Court Hall estate.

Training courses proliferated. In summer 1915 an egg and poultry demonstration train toured Devon, just as it had before the war. In Thorveton, Lapford and Barnstaple the two demonstration carriages were filled with poultry keepers and farmers who were regaled with up-to-date scientific and business approaches to enhancing output through mass-production methods of collecting, grading and transporting eggs, and breeding, feeding, killing and trussing chickens. The county council, too, employed an expert poultry instructor to travel around the county running courses on keeping chickens, ducks, turkeys and geese. Newspaper reports indicate that the courses, which lasted twelve days and cost 2s 6d, were popular, and during the war there was a marked increase in advertisements for poultry coops, equipment and feed. Several newspapers started weekly 'poultry columns' full of detailed advice.

Disease and pests seemed to multiply as production intensified. The late 1917 potato crop was dramatically hit by disease, accentuated by a very wet season. The Executive Committee secured 385 spraying machines, but the hundreds of small plots in schools and towns made timely and effective spraying difficult. Farmers around Totnes complained that it was no good tilling old fields unless the hordes of rabbits were eliminated, as they would eat half the crop. Trapping was deemed inefficient as the costs were greater than the wholesale price of the rabbit, and mass gassing and poisoning were called for. The situation was, perhaps, a little alleviated by Miss Buller's suggestion that war hospitals would welcome the provision of up to 3,000 rabbits each week. The alleged depredations of sparrows caused controversy across the county in 1917, when the County Food Production Committee sent a letter to all district councils asking them to kill as many of the birds as possible. Some councils agreed, and offered 3*d* for every dozen fully fledged sparrows' heads, but others did nothing, firmly convinced that rooks, rats, mice and bad weather were far greater threats to the crops. Presumably attempting to turn a wartime necessity into a sport, Sir Ian Amory suggested that rat and sparrow hunting clubs should be created in and around Tiverton. Early in January 1918 the County Food Production Committee agreed that wood pigeon shoots should take place across the county.

The South Devon Hunt continued to operate during the war, despite the enlistment of several key workers, and it took over the countryside of the Mid-Devon Hunt, which had had to give up its pack. Sixteen brace of foxes were killed in the 1916–17 season. Packs of foxhounds at Eggesford, Tetcott, Stevenstone, East Devon, Lamerton, Tiverton and Silverton continued to hunt, although with fewer staff and less public ceremony than hitherto. Their activities did not escape criticism, however much they were defended as the eradication of vermin and a contribution to the enjoyment of wounded soldiers. Sir Ian Amory had to endure public criticism when his horses avoided requisition, and also when a South Devon kennelman and whip was exempted from active service. Lord Fortescue, a keen huntsman, personally intervened in the difficulties experienced by the Devon and Somerset Staghounds, who were trying to cull wild red deer with a greatly reduced number of staff and horses. Indeed, news of the brief halt to its activities in autumn 1914 even reached the ears of *Punch*, which promptly declared that 'there is said to be a movement on foot among the local stags in passing a vote of thanks'. The vote was premature. As a temporary but (he argued) necessary expedient, Fortescue arranged for a few kennelmen with hounds to drive selected deer towards snares laid by an expert countryman. During the war a hundred deer were snared and sixty or so hunted each year, and Fortescue noted in his memoirs that 'This reduction of the herd combined with the liberal portions of venison distributed gave great satisfaction to the farmers' across whose land the deer and the hunters roamed – and sometimes damaged.

A HARD-WON RURAL VICTORY

In December 1917 Fortescue summarised the first year's work of the War Agricultural Executive Committee. There were, he said, many thousands of new acres of corn, while 162 farms had been surveyed as inadequate: 74 had been ordered to break up further grassland and 88 had been given special cultivation orders. Eventually seven had been taken over by the Executive Committee. In a typical prosecution that year, William Hooper of Chilverton Farm was fined £5 under the Defence of the Realm Act at Chulmleigh Petty Sessions for failing to thatch two ricks of wheat. The roofs were flat, the ricks rotten and 'swimming with rats'. No notice was taken of Hooper's defence that the land was too poor for wheat and there was no thatcher to be found.

The Executive Committee dealt severely throughout 1918 with farmers it considered inadequate and recalcitrant. In January it took over a 180-acre farm at High Chiverton, near Winkleigh. It should have produced 2,000 bushels of corn but managed only 20, ricks had not been thatched, horses and cattle were in abysmal condition, and the septuagenarian farmer had tried to kick the policeman who delivered the formal notice to improve output or face prosecution. In March a farmer at Knowstone was heavily fined £30 and £20 costs for wilfully ignoring an order to put 34 extra acres under the plough. In June Honiton court ignored a Southleigh farmer's defence that a soldier he had hired was a watchmaker and a hopeless labourer, and fined him for failing to plough up 28 extra acres. Heavy fines and confiscations were dealt out to other openly defiant farmers at Chudleigh, Membury, Plymouth, Stockleigh and Thorveton as the hard-line policy was implemented.

COPING WITH THE SHORTAGES

In 1917 and 1918 wheat, potatoes, meat and sugar became scarce. In summer 1917 the Food Production Department's 'travelling instructors' were busy across the country promoting the use of alternative sweeteners such as honey, and the neutralisation of natural acids with bicarbonate of soda when stewing fruit. Light pastries, muffins, crumpets and teacakes were barred from sale, and cakes, buns, scones and biscuits were severely limited in their permitted sugar and flour content. Teashops, which abounded in the rural and seaside resorts of Devon, were not allowed to serve any customers between 3 p.m. and 6 p.m. with more than 2oz in total of bread and permitted cakes.

In the autumn of 1917 a number of women, and a few men, were embarrassed to find themselves in court, and also named in detailed newspaper reports, for contravening the sugar regulations. Householders could obtain sugar for bottling purposes or jam but only if they possessed fruit trees or bushes. Bideford town council decided to prosecute all those who obtained sugar but had no trees, and the wives of the headmaster of Bideford Grammar School, the organist of the parish church, the proprietor of Bideford Ladies School and a missionary were among those ending up before the magistrates. They were fined about £1 each depending upon the amount of sugar they had fraudulently secured. Most pleaded that the application forms were confusing and the sugar was used to make jam, but the town clerk denied the first excuse and ruled out the second as irrelevant. Teignmouth UDC was more conciliatory. It sent cautionary circulars to all households with tiny gardens or no garden at all, and a substantial amount of sugar was handed back to the shops. Initially South Molton Town Council contented itself with issuing warnings that the applicants' gardens could be inspected. Needless to say the warnings proved inadequate, and Lord Fortescue himself chaired the South Molton court that shamed and fined seven local residents. At least twenty-four prosecutions took place in Exeter; the majority were found guilty and fined up to £2.

In spring 1917 potatoes were elusive. If any shops were suspected of securing supplies huge crowds suddenly appeared. On 2 March 1917 the *Teignmouth Post* reported, 'From early morning till late at night anxious housewives were pursuing the elusive tuber from shop to shop', and when shopkeepers could obtain supplies they were rationing each customer to 2–3lbs. In Brixham the long and anxious queues disintegrated into a mêlée in which several

Adults and children with their potato postcards, Exeter. (West Country Studies Library)

women fainted, and in Exeter 'a burly policeman regulated the crowd with difficulty' when news spread that a St Thomas trader had secured a half-ton load. A subsequent consignment in Exeter was reserved for the poor, and the distribution was controlled by the issue of 1,500 postcards guaranteeing a 5lb supply for each family.

Rumours – justified ones – flew around that farmers were holding back potato supplies until wholesale prices improved and the Food Controller's maximum retail price was raised. Several shopkeepers across the county were fined for selling potatoes above the permitted price of 1½d a lb, and court cases revealed the recriminations swirling around between traders and farmers as sales were negotiated in a market subject to tight government controls. In April 1917 several north Devon farmers and another from Widecombe were heavily fined – up to £5 and £15 costs – for selling potatoes wholesale above the official price. The shortages had nothing to do with German U-boats: they had been caused by the maximum retail price being fixed at a lower rate than the prevailing market price.

The chronic shortage of meat early in 1918 was also caused by a government decision that failed to take into account all its repercussions. In 1917 imports of frozen beef from South America for the armed forces declined as the U-boat campaign intensified, and it was decided that 200,000 cattle should be purchased from the home market. Outside this purchase, from the late summer of 1917 the government progressively lowered the maximum sale prices farmers could set for cattle, and ignored the storm of protest from all regions, including Devon. The inevitable shortages occurred. Meat was plentiful in the early autumn of 1917 as farmers had sold an abnormally large number of animals at good prices, but by December it was scarce, and chaos ensued until rationing was introduced in February 1918, wholesale prices improved and stocks could be built up again. The episode caused widespread alarm, especially as hitherto meat had been so readily available. Early in January 1918 Plymouth's *Western Evening Herald* reported that 'there were crowds – they could not be called queues – in the retail market clamouring for supplies'. Each day the few carcasses delivered to traders were snapped up by lucky early shoppers, leaving others angry and frustrated. Recriminations flew around the borough, with butchers blamed for favouring richer customers, wholesalers blamed for favouring particular retailers and extorting high prices, and the government blamed by some for too little centralised control and by others for too much.

There were complaints, too, that local herrings were being sent direct to London where higher prices prevailed, and even rabbits soared in price. Margarine became scarce, largely because of the problems of wartime distribution.

When one 7½ ton assignment suddenly reached a Plymouth shop the complete staff served 2,500 people with half a pound apiece in less than an hour. By the end of January local trades unions were protesting vociferously at the inefficiency of the supply chain and price controls, and resenting the inordinate time wives spent hunting down provisions and waiting in long queues, often to be disappointed as supplies quickly ran out. It took the introduction of rationing and far tighter food controls by the government to ensure that a fairer distribution of available foodstuffs and less volatile pricing gradually came about in the last months of the war.

Lord Fortescue and the 'Clean Cut'

In 1918 another draconian wartime measure struck the countryside. The government introduced what became known as a 'Clean Cut', aimed at scouring the nation for yet more troops for the intended Western Front offensive. It nullified all previous exemptions, and Devon was expected to find nearly 1,000 more men, largely from the rural communities, within a few weeks. In a typically tense event in May 1918 the Plymouth Appeal Tribunal faced 130 cases of young men engaged in agriculture whose earlier exemptions had been cancelled. The tribunal retained sympathy for some farmers faced with a sudden loss of key workers just when their farming practices and production targets were under severe pressure, but Captain Stirling, the military representative, was relentlessly opposed to any concessions, including delaying enlistment until a substitute worker could be found. During one vexatious case he said, 'A substitution case is no use to the quota, 950 men having to be obtained before the end of June. We have no time. You know there is another great attack on the Western Front, and we cannot delay the military programme for 950 men.' He won this case, and indeed most others, and if baulked he did not hesitate to remind the tribunal that military service took precedence over civilian occupations except in the most special of circumstances. He denied any shortage of labour existed as farmers still paid poor wages, and he condemned as unpatriotic but otherwise ignored one applicant's threats to close a dairy if any more workers were taken. The farmers' sole moment of satisfaction occurred when an incensed tribunal member asserted that 'some of us feel strongly that thousands of men in the Dockyard, infinitely less important than these men, are being sheltered by the Government'.

The target was achieved, but at a cost Lord Fortescue acknowledged. In a private memorandum, possibly to the Board of Agriculture, written just after the 'Clean Cut', Lord Fortescue acknowledged the primacy of military necessity but asserted that the exercise could not be repeated. Most Devon farms were small and run by single families, he wrote, and their members worked longer and harder than all substitutes whether women, young boys, older men, soldiers or prisoners. 'Unquestionably some are throwing up their farms,' he added ominously, and 'a very bad impression has been caused in many quarters by the way in which both time and man-power often appears to be wasted.' Nevertheless these thoughts did not stop him sending the following severe warning via the editors of local newspapers to farmers considering active opposition to the 'Clean Cut':

> Sir – It has been reported to me that some farmers who anticipate that they will be seriously inconvenienced by the calling up of sons or labourers under His Majesty's Proclamation of 20th April, are saying that they will put their cattle into the fields they had laid up for hay.
>
> People suffering from a sense of grievance are apt to say more than they mean, and I hope there is no occasion to take threats of this kind at all seriously; but if there should, unfortunately, be any farmers in this County who in resentment at steps made necessary by the requirement of National Defence have forgotten their duty to provide all they can for the food of the nation and its fighting men and their animals, I would remind them that under the powers entrusted to Agricultural Executive Committees by the Defence of the Realm Act, they can be compelled to farm as directed and are liable to a £100 fine and (or) imprisonment if they fail to do so.
>
> Fortescue

Through endless persuasion and constant pressure the required changes in output were achieved. In July 1918 a survey of the extra acreage showed Devon ranking high in the English and Welsh league table. Its exact position depended upon whether Yorkshire and Lincolnshire were counted as single entities (ranking list 1), or Yorkshire was divided into its three Ridings and Lincolnshire into Holland, Kesteven and Lindsey (ranking list 2).

Crop	Increase in acreage 1916–18	Devon ranking 1	Devon ranking 2
Wheat	38,000	3	1
Barley	8,000	4	3
Oats	58,000	2	1
Other corn	15,000	4	2
Potatoes	9,000	3	1

Lord Fortescue's memoirs, together with reports of his numerous speeches, reveal his determination to ensure that government policies were implemented as fully as possible within the county, and he did so in full knowledge of the particular pressures brought to bear upon the agricultural communities. Although privately he thought farming families had been pressurised to the point of collapse by the summer of 1918, in earlier years he had had little sympathy with their protestations of hardship and pleas for more lenient treatment, and it is reasonable to surmise he had thought their complaints had little substance. Even as late as March 1917 he did not endear himself to Devon farmers during an agricultural debate in the House of Lords by asserting they wasted the equivalent of 500 men's annual working hours gossiping at agricultural markets and doing little business.

RELATIONSHIPS CHANGE

Farm labourers, too, had their axes to grind. Early in 1918 wartime unrest over wages led to vigorous efforts being made to establish more local branches of the Agricultural Labourers' & Rural Workers' Union. A Broadclyst labourer named Christopher England was a prime mover. He was an aggressive speaker, and at a Tiverton Junction meeting attended by 200 farmworkers he claimed that his Broadclyst branch had been created in anger after a recent war economy meeting to which 'a rich landowner came and a few with him as his bodyguard' and urged everyone to economise and put money into War Bonds. How do you economise on 15s to 18s a week? England asked. He asserted that the great landowners still lived a privileged life in wartime, with male as well as female servants in evidence, and he did not fail to mention how farmers' sons had not responded to the national call to arms. All of them, he concluded, 'are like a lot of parasites sticking on you and sucking the life out of you'. His rhetoric fell on receptive ears, and branches were formed not only at Tiverton Junction but also at nearby Bradninch and Silverton.

A week later worried Tiverton farmers met to consider the threat of strikes. They agreed they had to recognise the union, but also had to adopt a united front in negotiations with it. Soon afterwards the Devon Farmers' Union met a deputation from the Agricultural Labourers' Union, led by England. In a mutually suspicious atmosphere several labourers recounted examples of low wages – one in Silverton had six children and worked a twelve hour day six days a week and part of Sundays for 23s 6d plus a cottage and 1s 6d for cider, and another from Exminster had six children under ten and received £1 a week. The farmers cried out 'Rot' and 'Bosh' when accused of long-term profiteering, and not surprisingly nothing was settled, partly because both sides knew that the National Wages Board was trying to determine a fair wage. The only moment of agreement was when a labourer lamented that his children could not leave school at the age of twelve.

A month later, in early May 1918, a 31*s* a week minimum wage, including the rental value of a cottage, was announced. It was a little above the 30*s* stated as a maximum by the employers and a lot less than the 40*s* sought by the union. Any hopes for a united rural community were premature.

CONCLUSION

War altered the work patterns of many families in the towns and villages of Devon, and not just those of men serving in the armed forces. Factories, shipyards and quarries had to adjust to sudden shifts in demand for their output, and to the pressures and opportunities presented to them by contracts linked to the war. This adjustment was rendered more acute by the significant loss of manpower through voluntary recruitment and conscription, and by the vagaries of tribunals trying to determine whether or not applicants for exemption had genuine family needs or occupational skills meriting sympathetic attention.

Several factors linked to the war deepened the tension that already existed between many employees and employers before 1914. The wartime cost of living rose significantly, and employers varied widely in their willingness to improve wages to a similar extent. If they did not, a unique combination of feelings was likely to induce industrial action, despite the fact that a bitter war was being fought around the world, and more likely than not involving relations and friends of the strikers. Indeed, the very fact the war was being fought, and a great number of ordinary men were dying or being maimed as a result, incited deep-seated feelings that the multiplicity of sacrifices merited rewards in terms of better wages, working conditions and welfare reforms. The prevailing attitude was that the country could afford it, as despite the huge financial cost of the war it seemed obvious that many employers were making unprecedented profits from their new contracts. Workers wanted recognition that they were key contributors to the success of their firms, just as they sought recognition that they were the key group within society fighting for military victory. Throughout the war, though, the working classes were not as unified as trades union leaders hoped. Not surprisingly many men already in uniform condemned strikers for blatant self-interest, a culpable lack of patriotism and cowardice — and actively disrupted strike meetings.

The rural communities endured similar pressures but reacted differently to them. By and large farmers profited by wartime demands for their produce, and despite the initial disappearance of men in the Volunteers and Territorials, and the compulsory purchase of hundreds of horses, their ability to manage their farms seems to have been little impaired, although great controversy raged around the exact degree of hardship they suffered as a result of the ceaseless call for recruits. On the one hand a contemporary survey, and the later estimates of historians, indicated that there was a relatively small diminution in the overall labour force and the number of understaffed holdings, while on the other hand farmers repeatedly claimed that dire shortages prevented them from undertaking any new initiatives. Certainly farmers aroused a great deal of enmity by what was perceived to be their uncooperative attitude, and this was compounded by a general suspicion that they would go to any lengths to ensure their sons stayed on their farms.

The farmers had strong views on the ways in which shortages could be resolved, and the employment of women was anathema to most of them. This hostility was not so much because women were incapable of working on farms, despite frequent accusations to that effect, but more because unknown women from outside their families were unwelcome on their farms, in their farmhouses and mixing in male company. Despite all the efforts of strong-minded proponents of female farmworkers, intensive training courses and the praise of a small number of farmers and landowners, relatively few farms employed women. Most women had to look to urban employment and voluntary work to contribute to the war effort. It was significant that cheap, malleable and untrained labour in the form of older schoolboys proved particularly popular, and even conscientious objectors were employed with little overt hostility. With an enormous amount of effort and organisation, prisoners of war and soldiers reluctantly released from military duties had to be imported into the county to make up numbers.

Much of the county's landscape was changed by the demands of war. Devon's forests were eroded to satisfy the insatiable demand for timber by industry and the army, and many thousands of acres of grassland of varying quality were reluctantly put under the plough. Towards the end of the war centralised control was implemented with a severity that must have surprised many farmers, especially those who ended up being surveyed and subsequently condemned as inefficient or recalcitrant. It seems fair to say, as Lord Fortescue himself admitted, that farmers were enduring a multiplicity of pressures by 1918 – an alarming diminution of skilled labour, continuing shortages of skilled craftsmen such as thatchers and engineers, and relentless demands for extra acres to be put under the plough. Relationships all round were poor, and not least those between the more militant members of the rural workforce and their employers. The war ended with the scene set for continuing tension in the countryside.

CHAPTER SEVEN

INTO THE 1920s

Aspirations and anxieties

The 1920s were a volatile decade. The economy boomed for a year or so after the Armistice as domestic production increased to offset wartime shortages, and it seemed that full employment, high wages, consumer confidence, sound welfare reform and continuing political stability were in sight. It was, though, a false dawn, and before the end of 1920 over-production led to a sudden crash as orders ceased, factories stockpiled, profits declined, wages were restricted, employees were laid off and disillusion spread across the country, but particularly in the major manufacturing centres of the Midlands, North of England and South Wales. Protest marches and strikes became frequent occurrences. In 1922 the Conservatives ended their wartime alliance with Lloyd George's Liberals, and the nation endured a series of short-lived governments and startling election results. In the next two years first the Conservatives held power, and then – to many people's horror but many other's joy – a minority Labour government was sworn in, only to be replaced a few months later by the resurgent Conservatives. From 1924 onward things gradually settled down politically, if not socially, and Stanley Baldwin's Conservative government survived until 1929, when it was replaced by another minority Labour administration, which in turn merged into a National Coalition government in 1931 in the face of another deep depression.

Throughout the decade there was deep working-class unrest across most industries at the opposition to pay rises, the attempts to impose wage cuts, the stubbornly high level of unemployment and the bare subsistence level of state benefit payments. Employer-employee relations foundered in a continual whirl of mutual suspicion and recrimination, and to many people the nation seemed to have been hovering on the brink of a Russian-style revolution since the end of the war. In May 1926 swelling discontent, especially among miners but also among railway and dockyard workers, erupted into the famous National Strike – which paralysed the country's supply network, filled many people with fears that violent revolution was among them and then collapsed after nine days, when Baldwin stood firm and the unions ran out of money and resolve.

The National Strike has entered into national folklore as evidence of the huge divide between the social classes, and has become the iconic image of an apparently deeply depressing decade. It is, though, only one image, and for many who remained in work – and they were the majority of people – the decade brought slowly accumulating prosperity. Wages rose a little but prices fell a lot, and there was money to spare for visits to the cinema, dance hall and seaside, for a few extra tinned or packet delicacies on the table, and for some of the decade's new mass-produced clothes that were advertised in magazines and shops. Across Devon, as elsewhere, poverty and prosperity existed alongside each other in town and village alike, with some families seeing the post-war world as an era when briefly held high hopes of a better life were cruelly dashed but others as a time when unprecedented opportunities existed for advancement and excitement. In a clear example of the dichotomy of the times, disgruntled railway workers from Exeter, Newton Abbot and Plymouth took part in the decade's strikes, including the National Strike, and angry groups of unemployed men from these towns joined the nationwide protest marches, but each summer crowded passenger trains brought thousands of holidaymakers with money to spend in the still prosperous seaside towns of north and south Devon.

The Armistice

Hostilities ceased at eleven o'clock on the morning of 11 November 1918, but the war maintained its malign influence for many years to come. Celebrations held in villages and towns across the nation provided a desperate moment to release all the pent-up emotions of the previous four years, but the laughter, embraces and dancing in the streets belied the lingering personal grief and the fears of what the future might bring for multitudes of families living without husbands, sons and brothers.

The celebrations that the killing had stopped were widespread. They occurred spontaneously as the news filtered through to surprise each locality that morning. The *Torquay Times* reported that 'The glorious news of the signing of the armistice came through the harbour or rather the ships in the harbour to a half-awake Torquay. It had travelled on air waves from the Admiralty at Devonport and its arrival was signalled to those who were rubbing sleep from their eyes by a chorus of screaming sirens from the naval craft snugly moored alongside the piers.' Soon afterwards people came out on the streets, some banged drums or dustbin lids, others waved flags or draped them around their shoulders. 'The composition of the street crowds was unique. American soldiers, Belgian soldiers, and New Zealand soldiers in khaki, convalescent soldiers in blue, naval air men, and land girls mingled with civilians and children in hundreds.' A little later, crowded motor cars and horse-drawn buses and wagons appeared arrayed in red, white and blue, ships were decorated as though for a review, a seaplane slowly circled the town, and the mayor hurriedly arranged a civic procession and speeches. 'At night, wonder of wonders, the lamps were turned on … maroons were discharged, coloured fires burnt, and occasionally a rocket dashed across the sky … the bells rang out again once more, and a day of real harmless fun and frolic ended without trouble or casualty.' Amid all the excitement, though, 'others … wept silently as they thought of their heroic departed ones, but strove to keep the tears back at the sight of the cheerful faces of those who had not suffered as they had.' Plymouth was equally jubilant, with crowds of singing and cheering British and Australian servicemen, workers from shops, offices and factories, and children milling around the main streets or forming noisy *ad hoc* processions. Bands from the barracks and across the borough rivalled the ships' hooters and sirens. In both Torquay and Plymouth that evening, as elsewhere across the nation, churches hurriedly organised thanksgiving services.

Hospitals and casualties

Wounded and sick servicemen continued to die, though, and the virulent influenza epidemic was at its height that November, killing 230,000 men, women and children across the country before finally petering out in the middle of 1919. It struck its victims quickly and spread rapidly; and there was no medical remedy, as the virus remained unidentified until 1933. Private James Bale, a farmer's son from Mortehoe, died at Rouen aged twenty-two on 12 November 1918 from wounds he had received the day before the war ended, and Bombardier G.H. Hewitt, aged twenty-five, who served all through the war after volunteering in August 1914, died at home in Ilfracombe in February 1919 from pneumonia contracted after succumbing to influenza.

Most of the emergency war hospitals stayed busy for several months after the Armistice, and only gradually closed as their final patients were discharged or sent to permanent military hospitals during 1919. Their surplus equipment was usually donated to worthy causes, and the properties were handed back to their owners. When the Torquay Town Hall Hospital closed on 31 March 1919 the complete outdoor ward was donated to the town council as an open-air school, and other equipment and furniture went to local children's hospitals, nursing associations and convalescent homes. In Budleigh Salterton the balance of the hospital Comforts Fund – £36 11s 4d – was donated to St Dunstan's Home for Blinded Servicemen, in Paignton most of the donated wartime goods were auctioned and £455 8s 7d was divided between the local Red Cross branch and the County VAD Fund, and in Exmouth substantial gifts of clothing, bedding, furniture and equipment were made to local hospitals, district nurses and the Serbian and Belgian Relief Funds. Alderman Stocker, the chairman of Exeter Education Committee, was angry that the military authorities held onto the Episcopal Girls' School, the Children's Home in Heavitree, the College Hostel in Castle Street and the Eye Hospital into 1920, but other city councillors disagreed. They welcomed the extra trade and employment that the emergency hospitals had brought into the locality, and the beds remained needed as many soldiers were brought home with long-term illnesses such as malaria, tuberculosis and venereal diseases.

THE SOLDIERS RETURN

Military units were gradually demobilised, although not nearly as quickly as the men wished, and the delays caused significant unrest, even the occasional mutiny, in camps and barracks around the world. Slowly, though, towns and villages welcomed their men home. In Ilfracombe, for example, a special reception and social evening was arranged for the town's returning servicemen on 25 February 1919. A less palatable incident occurred in Bideford when a conscientious objector returned to his teaching post, which encouraged the boys to strike. 'About 50 or 60 ran out of the school,' reported the *Devon & Exeter Gazette*, 'and, forming a procession, marched around the town singing patriotic songs. They went back to the school after it had been closed, and waited for Mr Guard's appearance, and escorted him, amid much booing, to his home.' Stones were thrown at him, and a crowd, including parents, 'watched the demonstration with seeming approval'. The managers regretted that he had not been moved to another school.

For the servicemen themselves, the first club rooms of the Comrades of the Great War Association, one of several precursors of the British Legion, were being planned in Devon. In January 1918 Lord Fortescue put in motion plans for a Devon division of the new Association. Some aspects had an egalitarian ring. All ranks and sections of the armed services were eligible for membership. In addition, each branch within the county would be self-governing within the Association's constitution and rules. Another rule ensured that branches were kept free from any political affiliations, although the lure of the ex-servicemen's votes attracted several Devon parliamentary candidates to early Association meetings.

The Association was supposed to be non-partisan, but different people saw it as serving different ends. At Exeter's inaugural meeting Lord Fortescue proclaimed that the pre-war ill-will between the social classes had not stopped all those classes coming together to defeat the Germans, and he asserted that the 'hardships and dangers shared together, victories won together, had taught that all the wretched suspicions and clash of interest which divided them in the past were now no barriers to good fellowship or united work in a great cause'. He saw the Association actively promoting the cause of empire, and strongly implied that the branch members should be dedicating themselves to the maintenance of the existing social and political *status quo*. The Devon's Comrades of the Great War Development Committee rested firmly and exclusively in the hands of Sir Henry Lopes, Admiral Sir William Acland, Miss Georgiana Buller, Major J.S.C. Davies, Major Chichester and other county dignitaries.

In February 1918 a meeting in Ilfracombe dedicated itself to creating a branch. There were already eighty members, and the visiting speaker, the airman Captain Valentine Baker, said that the aim was essentially social and humanitarian, and 'to see that no man who had fought for his country should be allowed to eke out an existence travelling with a barrel organ or selling matches in the street or to go to the workhouse'. A few days before the Armistice Vice-Admiral Archibald Stoddart opened the Association's first clubhouse in Devon, in Teignmouth, and added another perspective. He hoped that the men's relaxation would be complemented by their determined efforts to ensure succeeding generations remembered the inspiring victories and the heroic sacrifices so many families had made to protect the British way of life.

FORMAL COMMEMORATIONS

There were many events to commemorate wartime service and sacrifice. In February 1919 Victoria Hall in Exeter witnessed a ceremony led by Miss Calmady-Hamlyn and Mrs Mildmay, celebrating the work of the Devon Women's War Agriculture Committee and its Land Army personnel. Sixty women received their good service ribbons, letters were read from farmers praising their female employees, and the work of the seventy women engaged in forestry and the team running Great Bidlake Farm was publicly acknowledged. It was a final assertion of the triumph of the committee and the Land Army volunteers over male prejudice and the vicissitudes of agricultural life.

That summer a more submissive tone was discernible when Lady Fortescue attended a final inspection and celebration of Great Bidlake Farm. A military band played and a highlight was a 'Victory March' by Miss Calmady-Hamlyn and farmworkers dressed as representatives of Allied forces, British historical figures, and allegories of War, Famine, Patriotism, Justice and Peace. Miss Calmady-Hamlyn said her only aim had been to help the men win the war, and 'the last thing in their minds was to keep out the men when they came home. She believed all the members of the Land Army were longing to hand back the charge to the men when they came back.' The women workers had done their bit, and they were determined to ensure a trouble-free transfer of responsibilities. Soon afterwards Miss Calmady-Hamlyn turned her abundant energy and extensive social network towards the successful promotion of Women's Institutes and their numerous voluntary activities across the county.

The signing of the major peace treaties in the Palace of Versailles prompted Peace Day celebrations on 19 July 1919. Events incorporated the whole community, but focused in particular upon children. In a typical list of activities the children of Combe Martin received flags to wave, and then processed through the village singing patriotic songs accompanied by the brass band to attend a public tea party in the Town Hall, enjoy a sports gala, and watch a bonfire and fireworks display in the evening. Heavy rain in places impeded many activities, and several communities had to cancel their sports days. Nevertheless in wet Kenton and Powderham the Earl of Devon treated the returning soldiers and sailors to 'a capital dinner' and the schoolchildren to 'a capital tea', and in nearby Exminster an empty ward of the mental hospital was turned into a village tea room, and the weather cleared sufficiently to allow games on the hospital cricket pitch. In Crediton the procession included the police, firemen, Friendly Society staff, disabled servicemen and the VAD. They went on enjoy their sports between the showers. A major event was the victory march through the damp and misty streets of Exeter. Headed by military bands and infantry and artillery units from the local barracks, it was joined by 1,500 children from the city's various schools. At its end the children attended a special service in the cathedral.

Children and the Victory Arch, Aveton Gifford. (Cookworthy Museum)

Children in uniforms and costumes prepare for the Peace Day procession in Kingsbridge. (Cookworthy Museum)

"Greater love hath no man, than this that he lay down his life for his friends."

ROLL of HONOUR.

Henry Copland
William Copland
James Luxon
Charles Trout
Rupert Trout
George Taylor
Frank Bond
Charles Garnsworthy
Tom Sercombe
Sidney Whitty
Alfred Polglass
Sidney Trout
William Osborne
Cecil Palmer
Walter Wills
Henry Denham
George Hurford
John Newman
Fred Edworthy
Sidney Wannell
Ewart Wilson
Sidney Rowe
Cecil Kentsbeer
Francis Newman
George Wannell
John Mudge
Fred Puddicombe
William Durrant
William Mills

Frederick Rowery
John Roy
Henry J. Rowe
Wallace Anstey
R. Pike
Herbert Kentsbeer
William Baker
Henry Rustell
Maurice Hill
Frank Wannell
Albert Mills
William Chambers
Frederick Dunscombe
James Dunscombe
James Matthews
Reginald Kerslake
William Bolt
Herbert Manning
Sidney Gale
Harry Squires
Alfred Cobley
Phillip Cornish
Archibald Longridge
Albert Mingo
Sidney Salway
Richard May
Lewis Mogridge
Frederick Hawkings
George Howard

TOPSHAM
PEACE CELEBRATIONS
JULY 19TH. 1919.
OFFICIAL PROGRAMME

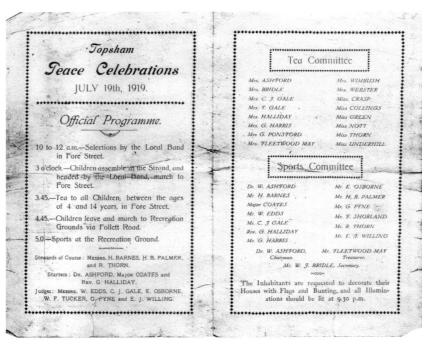

Topsham Peace Celebrations
JULY 19th, 1919.

Official Programme.

10 to 12 a.m.—Selections by the Local Band in Fore Street.

3 o'clock —Children assemble at the Strand, and headed by the Local Band, march to Fore Street.

3.45.—Tea to all Children, between the ages of 4 and 14 years, in Fore Street.

4.45.—Children leave and march to Recreation Grounds via Follett Road.

5.0 —Sports at the Recreation Ground.

Stewards of Course : Messrs. H. BARNES, H. B. PALMER, and R. THORN.

Starters : Dr. ASHFORD, Major COATES and Rev. G. HALLIDAY.

Judges : Messrs. W. EDDS, C. J. GALE, E. OSBORNE, W. F. TUCKER, G. PYNE and E. J. WILLING.

Tea Committee

Mrs. ASHFORD	Mrs. WIMBUSH
Mrs. BRIDLE	Mrs. WEBSTER
Mrs. C. J. GALE	Miss CRASP
Mrs. T. GALE	Miss COLLINGS
Mrs. HALLIDAY	Miss GREEN
Mrs. G. HARRIS	Miss NOTT
Mrs. G. PONSFORD	Miss THORN
Mrs. FLEETWOOD MAY	Miss UNDERHILL

Sports Committee

Dr. W. ASHFORD	Mr. E. OSBORNE
Mr. H. BARNES	Mr. H. B. PALMER
Major COATES	Mr. G. PYNE
Mr. W. EDDS	Mr. F. SHORLAND
Mr. C. J. GALE	Mr. R. THORN
Rev. G. HALLIDAY	Mr. E. J. WILLING
Mr. G. HARRIS	

Dr. W. ASHFORD   Mr. FLEETWOOD MAY
Chairman.   Treasurer.
Mr. W. J. BRIDLE, Secretary.

The Inhabitants are requested to decorate their Houses with Flags and Bunting, and all Illuminations should be lit at 9.30 p.m.

The Peace Day Programme, Topsham (cover and inside). (Topsham Museum)

That July an impressive Thanksgiving Day service was held in Exeter Cathedral. Not surprisingly, Bishop Cecil chose to preach from the verse 'Remember the marvellous works that He hath done' from Psalm 105, and asserted that 'the bravest troops and the most skilful generals would have been useless in the war if we had not had God's Blessing'. He told his congregation that Germany's perfidy must never be forgotten and its punishment, strict but falling short of vengeance, must ensure it never presented a threat to the world again.

A few days later the cathedral hosted a service commemorating the work of the VAD units in the county. The dean praised the members' long and devoted service, and the often humble tasks they undertook without complaint. After the service Earl Fortescue inspected the VAD contingent, and in his farewell speech suggested that their labours were not over, as so many nursing associations and child welfare clinics would welcome their expertise.

At the 1919 Annual General Meeting of the Devon Red Cross Society Major J.S.C. Davies, the county director, received great praise, especially from Lady Fortescue, and was presented with several substantial gifts, including a motor car and an inscribed silver salver. In January 1920 many county dignitaries, including Earl and Countess Fortescue, Sir Ian and Lady Amory, Lady Florence Cecil, Mrs Mildmay, the Mayor of Exeter and Sir Henry Davy, who was the wartime Southern Command's consulting physician, came together to give Miss Georgiana Buller a presentation in public recognition

Peace Day ceremony at Ilfracombe. (Ilfracombe Museum)

of her work at the Exeter military hospitals. Sir Henry Davy remarked how much 'the generals and other superior officers' appreciated her organisational skills and efficiency, and Mrs Mildmay said that the wounded men transferred from Exeter to the VAD hospital in her mansion at Flete were 'full of praise and appreciation for their treatment ... Men talked of the Exeter hospitals as "Paradise".' Worn out, Miss Buller had collapsed soon after the Armistice, but in due course as Dame Georgiana Buller she became chair of the Devonian Cripples Care Association and was instrumental in building Exeter's Princess Elizabeth Orthopaedic Hospital for forty-eight children, which opened in 1927, and the St Loye's Training Centre for Cripples ten years later.

WAR MEMORIALS

The 1920s witnessed the unveiling and dedication of numerous war memorials. Usually local decisions regarding the most appropriate form of memorial, and its site and inscriptions, were reached after numerous meetings, a host of ideas and a variety of hotly contested arguments. In some towns and villages there was opposition to memorials being associated with particular religious denominations, or indeed any denomination at all. Where crosses or victory columns were chosen, some were placed within consecrated ground and some were not.

Plaques within parish churches were common, such as the one in St Petrox at Dartmouth Castle mentioned in the opening lines of this book, even though its level of detail is unusual. Equally common were the high granite crosses, often Celtic in design, placed on pedestals in prominent outdoor positions. Some identified the ranks of the fallen servicemen, and some added any bravery awards, while others listed the names alphabetically without any further details, marking the men's equality in death. Different parishes reached different decisions. At Whimple in south-east Devon a cross inscribed '1914–1919 – in memory of the fallen' followed by the names and ranks of twenty-two officers and men in alphabetical order was placed in the Anglican parish churchyard. The date 1919 is common on Devon war memorials, as it refers not only to the signing of the Peace Treaty in Versailles but also to Devonshire Regiment soldiers who died in Russia that year when units were sent to join the White Russian armies fighting the Bolsheviks. The Whimple memorial was dedicated in March 1920. Relatives and friends placed flowers at its base, and children from the school provided bunches of primroses they had collected from the hedgerows. The rector and the Congregational minister – who could see the names of two of his sons on the cross – shared the service, and the rector poignantly recalled pre-war days when the lost men had walked down the village street and worshipped in the church or chapel with their families.

A few miles away in Broadclyst it was the rector of the parish, the Revd Charles Whitaker, who would have seen his son, Captain Arthur Cecil Whitaker, among the many names on the memorial plaque inside the church. The Whitaker family also placed a large stained-glass window at the eastern end of an aisle portraying their son in uniform, and also their daughter, Ruth, who became the VAD nurse mentioned in Chapter Four, kneeling in prayer before a vision of angels and Christ in glory. The window was a signal act of family faith and firm belief in the rightness of the Allied cause. Significantly, too, the bronze Devonshire Regiment plaque in Exeter Cathedral portrays an ordinary soldier crouching 'at arms' in a ruined building, with a crucifix immediately behind him.

In the small village of Sowton outside Exeter officers and men were remembered separately. Three brass memorial plaques were placed near each other in the parish church and dedicated in August 1920. The first was the parish memorial and recorded the names and ranks of six men – a sapper, gunner, private, two lance-corporals and a corporal. The other two plaques were privately funded by families of fallen officers, and contained greater detail. One commemorated the death of a nineteen-year-old second lieutenant on 28 April 1917 in France, and the other listed the earlier battles and eventual death of a twenty-seven-year-old major at Arras on 26 April 1917.

Crosses and plaques were not always the first choice of local residents. When ideas and opinions were sought in Ilfracombe, most votes, 587, were received for an X-ray unit at Tyrrell Cottage Hospital, with a town library coming second with 433 votes; other projects, including renovating the almshouses, building a

The Devonshire Regiment memorial in Exeter Cathedral. (Author's collection)

The Whitaker memorial window in Broadclyst parish church. (Tony Ovens/Broadclyst Church Council)

municipal centre, providing a recreation ground and erecting various obelisks and crosses, were far less popular. Nevertheless, in a heated public meeting to discuss this expression of local views the X-ray unit and the library were criticised as too costly to purchase and maintain, and a memorial library was further condemned by a commentator who believed most borrowers only sought debasing works of fiction. Soon afterwards the Cottage Hospital itself declined the offer of the X-ray unit, as it had no funds to maintain it indefinitely. In the end a memorial cross was erected, and 157 names were cut into the granite.

A community facility did reach fulfilment in Tiverton, however, where Mayor Gregory took the lead in planning a memorial that he said 'would appeal to the whole community, and be for the benefit of all'. He went on to assert, 'What they really needed was a public library', and added that the perfect building, the redundant Angel Hotel in the centre of the town, was up for sale. The idea met with general approval, especially as Sir Ian Amory and several other notable residents made generous donations to the fund. The ambitious project took a decade to complete, and the memorial library was not opened until 1929.

Unrest and fears of unrest

After the Armistice there was an understandable urge in some sections of society, mainly the middle and upper classes, to recreate what they remembered as the more stable and comfortable aspects of pre-war British life – cheap and plentiful servants, the deference of the lower orders, the reasonably buoyant economy, low taxation, the comforting supremacy of the British Empire protected by the Royal Navy, and the apparent permanence of the Liberal and Conservative parties. Of course such features of life were far from stable before the war, with servants frequently condemned as unreliable and rude, the lower orders prone to dissent and strikes, the economy subject to alarming highs and lows, taxation increasingly perceived by radical Liberal politicians as a weapon to beat wealthy landowners, the British Empire seen by many as an unnecessary national burden rather than a sign of divine approval, and the growth of the Labour Party applauded as the means of achieving wide-ranging state-funded social reform.

As the economy faltered and then floundered at the beginning of the 1920s, social and political conflict loomed on the horizon and Devon was not immune to swirling currents of discontent. To the working classes it seemed that the enhanced social reforms talked about during the war were grudgingly given, and that rises in wages were unlikely to exceed the rising cost of living by very much. It seemed, too, that those in positions of political, social and commercial influence before the war were determined to ensure those positions of influence remained intact, with minimal concessions made to working-class aspirations.

The talk of greater understanding between the classes and a fairer distribution of the nation's resources, which permeated the thanksgiving services, was widely reported but widely ignored. The earldoms and £100,000 granted to Field Marshal Haig and Admiral Beatty and the viscountcies and £30,000 to army commanders seemed to confirm this view. They seemed excessive and tactless rewards in comparison with the tiny gratuities handed out to millions of ordinary servicemen as they faced an uncertain future.

In 1922 there were 200 unemployed men in Newton Abbot, and they lobbied angrily for work rather than relief. A flag day, a concert and a football match to raise funds for the men were all that was achieved. In Ilfracombe, after much debate, an Unemployment Grants Committee helped towards the local council's costs of laying out the Victoria Pleasure Gardens in 1922, on condition that preference was given to unemployed servicemen applying for jobs. In 1924 there were still 130 men out of work, a considerable number for a small seaside town.

In Exeter there were 1,206 unemployed ex-servicemen in 1921, together with 215 other men and 312 women and girls. A conference called by the city's Employment Committee suggested increasing the number of road improvement schemes, extending the waterworks and starting housing schemes early, but all these ideas were confounded by complicated government regulations regarding loans, grants and dates. Some people were less sympathetic. They argued that many of the unemployed were not destitute as they 'had money coming in from trades unions and other sources', and although many of the women had been 'clerks who had been thrown out of various Government offices' they 'refused to listen to reason' and go back to their pre-war work as domestic servants. Nothing much was achieved, and certainly nothing reassuring was said to preserve the much-vaunted wartime unity of the nation.

Many politicians and senior officers feared that a significant proportion of ex-servicemen would be enticed into active subversion by the supposedly egalitarian creed of 'Bolshevikism' currently sweeping across Russia and parts of defeated Germany. Their fears were unfounded: Devon ex-servicemen displayed little sympathy towards Bolshevik agitators. In April 1921 their constant interruptions, including singing the National Anthem, completely wrecked two poorly attended Bolshevik meetings in Exeter that were led by a couple of engine drivers derisively nicknamed 'Comrade Lucy' and 'Comrade Porter'. After the meetings groups of ex-servicemen roughly handled the two men as they tried to escape home. The anger arose because the 'revolutionaries' had not served in the armed forces and were perceived as discrediting the country in whose name so many soldiers had died. Most ex-servicemen wanted a fairer country, but not through violent revolution. When the popular Prince of Wales stayed at Bicton

House with Lord and Lady Clinton a few months later, ex-servicemen flocked to cheer him as he toured the local villages. Two years earlier there had been equally welcoming crowds surrounding the prince when he cut the first turf of a new council housing scheme at North Prospect in Plymouth.

PEACETIME TRADE AND OCCUPATIONS

Despite the peaceful settings of many war memorials, they were the tangible signs of the traumas that so many families had endured for so many years. Yet, superficially life across the county seemed unchanged. As always, age-old sights and activities intermingled with signs of modernisation. Both coastal and ocean-going trade remained busy. Fishing carried on from Brixham and Plymouth, although the industry was in slow decline. Appledore secured further ship-building contracts, Ilfracombe regularly unloaded coal from coastal colliers, and the docks in Teignmouth and Exmouth continued to handle a variety of goods, including timber, wood-pulp, cement, china clay, animal feed and fertilisers. In south Devon at Tuckenhay, several miles up the Dart River, the tiny quay still unloaded coal and materials for an ancient paper mill, while at Fremington on the river Taw in north Devon coastal steamers brought coal in and took china clay out for several more decades. Plymouth's Millbay docks saw the comings and goings of numerous mail and passenger liners, and Devonport remained a major naval base, and went on to build a series of oilers, sloops, frigates and destroyers as well as the large cruisers HMS *Frobisher*,

The Barbican Fish Quay, Plymouth. (Author's collection)

Cornwall, Devonshire and Exeter in the 1920s, and HMS Leander, Orion, Apollo, Birmingham and Gloucester in the 1930s. The yard also converted the light battle-cruisers HMS Furious, Courageous and Glorious into aircraft carriers. In 1928 two RAF flying boat squadrons reoccupied the wartime base at Mount Batten.

Remnants of Devon's mining industry remained alive, although often faltering. Tin and arsenic were still extracted at Owlescombe near Ashburton and at Peter Tavy. A barites mine existed at Bridford, and Haytor mine still provided iron ore, as did other workings near Moretonhampstead, Bovey Tracey and Hennock. Umber was dug from open pits near Ashburton, and ochre at Whitstone, Brentor and Chillaton for use in camouflage paint. The quarries in the Teign valley continued to be highly active. The paper mills at Stoke Canon, Hele and Silverton in the Exe and Culm valleys, and the textile mills at Uffculme, Buckfastleigh and Tiverton also remained profitable.

HORSES AND HORSE POWER

Riding horses or being pulled by them in a variety of carriages, traps, carts and wagons were still the most common forms of transport in rural districts, and indeed in most towns. Horse troughs with inscriptions commemorating the thoughtful donors remained welcome urban facilities, often in the middle of crossroads, for some years to come. Some wealthy families could still be seen in carriages pulled by two or even four horses, driven by retained coachmen, but increasingly they preferred luxury cars and a uniformed chauffeur. After the war the sight and smell of horses were rivalled by the sight and smell of vehicles powered by internal combustion engines. In the 1920s the pre-war exclusivity of the motor car owner began to be eroded by the introduction of the mass-produced Austin 7 and Ford Model T, but the overwhelming victory of cars and lorries over horses and steam engines lay another world war away. Nevertheless, signs of the surge in mobility were there, and the number of cars soared from 132,000 in 1914 to 1,056,000 by 1930. For hundreds of years all traffic on the main road from Bristol to Plymouth had passed through the middle of Exeter, but in 1936 the huge traffic backlogs in the city finally prompted the opening of an inner bypass.

There were other transport opportunities. Plymouth and Exeter kept their trams, which clanked and sparked their way through the central parts of the towns until gradually being replaced by buses in the 1930s. Bicycles were proliferating in the towns and also in the country, despite the damage rough roads could inflict on wheels and tyres. Shops prided themselves on delivering goods to customers' doors, and errand boys with large baskets on the front of their bicycles remained ubiquitous urban sights. Tradesmen's lorries and vans, many still harnessed to horses but some steam-powered and an increasing number petrol-driven, toured villages regularly to deliver a huge variety of household goods from coal to bread and meat to milk. The sale of thousands of motor vehicles by the army soon after the war provided a sound business opportunity for many firms to refit cheaply purchased lorries and vans for commercial use. And, of course, many servicemen had been trained as drivers and mechanics.

Despite the appalling country roads, with their steep hills, blind corners, narrow bridges and potholes, and despite the unreliability of vehicles' brakes, carburettors, radiators and gearboxes, the use of lorries to transport animals to markets and railway goods yards and to bring supplies back to farms became increasingly common. They proved much speedier than horses and carts, and more convenient than driving sheep and cattle for miles on foot. In addition milk started to be collected from farms in churns each day for transportation to bulk milk factories or creameries, and farm-produced dairy produce declined as a result. Writing a quarter of a century later, Nellie Drake recalled the 'great milk lorries' grinding along the country lanes to and from the Ambrosia creamery in Lapford in the mid-1920s.

Life undoubtedly became more dangerous for all other road users. There were few road signs, few trained drivers, no obligation to have vehicles tested for roadworthiness, and, historian Martin Pugh asserts, wealthy young women as well as young men drove cars with unthinking contempt for any speed restrictions or the safety of pedestrians. There were many accidents and court cases, and in 1925 belated warnings were issued to farmers to take care when driving out of fields onto the public highway, and also to motorists to be watchful for the sudden appearance of farm vehicles in front of them. The 1920s saw a few Devon main roads widened and asphalted, a few dangerous corners redesigned and a few hump-backed bridges rebuilt, but earth compacted with stones from local quarries still served most routes.

TOURISM PROSPERS

The tourist trade had faltered but not collapsed during the war, and quickly revived. The heavily worked railway system ceased to be dominated by trains transporting troops and military supplies, and settled down again to the routine passage of local and long-distance passenger and goods services. Trainloads of apples, soft fruit, milk, sheep and cattle continued to rumble eastwards out of the county, and so frequent were the packed holiday trains coming down to Devon and Cornwall that Newton Abbot became a bottle-neck, with some services enduring long waits to pass through the station. Several major stations, especially at junctions such as Cullompton, Newton Abbot, Exeter St David's and Exeter Queen Street, were completely rebuilt in the 1920s. The inter-war years were the high point of rail transport in the south-west.

The surviving paddle steamers were returned to their commercial owners by the Admiralty, and duly renovated they enjoyed many more years of peaceful pleasure cruises along the northern and southern coast. In Ilfracombe the Harbour Committee was delighted that by 1920 the renewed visits of the White Funnel and Yellow Funnel steamers had converted its wartime deficit of £2,000 to a peacetime profit of £700. River boats continued to bring tourists up the Tamar, where the valley's farmers still profited from the strawberries and cream the visitors enjoyed at their stopping-off points. Seaside hotels and guesthouses prospered, beaches were crowded, and inland roads, beauty spots and cafés witnessed a new influx of charabancs, many of them motorised. It was the 1920s that saw the larger hotels advertising that they were approved by the Automobile Association or Royal Automobile Club, and possessed garages. Times were changing in other ways too. Victorian decor was fast becoming unfashionable. The renowned Ilfracombe Hotel, the epitome of Victorian luxury with its elaborate mock-Gothic finery, was fifty-two years old in 1919, and it was to endure a sharp decline in popularity after the war as more modern establishments with sleeker clean-cut lines offering equally high standards of service took centre stage.

Health issues

In 1927 Dr Adkins reported that the overall percentage of elementary school pupils identified with 'defects' meriting treatment had fallen from 45 per cent in 1914 to 25.6 per cent. Nevertheless major problems persisted. Two years earlier Dr Adkins reported that the 'many-headed monster (in more sense than one) of uncleanliness still defies extinction', with a stubborn minority of children's bodies and heads, and indeed homes, thoroughly infested. Influenza still mystified doctors and continued to close many schools each year.

In 1920 a government inspector criticised the absence of facilities in Devon's elementary schools for the health-giving and character-building team games so beloved of secondary and public schools. Most elementary schoolchildren, he wrote, 'simply romp and shout in the playground'. Some schools benefited from fields loaned by local farmers and landowners, in others teachers walked classes to distant public pitches, but many could do nothing. In 1926 there was a sign of hope in the creation of a Devon branch of the National Playing Fields Association.

In 1923 an alarming report from one school medical officer, Dr Corkery, caused a major furore across Devon. He claimed to see a distinct degree of physical and mental 'decadence' in country children, and blamed decades of intermarriage in isolated communities together with poor housing, low wages and large families. No doubt he was influenced by the strong eugenics movement in Britain. This sought to combat what its advocates believed to be the racial degeneracy of the lowest social groups by seeking ways, through education and even segregated living, to prevent them bearing offspring. Dr Corkery's extreme conclusions were strongly challenged by rural county councillors and education committee members. Villages were no longer isolated, they said, housing was far worse in the past, wages had more than doubled in the last decade, and families were much smaller than a generation ago. Others, though, agreed with him, and there were calls for more physical education, and laments that so many country children walked long distances to school and had grossly inadequate midday meals. Lord Clinton told the Devon Federation of Women's Institutes that the countryside with its purer air and greater space was 'infinitely better' for bringing up children than the towns, but he acknowledged that slums existed in many 'over-congested villages'. As part of a nationwide survey of the health of country children, Sir George Newman, the chief medical officer, inspected a Devon village school in 1925 and found '17 out of 19 children with severely impaired physique'. Village life, though, continued much as it had done for many decades past.

THE POOR

Poor Law reform was in the air after the war, and the wartime workhouse scandals were not forgotten. Speaking in January 1920, Sir Robert Newman, MP for Exeter, said that poverty was not a crime but a misfortune, and children, the elderly and the infirm should be removed entirely from the Poor Law system. Boards of Guardians should be abolished, he said, because the taint of pauperism was forever associated with their names, and they had little choice under the regulations to do anything but relieve cases of destitution as frugally as possible. A few years later Bishop Cecil roundly condemned the Poor Law, first as 'unjust' because relief varied widely from Board to Board, second as 'harsh' because it humiliated people, and third as 'extravagant' because of the proliferation of officials. In 1929 the numerous Boards were abolished and relief was placed in the hands of new Public Assistance Committees set up by local authorities, such as Devon County Council. The names changed, but viewed from the general public's perspective the essentially Victorian buildings stayed much the same, and so did the stigma. Benefits paid to the unemployed rose, but never above subsistence level.

In 1920 an alternative system was considered to create greater opportunities for local orphan and destitute children. In 1912 Kinsley Fairbridge, then a Rhodes Scholar at Oxford University, took thirty-five children to his farm

Minesweepers at Ilfracombe, 1919: the paddlesteamers return. (Ilfracombe Museum)

in Pinjarra, Western Australia, where they were lodged, trained in a variety of skills until the age of sixteen and then apprenticed. Fairbridge returned to England after the war and spoke at Exeter, and Sir James Owen, the ex-mayor, heartily commended the growing work of his Child Emigration Society. It took children at the age of seven, promised to house them in small groups of ten under carefully selected house-mothers, and ensured that they were paid for their work as well as being trained in farm work or domestic service. Australians, Fairbridge asserted, attached no stigma to these pauper children, and as land was cheap many skilled boys could become farm owners in their own right. Although nothing was done immediately, in due course the controversial child emigration scheme got under way in Devon. Sadly the numerous scandals associated with it lay hidden for many decades to come.

EDUCATIONAL OPPORTUNITIES AND RESTRICTIONS

Almost all of Devon's villages and towns kept their Victorian school buildings throughout the 1920s, despite their age, limited facilities and hard use. The much-debated post-fourteen continuation schools and classes never appeared in Devon because of the sudden economic downturn in 1920–21. In addition, vital school repairs were often postponed as government grants were cut, and several small schools such as Buckfast, Powderham and Holwell had to be closed in the early 1920s. In some compensation, when the Treasury loosened its purse strings a little in the mid-1920s a slowly growing number of schools received electric light, new hot water heating systems, better opening windows and tarred playgrounds. These novelties were well received by teachers. However, a combination of the wartime backlog of repairs, the increasing building standards demanded by the Board of Education and the declining financial resources of Anglican parishes meant that church schools fell more and more behind council schools in the quality of their buildings and facilities. In 1925 the Bishop of Exeter launched a desperate appeal for £20,000, arguing that 'every child should be brought up to believe in the faith of his father' and asserting that this was only achievable in an Anglican school.

Practical education for the working classes received a significant boost. The county council continued to provide courses in butter-, cream- and cheese-making, bee- and poultry-keeping, and farriery as a matter of routine, and in thatching, fence-making, hedging and ditching, and hurdle-making where an obvious demand existed and instructors could be found. It also supported Women's Institutes in their provision of lace-making and willow-work classes. In 1927 Devon Education Committee agreed that handwork instruction should be promoted far more in schools, with syllabuses closely linked to the local environment and occupations. It is difficult to avoid the conclusion that an opportunity had been spotted to tie the elementary school curriculum more tightly to the needs of local urban and rural employers. Rural education was also encouraged with new grants, avowedly to offset the lure of urban occupations, especially it seems in garages, among village children. A new rural syllabus was adopted which involved the complete immersion of schoolwork in the geography and history, flora and fauna, agriculture and crafts, buildings and traditions to be seen and experienced in the locality. In 1928 the first schools, in Uffculme and South Molton, embarked upon this dramatic new bias in their teaching.

Nevertheless the education system continued to mirror the social classes. For all the much-lauded attention given to the slow spread of socially prestigious secondary schools and the rising percentage of scholarships to them, secondary schools remained relatively few in number, and small. For the year 1928–29 the total number of pupils in secondary schools maintained by the county council was 3,274, with a further 585 in schools grant-aided by the county. It amounted to about 15 per cent of young people aged twelve to sixteen, and just a quarter of these pupils were county scholarship holders or had achieved places through local bursaries.

Plymouth, though, nearly achieved something radically different. Soon after the war Ernest Chandler Cook, its education secretary, secured widespread support for the reorganisation of all elementary schools into separate junior and senior schools, through which greater opportunities would be created for more single-age classes, better targeted lessons and, particularly important, a voluntary extra year at school. Even more dramatically, fees would be abolished in all secondary schools, and the criterion firmly established that admission should be based solely upon children's ability to profit from the syllabuses offered by the school. Plymouth was well on the way to achieving these aims, and to allaying all the fears of costs and the erosion of social divides, when the whole scheme was fatally damaged by the recurring cuts in national educational expenditure, culminating in the depression of 1930–31.

In 1928 the government introduced *The New Prospect in Education*, which required all local education authorities to work out how they could divide elementary schools in each town and rural district into junior and senior schools, or departments within a single school, over the next few years. This, and not any deep egalitarian erosion of the elementary-secondary school divide, was the major inter-war change in education. In 1929 Devon Education Committee got started on the mammoth task, and its first scheme centred on Paignton. Curledge Street Boys' and Girls' School would be converted to a Mixed Senior School, with huts for boys' woodwork and girls' cookery, the other elementary schools in the locality becoming its 'feeder' junior schools. The changes were still grinding on when the Second World War broke out, and they were superseded by the 1944 Education Act and the modern sequential primary-secondary school system.

AGRICULTURE

The county war agricultural executive committees were wound up in 1919. Normal market forces started to operate again, land taken over by the committees was returned to its owners, and the horses and tractors controlled by the committees were put up for sale. In 1919 the Forestry Act set up the Forestry Commission, with powers to buy land and plant trees, and under Lord Clinton, the county's new Forestry Commissioner, Devon witnessed the nation's first plantation on the slopes of the Taw valley near Eggesford. In due course others followed, to fill the hundreds of acres denuded by wartime logging.

Most farmers were pleased to return to pasture the fields they had been forced to till, although many were merely abandoned to become weed-strewn rather than rich grassland. By 1921 the corn acreage in Devon had decreased by about 10,000 acres from its 1918 high point, and another 52,000 acres were lost by 1927. However, flocks and herds were rebuilt, and both lambs and cattle were often sent by rail to the Midlands for fattening. When the war ended both farmers and their labourers had some degree of protection, farmers from the guaranteed prices for wheat and oats and labourers from the minimum wage legislation. In 1920 guaranteed prices were raised, but the wartime period of high profits suddenly ended when the government reneged on its agreement during the 1921 slump. The views of farmers counted for nothing against wider national arguments in favour of free trade and cheap food. Indeed, with a few vocal exceptions such as George Lambert, South Molton's Liberal MP from 1891 to 1924 and 1929 to 1945, farmers and landowners possessed little influence in Parliament. As farming profits fell, so some families returned to farmhouse production of dairy produce for local markets, and to the rearrangement of domestic life in order to take in bed and breakfast guests.

Tractors gradually increased in number and working farm horses slowly decreased, and the mechanical threshing engine became a far more common sight. Some energetic entrepreneurs seized the opportunity to take advantage of mechanisation. Percy Bailey of Marwood in north Devon was one. He had become fascinated by tractors on his father's farm, and after the war he established a successful contract ploughing and harvesting business. In due course he developed a tractor and agricultural machinery sales department, and the firm of Messrs Baileys Engineers based in Pilton prospered into the 1930s. Many fields, though, became the graveyards of the tractors purchased cheaply after the war. Their unreliable frames and engines, and the scarcity and expense of spares, rendered them useful only if their owners were mechanically minded, which many farmers were not.

The decrepit nature of much rural housing was frequently criticised, although little headway was made in improving it during the 1920s beyond a few scattered council houses. Nevertheless primitiveness did not necessarily mean squalor. In 1993 an elderly resident recalled her family's tied cottage on Lord Clinton's estate at Weare Gifford seventy years earlier. It was made of cob, like countless others, and had a corrugated iron roof and concrete floors. It had no labour-saving devices but was 'always spotlessly clean'. Water came from a well, in which a lump of limestone was kept to keep the water pure. A kettle and stewpot were suspended from 'a large saw-like contraption' in front of an open fire. 'Our table was white wood which was constantly being scrubbed to keep it clean.'

THE GREAT ESTATES

Land ownership continued to change as yet more large estates across Devon were broken up and sold. In June 1920, 2,000 acres, including six farms with their labourers' cottages, which formed part of the Sidbury Manor estate owned by the Cave family, were sold for £16,000. In August farms, cottages and woods from Mrs Penn-Curzon's Watermouth estate were divided into ninety-five lots and sold for £82,000. In September farms totalling 1,600 acres around Sandford, Stockleigh Pomeroy and Cheriton Fitzpaine belonging to Sir William Ferguson-Davies were sold for £25,000. In January 1921 much of Captain Templar's Lindridge estate between Newton Abbot and Teignmouth was put under the hammer. Reporting the sale, the *Western Times* commented that a few years earlier no-one would have thought that this prosperous estate would be sold, but now it was merely following a clear trend. As farming profits declined so the price of land plummeted, and when the 1,975-acre Stuckeridge estate near Bampton came on the market in 1926 many lots did not reach their reserve price and were withdrawn. So many farms were coming into new ownership – either because tenants could not afford the auction prices or decided to leave the land for other reasons, including the rigours of wartime directives – that the county council held courses in soil analysis and field experiments for the newcomers. In 1919 it was calculated that there were 385 new farmers in the county.

Many notable families, though, retained their mansions and rural estates, even if some distant properties were sold as part of consolidation campaigns. For example, during the inter-war years Sir Charles Dyke Acland and his successor, his brother Arthur, kept the Killerton estate, Sir Gilbert Acland-Troyte kept Hunstham Court, Sir Ian Heathcote-Amory kept Knightshayes Court, the 10th Lord Clifford of Chudleigh kept Ugbrooke, the 21st Lord Clinton kept Bicton House and widespread estates across north and east Devon, Miss Rosalie Chichester kept Arlington Court, the 14th and 15th Earls of Devon kept Powderham Castle, the 4th and 5th Earls Fortescue kept Castle Hill, Lieutenant-Colonel (later Baron) Mildmay kept Flete and his prize herd of South Devon cattle, and the 4th Earl of Morley kept Saltram. The 4th Lord Poltimore kept Poltimore House, a few miles outside Exeter, but only until 1920, when the land was sold and the house let as a girls' school, and he made Court Hall, North Molton, his primary residence. After the Second World War the estates had very different futures. Killerton House, Knightshayes Court, Arlington Court and Saltram House are now National Trust properties, Huntsham Court and Court Hall are hotels, Flete is divided into retirement apartments and Poltimore House is ruinous, but the subject of a major conservation project. In 1958 the 5th Earl Fortescue left Castle Hill to his daughter, and it is now the home of the Earl and Countess of Arran. However, Lord Clifford of Chudleigh still owns Ugbrooke, the Earl of Devon still owns Powderham and the Clinton estate still extends to 25,000 acres of productive dairy farms and managed forests.

These mansions and their surrounding land still employed many servants – cooks, housekeepers, butler, lady's maid, kitchen maids, laundry maids, chauffeur, grooms, gamekeepers and gardeners – and major social events such as coming-of-age parties, society weddings and Christmas balls were still reported in detail in county newspapers. Stag- and fox-hunting got into their stride again. In 1920 Sir Ian Amory furiously complained about the shortage of foxes. Fox fur had become immensely fashionable and many more animals than hitherto were being trapped. Sir Ian vehemently urged local farmers to 'play the game' and support the hunt. Another challenge to the lifestyle of the wealthy was on the horizon, though. The 1920s saw the rise of the League for the Prohibition of Cruel Sports, and in 1926 a well-reported meeting in Exeter highlighted the 'terrible, agonised noises' of the cornered animals and the evil of men 'who find their pleasure in other creatures' pain'.

CONCLUSION

The post-war decade brought mixed fortunes to the towns and villages of Devon. The war heightened the need to introduce greater welfare reform, and families undoubtedly benefited from more readily available maternity care and treatment offered through the school health service. Improved working-class housing also took its first hesitant steps forward, as local councils and private builders took advantage of the modest aid offered by the government. The ports, mines and factories across the county survived into the 1920s, although with varying degrees of prosperity, and seaside resorts attained great popularity again as a new era of holidaymaking got rapidly under way. The railways flourished as goods and passengers flowed in and out of the county, and the smell of petrol and exhaust fumes from lorries and motor cars increasingly mingled with the centuries-old odour of horses.

Farming, though, entered another period of decline as government protection was withdrawn and agricultural wages failed to match those offered in towns. Wartime profits were replaced by peacetime anxieties. As the rural population continued to decline there were signs that medical officers suspected the overall physical and mental health of working-class families remaining in the countryside were at risk. Desperate efforts were made to match the curriculum of rural elementary schools to the needs of employers, and make country crafts more attractive to school leavers. Many thousands of acres and hundreds of farms were sold, many by major landowners who decided to raise funds and concentrate their holdings nearer their chief residence, or else had lost interest in landowning as a source of steady income, social status, political power and local influence. Nevertheless Devon retained a considerable number of great estates throughout the inter-war years, and the activities of the noble and landowning classes continued to occupy columns in the local newspapers alongside reports and articles on the problems of local unemployment, the evils of slum life, strikes and the fears of civil unrest. Not too far away from these contrasting columns were numerous advertisements for the host of tourist resorts, hotels and places of interest across the county to be reached by rail, motor car and charabancs. And those thousands of tourists could not fail to note the growing number of stark granite columns with neat lists of names inscribed upon them.

BIBLIOGRAPHY

NEWSPAPERS

Brixham Western Guardian
Crediton Chronicle
Devon & Exeter Gazette
Devon & Somerset Weekly News
Exeter Express & Echo
Ilfracombe Chronicle
Ilfracombe Gazette & Observer
Mid Devon Advertiser
Mid Devon & Newton Times
North Devon Herald
North Devon Journal
Paignton Observer & Echo
Paignton Western Guardian
Salcombe Gazette
Sidmouth Observer
South Devon Gazette & Kingsbridge Times
South Molton Gazette
Teignmouth Post
Times Educational Supplement
Tiverton Gazette
Torquay Times
Totnes Times & Devon News
Trewman's Flying Post, Exeter
Western Evening Herald
Western Morning News
Western Times

COUNTY AND PRIVATE PAPERS

Barnstaple & North Devon Museum

Royal Devon Yeomanry Papers
Captain Gamblen's Memoirs

Bovey Tracey Heritage Centre

Wallace, J. (no date) Research Notes on the House of Mercy

Devon Record Office, Sowton, Exeter

DRO 63/5/2/7 Maynard School Magazine 1914
DRO DCC 148/6 Devon County Council Minutes

DRO 149/1/1/2 Devon War Agricultural Committee

DRO DCC 150/4/1/11-17 Devon Education Committee and Sub-Committee Minutes

DRO DCC 153/5/7-8 Mental Deficiency Committee Minutes

DRO DCC 1/3/1 and 157/5/5/1 Maternity & Child Welfare Committee Memoranda and Correspondence 1913-1919

DRO 1037M/LG3/2 Ford of Branscombe Papers (including 1915 Report of County Medical Officer)

DRO 1037M/LG4/4 Copies of *The National Food Journal*

DRO 1262M/L112 Lord Lieutenancy 1914–19 Files (including various Red Cross Files)

DRO 1262M/L141 Women and War Service Files

DRO 1262M/L117 and L139 Belgian Refugees Files

DRO 1262M/O/LD/141/1-60 Devon County Executive Food Committee Minutes and Reports

DRO 1148M/add14/Series II/34 & 123 Includes various Acland family documents concerned with food production

DRO 2065M/add/F357 File of newspaper cuttings on Miss Georgiana Buller

DRO 2667M/F1 Ruth Whitaker's Memoirs

DRO 4711Zadd/Z30 Messrs Willey's War Work

DRO DCC 5189M/Z1 Pamphlet 'A Talk to School Children on Our Daily Bread'

DRO 3252Z/Z1 Ilfracombe Holidaymaker's diary

Devon Family History Society, *Homes for Friendless and Fallen Girls*

Plymouth & West Devon Record Office, Plymouth

1306/20-26 Diary of Miss Edrica de la Pole

Topsham Museum

War Diary of G. May, 1st Devon Battery, RFA

Copy of J.D. Pym, *Dick 'Pincher' Pym Memories* (Alexander Pym, 1999)

West Country Studies Library, Exeter

Census of England & Wales for 1901, 1911 and 1921 – County of Devon, HMSO

SCHOOL LOGBOOKS

Devon Record Office, Sowton, Exeter

68/3/1/7 Exeter, Rack Street Central

68/4/2/4 Exeter, St Thomas's Council

72/15/1/6 Exeter, Episcopal CofE Girls

75/15/1/2 Exeter, Episcopal CofE Boys

76/5/1/1 Exeter, Cowick Street Council

76/7/1/3 Exeter, Heavitree CofE

76/8/1/3 Topsham Council Boys

76/16/2/2 Exeter, Newtown Council Boys

76/41/7 Alphington Council

431C/EAL1 Germansweek Council

456C/EFL1 Westwood CofE

624C/EFL1 Ashcombe CofE
695C/EFL1 Manaton CofE
699C/EFL1 Meeth CofE
725C/EAL1 Peter Tavy Council
733C/EFL1 Sheepstor CofE
792C/EFL5 Tavistock, CofE Girls
792C/EFL6 Tavistock, CofE Boys
1275Cadd/EAL2 Lustleigh Council
1276C/EFL1 Cornworthy CofE
1287C/EFL1 Harbertonford CofE Girls
1510C/EFL2 Crediton, Haywards Voluntary Girls
1510C/EFL8 Crediton, Haywards Voluntary Boys
1934C/EAL1 Loddiswell Nonconformist (from 1916 united with the CofE School)
2066C/EAL1 Throwleigh Council
2160A/PE4 Bovey Tracey CofE
2252/EFL1 Clyst St Mary CofE
2265C/EFL1/2 Exmouth, Exeter Road Council Boys
2267C/EAL1 Upottery Council
2269C/EFL2 Beer CofE
2300/EFL1 Moretonhampstead, Greenhill Council Girls
2301C/EFL1 Princetown Council Boys
2305C/EAL1 Tavistock, Plymouth Road Council Girls
2305C/EFL6 Tavistock, Plymouth Road Council Boys
2324C/EFL2 Hatherleigh Council Girls
2324C/EFL3 Hatherleigh Council Boys
2437C/EAL3 Ugborough Council
2438C/EAL2 Aveton Giffard CofE
2440C/EAL7 Totnes, Grove Council Boys
2574C/EFL1 Cotleigh CofE
2634C/EFL2 Christow Council
2635C/EFL1 Torquay, Ilsham CofE
2745C/EFL2 Tiverton, Heathcoat Council Girls
2934C/EAL4 Newton St Cyres CofE
2972C/EAL1 Thorveton Council
3029C/EFL2 Tiverton, Heathcoat Council Boys
3426C/EFL4 Kingskerswell CofE
3529C/EAL2 Yeoford Council
3655C/EFL1 Torquay, Homelands Council
3666C/EFL4 Torquay, Warberry CofE
3675C/EFL8 Torquay, St Saviour's & All Saints CofE Girls
3683Cadd/EFL4 Kingswear Council
3823C/ESL1 Okehampton Council Boys
4072/EFL2 Honiton Council
4468Cadd/EFL1 Woodbury CofE
6020C/EFL3 Ashburton Council
7201C/EAL1 Widecombe-in-the-Moor Council

North Devon Record Office, Barnstaple

631add/EFL1 Atherington CofE

632C/EAL2 Bishops Nympton Council
682C/EFL5 Ilfracombe, St Philip & St James CofE
710C/EAL2 North Molton, Heasley Mill Council
721C/EFL1 Roborough CofE
1447Cadd/ESL1 Barnstaple, Ashleigh Road Council Senior
2485C/EAL2 Great Torrington, Council Boys
2485C/EAL6 Great Torrington, Council Girls
3074C/EFL2 Great Torrington, Blue Coat Mixed
3079C/EFL2 Combe Martin Council Boys

Plymouth & West Devon Record Office, Plymouth

423/1/2 Plymouth, Grey Coat Boys
604/29 Plymouth, Charles Boys
1461/2 Tamerton Foliot, Mary Dean CofE
1532/1 Plymouth, North Road Girls
2065/1 Plymouth, Hyde Park Girls
2248/1 Devonport, Victoria Road Boys
2778 Plymouth, Eggbuckland CofE
2314/4 East Stonehouse, St George's CofE Boys
2314/7 East Stonehouse, St George's CofE Girls
2318/2 Plymouth, Ford Senior Girls
2324/5 Plymouth, Keppel Place Higher Elementary Boys

WEBSITES

www.british-history.ac.uk/report.aspx?compid=46089 (Duke of Bedford's Tavistock estates)
www.devonairfields.tripod.com/torq.html (airfields)
www.legendarydartmoor.co.uk (sphagnum moss)
www.mareud.com/Ferro-Concrete/british_construction_co.html (concrete ships)
www.onoto.com//ssmedina.asp (P&O liner SS *Medina*)
www.pastscape.english-heritage.org.uk (Okehampton Field Artillery
    Practice Camp, Dartmoor)
www.plymouthdata.info/Great%20War.htm (Major John McCrae)
www.rastall.com/conship.html (concrete ships)
www.wrecksite.eu/wreck.aspx?374 (submarine C16)

BOOKS AND ARTICLES

Acland, A., *A Devon Family: The Story of the Aclands* (Phillimore, 1981)
Allan, S.M., *Devon Mental Hospital, Exminster: Centenary Souvenir* (Devon Mental Hospital, 1945)
Andrews, L., *The Education Act, 1918* (Routledge & Kegan Paul, 1976)
Anon., *A Handbook for Travellers in Devonshire* (John Murray, 1879)
Anon., *Devonshire: Historical, Descriptive, Biographical* (W. Mates & Co., 1907)
Anon., 'In Memoriam, Dame Georgiana Buller 1883–1953' in *Journal of Bone & Joint
    Surgery, Volume 35B: Number 4* (1953)
Anon., *Royal West of England Residential School for the Deaf, Exeter: Historical Survey
    1826–1976* (Heavitree Publishing Company, 1976)
Barlow, F. (ed.), *Exeter and its Region* (University of Exeter Press, 1969)
Booker, F., *The Great Western Railway: A New History* (David & Charles, second edition, 1985)

Carter, P., *Newton Abbot* (Mint Press, 2004)

Collins, E.J.T. (ed.), *The Agrarian History of England & Wales: Volume 7 Part 1* (Cambridge University Press, 2000)

DeGroot, G.J., *Blighty: British Society in the Era of the Great War* (Longman, 1996)

Delafield, E.M., *The War-Workers* (A.A. Knopf, 1918)

Devon Federation of Women's Institutes, *Devon Within Living Memory* (Countryside Books, 1993)

Drake, N.J., *A North Devon Village* (Wessex Press, 1950)

Fielder, D., *A History of Bideford* (Phillimore, 1985)

Finch, G., 'Devon's Farm Labourers in the Victorian Period: the Impact of Economic Change' in *The Devonshire Association Reports & Transactions, Volume 119*: 85–100 (1987)

Fraser, R., *General View of the County of Devon with observations on its means of improvement* (C. Macrae, 1745, reprinted by Porcupine, 1970)

Freeman, R., *Dartmouth and its Neighbours: A History of the Port and its People* (Richard Webb, 1990)

Gilbert, M., *First World War* (Weidenfeld & Nicolson, 1988)

Gill, C., *Plymouth: A New History* (Devon Books, 1993)

Gregory, A.T., *Recollections of a Country Editor* (Tiverton Gazette, 1932)

Harris, H., *Devon's Century of Change* (Peninsula Press, 1998)

Harris, J., *Private Lives, Public Spirit: Britain 1870-1914* (Penguin, 1993)

Harvey, H., *The Royal Devon & Exeter Hospital 1948-1998: A Better Provision Fifty Years On* (RD&E Healthcare Trust/Halsgrove, 1998)

Hawkins, M., *LSWR West Country Lines: Then and Now* (Grange Books/Hawk Editions, 1999)

Hawthorne, P., *Oldway Mansion: Historic Home of the Singer Family* (Torbay Books, 2009)

Holmes, R., *Tommy: The British Soldier on the Western Front 1914–1918* (Harper/Vintage, 2004)

Hopkins, E., *Childhood Transformed: Working Class Children in Nineteenth Century England* (Manchester University Press, 1994)

Hoppen, K.T., *The Mid-Victorian Generation 1846–1886* (Oxford University Press, 1998)

Hore, P., *The World Encyclopaedia of Battleships* (Anness Publishing, 2005)

Hurt, J., *Elementary Schooling and the Working Classes 1860–1918* (Routledge & Kegan Paul, 1979)

Ireland, B., *The Illustrated Guide to Cruisers* (Hermes House, 2008)

Irvine, E.D., 'A Century of Voluntary Service: The Exeter Diocesan Association for the Care of Girls (St Olave's Trust)' in *The Devonshire Association Reports & Transactions, Volume 113*: 133–45 (1981)

Kelly's Directory of Devonshire 1914

Lamplugh, L., *A History of Ilfracombe* (Phillimore, 1984)

Lowndes, G.A.N., *The Silent Social Revolution* (Oxford University Press, 1969)

Maggs, C., *Branch Lines of Devon: Exeter and South, Central and East Devon* (Alan Sutton, 1995)

Marsden, G.Y., 'Paignton Pleases American Sailors' in *American Red Cross Bulletin* (c.1917)

Martin, E.W., 'Rural Society in Devon in the Twentieth Century: The Fate of the Rural Tradition' in *The Devonshire Association Reports and Transactions, Volume 132*: 233–48 (2000)

Marwick, A., *The Deluge, British Society & the First World War* (The Bodley Head, 1965)

Pack, S.W.C., *Britannia at Dartmouth* (Alvin Redman, 1966)

Parker D., *Hertfordshire Children in War & Peace 1914–1939* (University of Hertfordshire Press, 2007)

Porter, V., *Yesterday's Countryside* (David & Charles, 2006)

Pugh, M., *We Danced All Night: A Social History of Britain Between The Wars* (Vintage, 2009)

Pym, J.D., *Dick 'Pincher' Pym Memories* (Alexander Pym, 1999)

Radford, J.P. & Tipper, A., *Starcross: Out of the Mainstream* (The G. Allan Roehr Institute, 1988)

Reed, M.A., *Pilton: Its Past & Its People* (Vineyard Press, 1977)

Robinson, R.E.R., *Bloody Eleventh: The History of the Devonshire Regiment: Volume 1 1685–1815* (The Devonshire & Dorset Regiment, 1988)

Rowland A.B., *The Royal Western Counties Hospital* (published privately, 1985)

Russell, P.M.G., *A History of Exeter Hospitals 1170–1948* (James Townshend, 1976)

Simon, B., *Education & The Labour Movement 1870–1920* (Lawrence & Wishart, 1965)

Simon, B., *The Politics of Educational Reform 1920–1940* (Lawrence & Wishart, 1974)

St Leger-Gordon, D., *Portrait of Devon* (Robert Hale, 1963)

Stanes, R., *Old Farming Days: Life on the Land in Devon and Cornwall* (Halsgrove, 2005)

Stevenson, D., *1914–1918: The History of the First World War* (Penguin, 2004)

Stevenson, J., *British Society 1914–45* (Pelican, 1984)

Thomas, D.S., *West Country Railway History* (David & Charles, 1974)

Travis, J.F., *The Rise of Devon Seaside Resorts 1750–1900* (University of Exeter Press, 1993)

Van der Kiste, J., *Plymouth* (The History Press, 2009)

Wall, R., *Bristol Channel Pleasure Steamers* (David & Charles, 1973)

Wallace, J., 'The Devon House of Mercy at Bovey Tracey' in *The Devonshire Association Reports & Transactions Volume 133*: 191–216 (2001)

Walling, R.A.J., *The Story of Plymouth* (Westaway Books, 1950)

Waters, L., *GWR Then and Now* (Ian Allan, 1994)

Wilson, L., *Ilfracombe's Yesterdays* (A. & P. Oldale, 1976)

Whetham, E., *The Agrarian History of England & Wales, Volume VIII, 1914–39* (Cambridge University Press, 1978)

Woodbridge, R.F., *Historical Survey of the Royal West of England Institution for the Deaf and Dumb 1826–1926* (William Pollard, 1926)

INDEX